Endorsements

"Do you have access to better web-based productivity tools at home than you do at the office? Is your corporate email inbox polluted with well-meaning but productivity-draining administrative emails? Is corporate IT a help or a hindrance to serving your customers? Do your internal projects spend more time competing for resources and attention than serving the organization? If any of these apply to you, then you must read this book! *Far from the Factory: Lean for the Information Age* is a lively and fascinating read containing several lifetimes of wisdom, experience, and insights. This book is a must-read for today's knowledge worker, IT manager, project manager, Lean neophyte, or Lean guru. It is filled with thought-provoking and entertaining anecdotes, illustrations, and tips that highlight the problem of waste in information-intensive processes. The book is filled with many practical tools and ideas from the Lean Body of Knowledge and expertly outlines how they can be put to use in driving out waste and improving information flow. While earlier texts have done a good job of explaining how Lean techniques can be adapted from shop floor to office floor, this book is the first to truly make the leap to the knowledge-intensive, email-filled, and utterly chaotic Information Age."

— Tim McLaren, MBA, PhD Assoc. Professor of IT and Supply Chain Management, Ryerson University and Project Leader, Korva Consulting Ltd

"It's one thing to develop a concept. It's another to make it sing. This is the hymnal."

— Dr. Don V. Steward, CEO Problematics, Professor Emeritus Sacramento State University, inventor of DSM

"A very inspiring and thoughtful reading for me as a knowledge worker. It is addressing the lean principles for the Web 2.0 in a quest for higher value efficiency of our time, in a work context of overflow of email, RSS, Facebook etc. It is describing among others a Lean process in 5 steps for the Knowledge worker, as well as describing how to get to a Lean Culture and Lean time metrics."

— Leif Edvinsson, The World´s First Professor of Intellectual Capital

"Congratulations to all the readers holding this book! It is not only well written and entertaining, it confirms some of my own experiences as well as offering important new insights that give you, the reader, many new ideas to consider to drive success in your business. These Lean ideas must be an integral part of the daily operations of your business. I am going to get each and every one of my management team a copy of this brilliant book at the start for our own Lean journey."

— Lennart Käll, CEO Wasa Kredit. Former CEO of Ticket Travel Group, ICA Bank and SEB Finans

"I really enjoyed reading *Far from the Factory: Lean for the Information Age*. This is a book that I did not even know we needed, but we do. The book addresses the needs of modern companies in a way that no other Lean handbook does. It takes a fresh attempt to ineffective office practices that has evolved in most companies and it suggests methods, tools and inspirations to tackle the challenges. The book gives a good mix of proven lean thinking and modern tools like collaboration software etc. to help restore your competitiveness"

— Gert Moelgaard, VP, Innovation & Business Development, NNE Pharmaplan

"Applying Lean to the office has long been the "missing link" for consultants and practitioners alike. This book fills that void with well though out, coherent and provocative prescriptions. In an environment full of armchair Lean experts who peddle dubious wisdom, this book is a bright light, showing how good thinking can advance best practices.

— Jorge A. Colazo Professor of Operations Management at Universidad Torcuato Di Tella, Argentina Former Toyota Production and Maintenance Manager Founder and CEO – Lean Specialists – Consultants in Process Improvement

"This is a beautiful book knitting together the concepts of LEAN for the white collar knowledge worker to a practical guide of how to really get the benefits out of your LEAN-project. The authors has proved a very deep understanding of how to make a difference In applying the LEAN philosophy in the information age and also the importance to involve all parts of the organization on the change journey. I certainly recommend all my CIO collegues to read the book."

— **Ulf Tingström, former CIO for several financial institutions in Nordic, Skandia/Old Mutual and SBAB**

"We have used Value Stream Mapping as the primary tool for making process improvements in the office, but the business of applying lean thinking in this environment is relatively new. I find it encouraging to see that the authors have developed additional tools and methods and are leveraging new applications that can be used to identify and eliminate waste for the purpose of improving process performance."

— **Lou Farinola, Manufacturing Engineering Director, Global Industrial Engineering and GM Global Manufacturing System**

"George Gonzalez-Rivas and Linus Larsson describe the challenge of working in the knowledge economy: Knowledge workers wrestling with data and information overload, offices and projects working in traditional ways and failing to keep pace with the information revolution; IT departments lagging behind the shift to a Web 2.0 world. *Far from the Factory: Lean for the Information Age* provides timely insight into how Lean can be applied in the knowledge environment. Practical tools and approaches are given that take Lean out of its traditional manufacturing setting and apply it the Knowledge world. Excellent guidance for leaders and workers in office and project environments, and a 'must read' for CIOs everywhere."

— **Julian Amey, Principal Fellow Warwick University, former Vice President, Global Supply Chain at AstraZeneca**

"This book is packed with new ideas, and breaks new ground in so many directions, for a 'traditional' Lean thinker like me! I have been continually surprised, amazed, and delighted at your many new insights. It truly breaks new ground in areas as IT, knowledge management, project management, office lean, and more that have been very much under-thought-out in transferring thinking from the factory to the office."

— **John Bicheno, Director MSc in Lean Operations at Lean Enterprise Research Centre, Cardiff Business School**

"This is an excellent book that I experienced and enjoyed reading on several levels. It is very useful — filled with good practical advice and tools adapted and designed to suit business improvement in information-oriented areas such as research and development. I look forward to experimenting with some of the novel approaches described. It is thought-provoking — rich in new ideas and concepts bringing together classical Lean principles with the tools and capabilities of a modern Web 2.0 environment. It teaches us how to visualize the depth of hidden wastes in our complex information flows and the large opportunity for improvement that this suggests. Finally it was fun to read a book that so creatively integrates and weaves together such a diversity of ideas and approaches and instructive stories into a much needed fresh adaption of Lean for knowledge workers.... just like me and everyone I work with in Research & Development."

— **Keith Russell PhD, Global Continuous Improvement Leader R&D, AstraZeneca Pharmaceuticals**

"Very interesting view on operational excellence, helpful to readers without a background in this area of expertise."

— **Bert Nordberg, President and CEO, Sony Ericsson**

Far from the Factory

Lean for the Information Age

George Gonzalez-Rivas
Linus Larsson

CRC Press
Taylor & Francis Group
Boca Raton London New York

CRC Press is an imprint of the
Taylor & Francis Group, an **informa** business

A PRODUCTIVITY PRESS BOOK

Productivity Press
Taylor & Francis Group
270 Madison Avenue
New York, NY 10016

International Standard Book Number: 978-1-4200-9456-5 (Paperback)

Library of Congress Cataloging-in-Publication Data

Gonzalez-Rivas, George.
    Far from the factory : lean for the information age / George Gonzalez-Rivas and Linus Larsson.
        p. cm.
    Includes bibliographical references and index.
    ISBN 978-1-4200-9456-5
    1. Knowledge management. 2. Knowledge workers. 3. Information technology. 4. Project management. I. Larsson, Linus. II. Title.

HD30.2.G65 2011
658.4'038--dc22   2010012540

Visit the Taylor & Francis Web site at
http://www.taylorandfrancis.com

and the Productivity Press Web site at
http://www.productivitypress.com

Contents

Acknowledgments

We have had many mentors and clients and colleagues and challengers on our journey. Some of their lessons came with grace and some came the hard way. We thank them all. Many authors and vendors shared their wisdom and their products, and we are grateful for the material and the explanations. Donald Steward is particularly worthy of mention for his development of the Dependency Structure Matrix and for his coaching and suggestions.

Introduction

The Lean Information Age

We are at an exciting time in the development of business and management science—the nexus of process improvement methodologies and the information handling tools that can take them to another level.

At the beginning of the 20th century, we had an agrarian economy in which most workers were farmers, artisans, or shopkeepers. Factories were very small and peopled by unfortunates who received appalling treatment for meager pay. The term *wage slave* was no exaggeration.

Then early in the 20th century, several great innovators reshaped everything: Taylor taught us to improve activities; Ford taught us how to scale improvements to entire production lines; Sloan showed us how to efficiently organize the much larger companies made possible by these changes; Deming and Juran taught us how to measure, check, and improve these processes; and Shingo and Ohno reminded us of the underlying principles of Ford and Deming and showed us how to better apply them.

> **TWO KEY LEAN IDEAS**
> 1. Push innovation and the responsibility for improvement down to the direct contributors—the modern-day craftspeople who understand the details of their work and have a pent-up well of suggestions to deploy.
> 2. Look at the entire process including the upstream supply chain to improve speed, remove waste, and give customers what they value.

Overlapping the latter part of this timeline, starting in the 1980s, was the development of a computer-enabled workforce. The service sector of the economy became increasingly important and tremendous information wrangling power moved down into the hands of the direct contributors. White-collar workers with Internet and intranet access have market and corporate information resources at their fingertips, which was inconceivable a generation earlier. At the same time, management was still absorbing the lessons of the factory/physical world such as economies of scale, divisional organization, centralized purchasing, and shared services. As a result, as Lean works its way into the office, we find that central control and economies of scale come into direct conflict with the bottoms-up empowered workforce that is key to generating innovations and improvements. This new workforce is comfortable with the Web 2.0 backdrop and the context of accelerated evolution of tools and Web-based solutions. They emphasize collaboration and networking and embrace "the new" as opposed to "the approved standard." Lean philosophy dovetails with this new culture of technical change to shape the businesses of tomorrow.

The new economy of scale is based on the electronic connections to peers, seamless connections to the supply chain, and massive open innovation to the information and applications marketplace. This puts it on a scale far beyond any that can be fit into a particular factory or even giant corporation. The rationale for breaking central organizations into various divisions, which is span of control, is being replaced by information force multipliers, which give managers unprecedented ability to understand what's going on as well as demonstrable productivity from self-directed worker teams.

In *Far from the Factory* you will discover how to leverage the latest crop of tool sets to deliver on the promise of Lean for the modern, information-rich, white-collar office. This is an environment where distance between networked computers does not matter and the work product zips through uncontrolled webs in nanoseconds. Figure 0.1 provides an overview of the major ideas we hope to impart.

In *Far from the Factory,* we apply the Lean paradigms that allow us to see and recognize waste among the processes, tools, and habits of knowledge workers. We borrow techniques from design control and advanced project management toolboxes that allow us to measure, evaluate, and pinpoint these new expressions of waste. We also develop a new paradigm—the information element—the

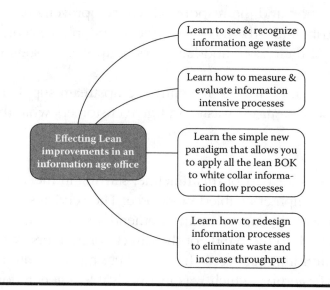

Figure 0.1   The four key ideas needed for Information Age Lean.

building block of documents and designs, which is the true index of information flow. This new perspective allows us to leverage Lean's vast body of knowledge and the theory of constraints to our advantage. It explains, for example, how the development of an entire new product can be held up by one simple piece of information in the same way that a sub-assembly in a factory can be held up for a single part. In addition, you will learn how to augment and kick-start your kaizen and problem-solving session by using the information matrix as a diagnostic and idea-generation tool.

Who Needs This Book

This book is for organizations and change agents or managers within those organizations who work with information. That does not mean only information technology companies and it does not reflect on the amount of information or information storage; rather it is for organizations that create, modify, and consume information electronically in their work. The more creative, one-off, or bespoke these projects or tasks are, the better. The larger and more complex the information usage is in any process, the greater the opportunity for improving that process using these ideas.

Our philosophy is that information *is* the work piece in this electronic age; it is not some form of metadata that accompanies the physical work item. Process flow has always had accompanying information flow. For example, the delivery date might be information used to schedule a machining operation. Value stream management is a great Lean tool that illustrates left-to-right process flow and right-to-left information flow governing a particular manufacturing process. From our perspective, it is less useful in the pure information world of today's high-tech office.

If you employ knowledge workers—resources who do most of their work on computers or with computers, access the Internet, utilize internal and external databases, use e-mail as their primary work transport system (when they're not using instant messaging [IM], file transfer protocol [FTP], Skype, Tweets, or any other new technology), and carry smart phones, and do not really know what that yellow interoffice envelope with the string closure is for—you need this book.

If you rely more on fax and Xerox machines than the Web, e-mail, or other modern means of communication, much of what we say may seem like a stretch to you. If you work on projects but utilize a waterfall or left-to-right Gantt chart and multitasked workers to manage them, this book can help quite a bit.

Who needs this book? In a phrase: any organization with a lot of Web DNA that wishes to cut costs and improve performance. And stay in business.

LEAN FOR THE KNOWLEDGE WORKER

Chapter 1

What Is Knowledge Worker Lean?

The fundamental difference between working with tangible assets and intangible ones, such as information, complicates the application of Factory Lean to the modern office. The focus of this chapter is to put Lean philosophy into the context of the new information age and the coming generations of information-pullers.

The Role of Lean in the Invisible Office

In the musical comedy *My Fair Lady* Professor Higgins vents his frustration with victorian women who only straighten up their hair as opposed to the mess that's inside.* One of the themes of this book is that we share the professor's frustration; in the modern office it is not a tidy desk or stockroom that matters but the efficient flow and use of "what's inside"—information.

The Lean for the information age office has some fundamental differences from what we call classic Lean. We do not deny the benefits of Lean for the office as currently described; we wish to add to it. Most of the Lean body of knowledge is directly applicable to the modern white-collar workplace. However, some aspects of it require translation and redefinition; others require an entirely new point of reference.

Our work is geared to the information age worker. The person we call the "knowledge worker," that is, a heavy computer user, adept at a number of applications, and a vast creator and consumer of information.

The current state of office Lean work and published material takes the factory analogy too literally. For example they take the Japanese workplace organization principles known as 5S and translate that into a tidy workplace. We see nothing

---

* Alan J. Lerner and Frederick Lowe, "A Hymn to Him," 1956.

wrong with that but believe it doesn't go nearly far enough.* In lean factories it is common to mark outdated or rarely used equipment with a red tag marking a probationary period. If that equipment is unused for a period of time it is considered unnecessary waste. There's nothing wrong with red-tagging old reference materials and unused office equipment. There's nothing wrong with standardizing workstations and adding visual performance feedback, such as progress charts or guiding office principles. However, these steps are not as important, today, as Lean information flow.

A tidy workflow strikes us as more relevant than a tidy storage room. One of the principles of 5S is that, once an area is clean and organized, it becomes easier to spot exceptions and we can understand and attack the root cause of the exception. This is great for solving the problem of toner spills around a centrally located copier, but not so great for understanding that the reason there is so much rework in a department is because some of the team members are still cutting and pasting from an obsolete data source. Visually, the correct and incorrect documents will look just the same.

The symptoms we would look for in the knowledge worker's information flow process are invisible to the eye in the workplace. We can stand in the hallway and observe as long and hard as we like, but we'll never learn to see them.

Mary and John can have spotless tidy cubicles with standard equipment located in a standard arrangement. It looks neat as a pin, but the real problem might be that Mary has several files on her hard drive that John doesn't even know exist and he'll spend the next two days recreating them.

What if, as happens more and more today, John and Mary don't work beside each other, or in the same building, or time zone, or they telecommute? The visual order and self-evident feedback that a 5S office system is supposed to provide is largely wasted unless we move it to the cloud.

A simple visual system cannot work in an environment where the key material—information—is largely invisible. To make Lean work in the modern office we need to make the invisible visible. We need to organize around the constantly evolving information flow, not the legacy process flow; we need to make it accessible to a distributed team, we need to develop effective visual management systems, and we need to do it all while adhering to the basic Lean principles of practical, bottom-driven solutions from the workforce.

To this end, a mash up of Lean principles and Web 2.0 collaborative technologies holds the key.

---

* Much emphasis is placed on the physical domain; for example, on how to organize your (actual, physical) desktop—phone here, keyboard there, pen cup here, and so forth. Examples abound about tidying up the filing cabinets and supply cabinets but practically nothing about knowledge management or file structure on servers.

Lean and Web 2.0

Modern-day offices rely less and less on paper-based work systems and more on electronic ones. Until the electronic age, office work-to-be-done was contained within documents or packages of documents. For example, a request for a quotation was received and logged; it was then routed to various workers to verify the current stock availability, pricing, terms, and other transactional details. A formal quote was prepared, perhaps legal and shipping terms were appended, and a salesperson followed up by mail or phone. The company resources add value directly to the work piece (the price quotation letter). This work piece could be physically tracked through the building from inbox to inbox, and much of the total response time was consumed by travel and waiting. To find the relevant information you needed to find the physical folder.

This is just a snippet of the overall process. On the front end, the customer first underwent an entire process to find appropriate vendors, develop some sort of product specification or service need before the request for a quote was ever typed up (with carbon paper copies, no less). On the back end, the selected vendors' responses needed to be compared and evaluated, financial viability needed to be established, delivery performance needed to be assessed, and all the follow-on sales discussions needed to take place. In addition, from a systems view, it is important to realize this work is replicated for every vendor the buyer contacted. Every one of them is manually retyping the specs into the quote. Every one of them is creating and filing these carbon copies. Every one of them is spending time to follow up and close on this prospect. And so on.

And think of the rework. The pre-electronic age office was ordering from a catalog (printed who knows when) or previous experience with the vendor. If the vendor has changed the product, he might suggest a substitute, which would trigger a whole new cycle of evaluation. The buyer might even learn that the substituted product incorporates features they had not included in their request for quotation. Therefore, to be fair and keep the pool of bidders broad, the buyer issues a revised request to each vendor. Now each vendor has to rework its quote. Let's hope that none of them decides to suggest even more features, else this process might never end!

There's a lot of waste here in the Lean sense. Rework. Waiting. Transport. Errors. How odd that seems today when we (generally) expect a very different approach.

Today, you might:

Google the product and evaluate far more offerings than paper catalogs could ever offer you.

View the product on the vendor's Web site. Gather a complete up-to-date description and educate yourself about the new advances or features available.

> *Purchase online* using your company's procurement card or by placing an electronic order. If you have an account, you can probably make the purchase with one click of your mouse.
>
> *Track your shipment* online or receive notification via email.

Records are generated automatically and stored electronically for retrieval as needed.

The whole process for a simple purchase certainly takes less time than typing a request for quote in the pre-electronic age. In addition, you are able to see exactly what you are getting (and might even have checked some blogs to get direct user feedback and customer satisfaction scores—something unheard of until recently). With shipping notification and package tracking, you eliminate delivery risk and enable effective planning since you know when your purchase will arrive. Your documentation time is negligible. Since only one vendor is involved, all the waste associated with the losing bids is eliminated and doesn't have to be absorbed into higher product prices.

Sadly, just because we can do the smart thing doesn't mean we do. An individual or an SOHO (small office/home office) worker can easily follow this speedy purchasing process. Most companies add layer upon layer of bureaucracy, budget control, and security to purchasing processes. Some of the reasons behind this practice are good: centrally evaluated and approved vendors help to ensure product quality, consolidated purchasing helps to lower negotiated rates, and the cycle time associated with accounting for widely distributed purchasing can contribute to budget overruns. These are reasoned arguments. However, most of the resistance is overreliance on legacy procedures and simple reluctance to change. We will show that Lean benefits trump legacy procedures and, because the same office workers become aware of them outside the confines of the official office toolset, become inevitable anyway.

Workers often view eliminating waste as a threat to employment, whereas management views it as a cost-cutting exercise. In Chapter 6, you will see why this interpretation is neither Lean, nor effective. Lean is actually geared toward redirecting work from wasted effort to high-value effort (see Figure 1.1).

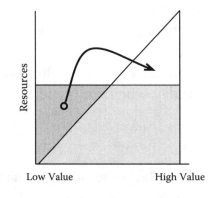

Low Value   High Value

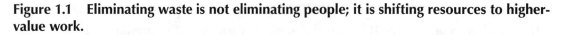

Figure 1.1   Eliminating waste is not eliminating people; it is shifting resources to higher-value work.

This increased high-value effort usually stimulates growth, not retrenchment. Increasing value to the customer should drive them to buy more or pay more. The goals are to:

■ Eliminate waste
■ Increase value
■ Add resources to cope with all the new demand

Key Point: Lean is not about cost cutting. Lean is about smart improvements. Eliminating waste allows you to redeploy attention and resources, and increase throughput. Eliminating waste allows you to lower price and increase quality, and spur greater demand to match your new increased capacity. Therefore, Lean is not a Plan B to deal with poor quarterly results or an economic crisis; Lean is a growth engine.

Increase Productivity: What You Can Learn from Bricklayers about Lean Improvement

The Internet marketplace is a network of companies and individuals buying and selling. The paths between these nodes are very heavily traveled and it makes obvious sense that their processes have been worn smooth. If you belong, say, to a gourmet coffee club, it is in the club's interest to make your purchase as easy to complete as possible. The cookie in your browser, the automatic login, the storage of your shipping address, the prompt if you want to use the credit card ending in 1234, and so forth mean that you don't have to remember anything— except that you need to buy coffee. From that point on, completing the process takes seconds.

On a larger scale, many modern enterprises have streamlined commerce via e-invoicing, electronic fund transfers, automatic reordering, and many other process improvements. The results are directly measurable and the business cases are as positive as they are easy to make.

If we have streamlined intercompany commerce, then why haven't we streamlined intracompany operations to anything like this level of maturity?

Millions of highly paid MBAs and researchers scattered throughout corporate America, Europe, and Japan spend a vast amount of their time cutting and pasting between Excel and PowerPoint when they're not managing inboxes bulging with low-priority email. These PowerPoint decks are e-mailed and e-mailed again for editing, which results in multiple copies, the introduction of version control errors, mutually contradictory edits, and delays due to late-arriving contributions. This process screams for improvement.

One of the first documented "lean" improvements is the story of the bricklayers. A young construction worker, John Gilbreth, noted that bricklayers building a wall bent over each time they picked up a brick. Every single brick required that they lower and then raise half of their body weight rather than just the weight of the brick. His idea of putting the bricks on a scaffold at waist height seems, in hindsight, a simple solution with a dramatic payback. Productivity increased threefold.

Gilbreth went on to elaborate on the concept of motion study and developed, among other things, the idea that nurses could hand instruments to surgeons so that they need not look away from the life-and-death business at hand. The combination of Gilbreth's work and Frederick Winslow Taylor's work on time led to the scientific management principle of time and motion study.

This work is the ancestor of Lean. Scientific management, the assembly line, and the total quality movement are all proto-versions of what we call Lean today.* The bricklayer example is so pure in the application of Lean principles that we think it important to stop and point them out.

> First, the suggestion starts at the workplace, with an employee and not an external source or expert.
> Second, there is no elaborate business case—it's a slap-your-forehead-why-didn't-we-think-of-this-before moment.
> Third, there is very little investment or capital expense, and the results arrive quickly. If it were to prove ineffective, the scaffolds could quickly be removed.
> Fourth, and last, it is a simple, limited idea that does one thing better. It is not a redesign of the construction process or a grand unifying theory of bricklaying. We will discuss in more detail later how the strength of Lean comes from the cumulative effect of many small improvements rather than a dramatic and risky redesign.

From the Lean perspective, the young Gilbreth, looking at bricklaying with fresh eyes, was able to "see waste" in a process that had been established for hundreds, if not thousands, of years (one doubts that the management team for the Hanging Gardens of Babylon took much stock in the extra efforts of their workers).† This example is already 80 years old. Have we fallen into the same trap? Have we just replaced bricks and mortar with spreadsheets and clip art? Why can't we do the same Lean breakthrough for our massive service and information economy?

E-mail, especially when used as part of a back-and-forth process, is a prime example of modern office waste. Everyone seems to be complaining about this drain to their workday and people seem to have a choice—they can do their work or answer all their e-mail, but not both. There are many tips and articles about using flags, tags, categories, and Personal Outlook mailboxes to tame your

---

* Frederick Winslow Taylor, *The Principles of Scientific Management* (New York: Harper & Brothers, 1911).
† Gilbreth was an interesting fellow. His son wrote the 1948 autobiographical novel *Cheaper by the Dozen*, which described how Gilbreth often enlisted his large family as guinea pigs to experiment with motion theories.

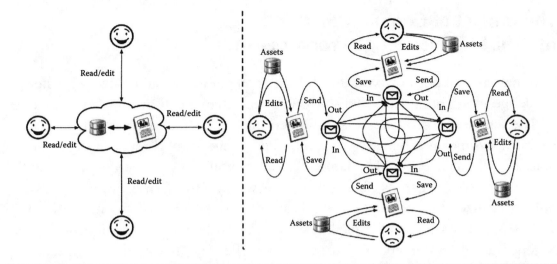

Figure 1.2 A Lean collaborative editing cycle versus the typical reply-to-all e-mail collaboration cycle.

inbox. E-mail has grown to the point that it either dominates your day, every day, or snowballs to unmanageability if you focus on other activities. Yet it need not be so.

Look at the diagram we call "the collaboration flower" (Figure 1.2; we will refer to it again in the e-mail-specific section), which represents two approaches to how a team can create a complex document such as an important PowerPoint presentation.* The collaborative Web 2.0 approach on the left is in marked contrast to the common practice (on the right) of e-mailing work-in-process back and forth, which is as inefficient as Gilbreth's bricklayers, but is a ubiquitous and unexamined part of almost every office's activity.

There are three main problems with "cutting and pasting bricks":

1. There are many extra steps.
2. There are several independent and private inventories (files on the users' hard drives) of electronic assets such as clip art, previously used diagrams/ photos, text from past presentations, and so forth.
3. This sequence of steps is unpredictable and it is likely that certain team edits will cancel each other out, will be duplicative, would have been better if synchronized, and so on. The simple elements of sequencing and delay drives error rates higher, increases rework, and significantly increases required time and effort.

Many improvements can be made in the high-tech office. Some of them are new but most already exist in young, smart companies. They need to be codified and distributed more broadly before we can see anything like the threefold improvement in bricklaying.

---

* This diagram was inspired from a presentation regarding the benefits of wiki's, which we cannot explicitly cite.

The Impact of Company Size and the Shift to Knowledge Worker Lean

Size matters, but not how you think. Large companies actually have a greater challenge in adopting Knowledge Worker Lean than small or midsize companies.

The Japanese word *kaizen* is translated into English as "improvement." Literally, *kai* means "change," especially the change management of the stakeholders is the challenge. Most large companies will see it written as KAIzen.

When Toyota began its phenomenal postwar industrial improvements, it quickly realized that it could not duplicate Detroit's degree of automation and scale with its lavish use of capital. It needed to find a way to do more with less. A generation later the student became the teacher and Toyota flabbergasted visiting Ford managers when they said, "We learned it from you."

In the same way, large companies have the large resource pools necessary to be inefficient. We've visited untold number of large sophisticated companies that conduct internal reporting by having managers and project leaders gather data, interview workers, and create a PowerPoint deck. This process can take weeks, the information is old before it is printed, and some of the sourcing is suspect or slanted. Worse, it is limited to whatever is on the slide; it's hard to query someone who answers "I'll have to get back to you" about any details.

Small companies, lacking the workforce to throw at a problem, often evolve quicker, technologically assisted means: a wiki for qualitative information, an intranet dashboard for quantitative information, and so on.

Smaller companies are less vested in their expensive enterprise resource planning (ERP) systems, they have a far simpler approval process, and, most important, they have a far simpler change management challenge because, well, they have far fewer people to change-manage.

Continuous Improvement: Theory Y, Generation X, and Info Pullers

The knowledge worker pool we are addressing has grown up with computers. Before computers became ubiquitous, managers wrote on yellow legal pads, which were then transcribed by secretaries, proofed, and retyped. Can you imagine? It took hours to get a memo out; today it takes each of us just a few minutes to do the same with e-mail (OK, maybe it shouldn't; more on that later). Now, modern managers may be doing their own typing, cutting and pasting, and perhaps even with more sophisticated analytics software. It may be hard to believe, but we expect that the current crop of office applications will go the way of the yellow legal pad just as quickly and their passing will go just as unlamented.

Consider the pace of change in our young managerial workforce. Seven of the top ten in-demand jobs of 2009 did not even exist as recently as 2004. Twenty-five percent of our knowledge workers have been with their employer less than one year. What might seem like a statistic pointing to mobility to the point of instability is actually great news for the performance improvement engineers and change agents out there. The resources they need to work with are far less vested in the legacy process than previous generations. They also are more accustomed to change. They have seen, and been part of, important changes just within the last few years. They have seen bedrock institutions, such as record stores and newspapers, become irrelevant or obsolete. It took radio 38 years to reach 50 million users, it took TV 13 years, but our knowledge workers adopted Facebook to that extent in just two short years.

More text messages were sent last year than the total population of the planet. Moreover, in the time it took you to read this far, four million songs were downloaded. The current crop of knowledge workers devours information like nothing ever seen before.

What's more, they are active. The tired image of the bureaucrat with an inbox, outbox, and a nonvarying process to push paper from one to the other does not apply. Knowledge workers today Google everything, at any time, including you as you are talking on the phone with them. They reach into the Internet to grab information 20 times per day. They can retrieve and reuse information and they value the ability to do so. You can think of them as information pullers, rather than paper pushers.

Often this unrestrained access to the ocean of information needs more managing than it gets. As we'll discuss, the out-of-sequence, multitasked, software-amplified use of information creates its own set of Lean wastes for knowledge workers and their employers. Much of our work hinges on developing a way to represent this fast-changing current state, analyze it, and improve it.

Finally, much has been said about the sense of entitlement that young workers have today. They have been receiving trophies merely for participating consistently since childhood. Many senior managers worry that they will fall apart at the first setback or failure. We don't buy it. More to the point, we don't care. We have found these Web-savvy workers to be stronger contributors to improvement programs than their seniors. As experienced consultants, we've learned that tenure is one of the biggest obstacles to the ability to accept change and adopt a philosophy of continuous improvement. Most entrenched company experts with 17 years of experience actually have 1 year's worth of experience repeated 17 times. They are so vested in their current way of doing things, they are unable to change. Worse, if they value experience, incumbency, and seniority more than the merits of the idea itself, they set the wrong tone for a Lean workplace. Lean workers, whether Knowledge Lean or Factory Lean, must be empowered to make suggestions, explain or defend their suggestions, and think for themselves.

Lean is highly vested in the so-called Theory Y* method of participative management. Knowledge workers don't need to be whipped into shape; they thoroughly enjoy their work and, on the surface, much of their leisure time is hard to distinguish from their paid time. Managers who understand this will allow them to take the responsibility and give them the authority to contribute toward projects they are committed to. The small scope, commonsense, and demonstrable improvement potential of Lean projects fit these resources like a glove. In addition, many knowledge workers are already vested in Web 2.0 philosophies such as collaboration, open innovations, knowledge-sharing forums, and so forth. Switching from an egalitarian Web world to a rigidly hierarchical office world is too much like the opening half of *The Matrix* for them. For best results, point them in the right Lean direction and step back.

If there is a key waste in the information age, it is a failure to capture all the intelligence and input and entrepreneurial power of the workforce. These men and women are smart. They will help your company evolve to new heights or they will help your competitors do so. Push them into the sclerosis of process conformity and company policy at your own risk.

Young knowledge workers today don't "use" the Web; they are perpetually "in" it. Entertainment, shopping, social connections, dating, and online gaming, not to mention information gathering and research are all ubiquitous activities. Their expectation is to find a detailed answer in near-zero time. They are quick to test and adopt tools; they swim in a Web marketplace that is continuously serving up new tools and techniques for review. The best asset a Knowledge Worker Lean (KWL) effort can have is smart, opinionated, young-in-spirit, information pullers—the kind who generate ideas like a fire hose that's broken loose.

How to Implement Lean in the Information Age

There are more Lean thinkers among us than you might imagine. A while ago, we were going through one of the most painful and inefficient processes that we are frequently subjected to: the airplane boarding process. So many things are wrong with this process, it's hard to know where to begin:

■ A broad front of passengers needs to be funneled through a very narrow opening.
■ The basic idea of boarding from the rear of the plane is largely ignored by passengers who are worried of losing out on the scarce overhead luggage space.

---

* In Theory Y, management assumes employees to be ambitious, motivated, and to exercise self-control. Employees gain satisfaction from doing their jobs well, not just from the desire for compensation or the fear of a rebuke from management. A Theory Y environment is characterized by open communication and certain amount of worker autonomy.

- There were so many turns so that the people collecting boarding passes had no visual cues as to the status of the actual boarding.
- There were duplicated steps. One flight attendant inspects your boarding pass at the beginning of the access ramp while another inspects the same boarding pass at the opposite end of this doorless, featureless tunnel, and so on.

As this progressed, the man next to us began one of those tentative conversations that grows as we noted similar interests and terminology. We spoke briefly, and, before we had actually gotten to our seats, we had come up with several Lean improvements for the boarding process:

1. It was obvious that the single biggest cause of delay was people placing their bags in the overhead and blocking the aisle. Therefore, we would give priority boarding for anyone without a bag. In addition, we would simply stress in the boarding instructions and perhaps with a couple of gentle signs on the gangway, to first step into your row and then put your bag up.
2. But worse, the control system in place was oblivious to the delays and exacerbated them. We were being rushed onto the plane by the gate attendant much faster than we could be seated. The result was a pileup in the gangway and aisle. What made sense to us was for the flight attendant, who was actually standing in the plane with a clear view of the cabin, to be the one calling the boarding for the gate from his or her microphone. This would "pull" us onto the plane rather than "push" us from the gate. Instead of filling spaces as they became available, we were crammed into a full access ramp and everyone's wait time increased dramatically.

The important part of the story is not that there are bad processes (we've been to airports, we knew that), but that more and more people see process change as their natural role. People are interested in innovation and change. Currently, this attitude is much more common in factories and assembly plants than it is in the white-collar office. There are explanations, if not justifications, for this:

First, factory workers in the Western world have been challenged by competition from cheap foreign labor for at least a generation now. The best way to fight back has been through productivity improvement. Some of this comes from the efficient use of capital equipment and some of it comes from process improvements such as reengineering or Lean efforts. Office jobs are also being outsourced of course, but this threat has not taken root as deeply as the loss of blue-collar work. There are some exceptions, such as call center work and various kinds of information technology (IT) development.
Second, and even more important, is the nature of the work itself. When Jim Womack and other early Lean authors wrote of the visual aspects of Lean,

they were drawing attention to the need to reinterpret activities and the evidence of these activities visible to us in the factory as waste. Stacks of excess inventory are not a safeguard against an uncertain supply so much as they are additional inventory carrying costs, additional space requirements, and a greater risk of unused or obsolete inventory. Learning to see waste and recognize it as such is a valuable perceptual shift or paradigm change for the physical process; but therein lies the rub. It is less help in the office.

How to Adapt Lean Methodology to Different Environments

As we continued to elaborate our office Lean techniques, we found that we were stretching Lean techniques more and more to make them fit. Frankly, we were valuing the theory more than the observed data—a common enough error. After a while, we developed the hypothesis that there are really three separate "Lean arenas," and, although all the fundamental principles of Lean apply for all of them, they do not all lend themselves to the same types of analysis. To be useful to each requires variations of the Lean tools and benchmarks.

Key Point: The three Lean arenas are:

Factory Lean—Classic Lean characterized by material flow and reverse metaflow information. Highly visible process and performance.
Paper Office Lean—The white-collar analog to Factory Lean. Characterized by material flow (in the form of documents, mostly paper but partly electronic). Largely visible.
Information Office Lean or Knowledge Worker Lean—No material whatsoever flows; documents are primarily electronic and can be printed if needed. Largely invisible.

The Lean arenas are all Lean in philosophy and approach, but there are some key differences. For example, in a factory environment, a workstation is typically dedicated to one activity at a time. Changing over to another operation or retooling is a key factor. That is why the conventional Lean tool single minute exchange of die (SMED) is such an important Factory Lean consideration. On the other hand, computer-based office workers are constantly multitasking. Their tasks shift simply by picking up the telephone, opening an e-mail, or hitting Control+Tab to switch applications on their computers. However, substituting second for minute (SSED) isn't the answer. This extreme multitasking (addressed at length in Chapter 4) is one of the key impediments to value stream mapping (VSM) for knowledge worker tasks. The data collection and quantification steps are very difficult to collect because the activities shift so frequently from one project to another. However, (later in that same Chapter as well as Chapter 5) we will describe ways to leverage technologies to capture this fast-moving data, which would be impossible to gather with a stopwatch and click counter.

In addition to multitasking, other office processes do not have a clear analog in the physical processes of a factory environment. Although it may not be immediately obvious, Lean methods can be applied to creative, iterative, and just downright fuzzy activities, such as engineering design. In fact, the benefits of Lean and the theory of constraints are greatest when the dependencies and statistical variation in the processes are high—conditions present in creative white-collar work, what we call knowledge worker activities. What's more, electronically supported information flow can take many paths, including simultaneous parallel paths, which paper-based information flow cannot. In addition, information flow is far trickier. Information can flow backward. The worker in step 12 for example, in order to get a head start on the project, might assume the value of the output in step 7 before the project reaches that step. Of course, if the actual results at step 7 are different, all the preparatory work done by the worker in step 12 is waste. Worse, the worker in step 7 can assume the value of the output in, say, step 12, in a common situation of mutual dependency. Now all the work in the intermediate steps that build on step 7 is at risk.

This is a new kind of waste, the waste of rework, which is different from the waste of defects. The work done in step 7 or 12 was not done incorrectly; it was done in the incorrect sequence. Something that is often impossible in factory-style physical assembly processes but is extremely common in white-collar work. Worse, computerized technologies magnify this problem by moving the information so quickly.

We will examine white-collar waste through the lens of the Lean philosophy. In a paper-based office environment, the analogs to a factory process are apparent and more or less readily applicable. The examples are different, the terminology is different, and there are some interesting discoveries, but traditional Lean thinking still applies.

The key difference is in the Lean concept of "learning to see,"* the technique of directly observing the work and shifting paradigms to recognize activities or assets that should actually be seen as waste. From this new perspective, things like in-process inventory don't represent a safety cushion; they represent inefficiently allocated resources. You can learn to see factory waste; you can learn to see waste in a paper-based office environment; but electronic information, the lifeblood of the high-tech office, is largely invisible. This makes information age waste different in several key ways from traditional wastes.

What is essential is invisible to the eye.

—Antoine de Saint Exupery, *Le Petit Prince*

---

* Made famous by Mike Rother and John Shook, *Learning to See: Value Stream Mapping to Add Value and Eliminate MUDA* (Cambridge, MA: Lean Enterprise Institute, 2003).

Some wastes, such as excess travel time, are not nearly as important in Information Lean as they are in Factory Lean. Electrons move so fast that physical distance per se is irrelevant. A more direct analog to travel time as it relates to information age waste is the number of handoffs: the distance is not important but the handling and time spent waiting in multiple inboxes is. Other wastes, such as the direct waste of time, become more important in a high-tech office. It is easy to see that a factory worker playing with a yo-yo is goofing off, but an office worker staring intently at his or her computer monitor might be engrossed in project accounting or surfing the Web for the latest viral videos on YouTube.

Figure 1.3 illustrates the idea of being "far from the factory." In the physical world of material handling and manufacturing, visibility is implicit—the work piece lies there before you or it doesn't. The paper-based office is in the business of "document assembly," which in a way is very similar to the factory environment. The electronic office is in the business of assembling and adding value to "bits" of information, not "atoms" of "stuff" that fly about at high speed accessed by a wide array of devices, which evolve and multiply at a dizzying rate. Not too long ago the phrase, "I got an RSS but couldn't text you so I sent a tweet before editing the wiki" would have made Lewis Carroll's "Jabberwocky" seem normal. Yet these are all commonplace terms now. The elusiveness axis in Figure 1.3 refers to the variability and unpredictability of the work. The metadata (delivery date, price, etc.) of a physical part may change but the part itself doesn't. However, when information is the work item, you have to plan on it changing even while it is being worked on. The old adage about changing the tires on a moving car is true for knowledge workers.

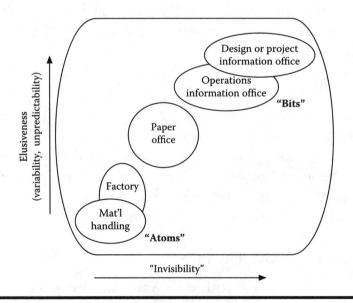

Figure 1.3 The Lean challenge is made harder the further from the factory environment you go because information flows tend to be elusive and invisible.

As we move on, we will describe wastes and drivers of waste that are of particular concern for high-tech offices that traffic in information. We will describe analytical techniques useful to address the major challenges of invisible and complex information flow. We highlight tools that may be valuable in these efforts. We will try to make the invisible office visible.

Chapter 2

It Came from the Factory: The Origins of Lean

Lean has spread from the factory into the office environment, but too literally and superficially. In this chapter, we describe the common elements of Factory Lean, its application to the paper-based office, and then focus on Information Age Lean and the implications of today's modern office tools.

From Factory Lean to Information Age Lean

Lean as we know it is usually considered a factory methodology, largely an adaptation of the Toyota production system, developed and improved throughout the second half the 20th century. Much scholarly work has been dedicated to show that many of these principles actually originated with either Henry Ford in the United States in the early 1920s or with the concept of takt time in Germany in the prewar buildup of the 1930s. However, from a practical perspective when people hear Lean, they think of a Japanese factory and its imitators. The frequent use of terms like *kaizen* and *poka yoke* does nothing to dispel that idea. The success and rapid adoption of Lean methodologies for factories and supply chains worldwide have been well documented. In much of the Western world, including the United States, legions of consultants and business authors have labored to bring these factory-spawned ideas into the office workplace.

The success and spread of what we now call Lean concepts in the factory (often mingled with ideas and approaches from business process reengineering, statistical process control, and the theory of constraints) have fostered the movement to capture these benefits in the office and service industries. However, as we pointed out in Chapter 1, the differences are significant enough that the study and application of Lean should be segregated along these lines:

1. Factory Lean (process flow)—This involves the physical movement of material. The information flow is metadata. The process is highly visual.
2. Paper Office Lean (paper flow)—This involves document flow and processing. Many analogs exist between it and Factory Lean although there is more multi-tasking and less visibility.
3. Information Age Lean (pure information flow)—This is typical in modern offices where most information moves electronically, and, therefore, invisibly. Multitasking is commonplace.

These three types of Lean roughly represent movement away from the physical factory floor to a level of greater abstraction and sometimes confusion. You can think of it as climbing from the factory floor, through the accounting department, to the product design group. We represent this in three tiers in Figure 2.1.

Visualizing Waste: The Factory Process

Let's start the journey that will take us into this third class of Lean for the knowledge worker with a basic factory example. In Figure 2.2, you'll see a stylized representation of the factory process. This factory uses a combination of machining tasks (represented by the gears symbol), manual assembly tasks (represented by a hand), and an outsourced activity to produce a final product (represented by the four-puzzle piece on the far right).

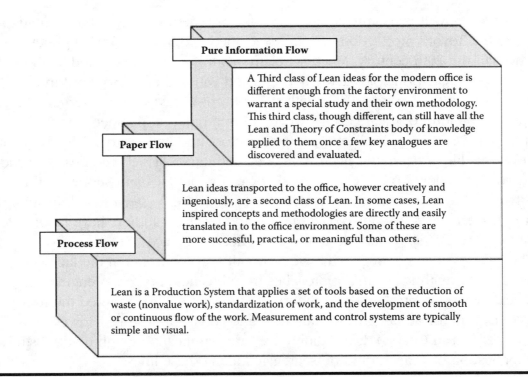

Figure 2.1 Evolution from process flow to pure information flow.

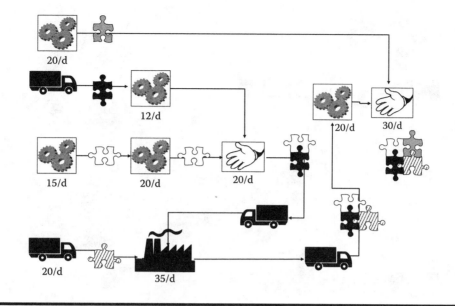

Figure 2.2   A stylized view of a typical value stream for production and outbound logistics describing four separate subassemblies.

Let's take a quick walk through this factory. On the first manufacturing line, we "machine" the gray puzzle piece. That piece, after what seems like a long trip, is manually connected (the hand icon) to the final assembly toward the end of the process. The numbers below the gears icon, which represents a machining operation, quantify that activity's output, which is 20 pieces per day. The same holds true for the production rates elsewhere in the figure. The second manufacturing line receives the black puzzle piece from a supplier and applies some machining steps to it before it goes to an assembly step, where it is combined with the third piece. The factory makes the third piece, first machining it from the white material and then modifying it in a second machining step before it goes to the assembly step.

Next, the subassembly, the output of lines two and three, is shipped to an outside vendor. This vendor combines our subassembly with the fourth hashed piece, which it receives from yet another vendor, and ships the three-piece subassembly back to us where we perform a machining step and perform the final assembly, combining it with the original piece from the first production line.

Readers experienced with Lean line balancing or the theory of constraints will have little trouble finding problems with this factory flow. Can you spot the bottleneck? You need all four puzzle pieces to complete the final product but the black puzzle piece in production line 2 can only be machined at 12 pieces per day, the lowest rate in our factory. This is our constraint. No matter what else is going on in the factory, we cannot complete our final product at anything above 12 pieces per day.

Now look at Figure 2.3, which adds some of the visual clues you would get from touring a real factory. Now that you have learned to see waste in the factory, you will have no trouble identifying it in this picture. For instance, there

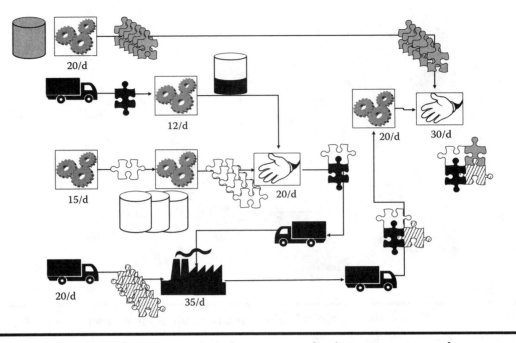

Figure 2.3 In a physical process you can learn to see classic Lean wastes such as excess travel, excess work-in-process, excess inventory, and line imbalance.

is too much gray and white raw material in inventory. There is significant over-production of both the gray and white puzzle pieces as they are stacked up idle and awaiting assembly, and, although this drawing is not to scale, it looks like we have transported an excessive quantity of the finished gray piece from where it is machined to the other edge of the diagram where it is assembled. It looks like there are at least two stacks of gray pieces either because they are moved in large batches or there just isn't enough receiving space at the assembly point. You might guess that you're paying top dollar for that 35 pieces-per-day outsource vendor and yet we're only feeding him 12 pieces per day. Pity since it looks like he's receiving and stockpiling the hashed pieces from another supplier at 20 pieces per day. Guess who's paying for all that unused material at our vendor's location? Chances are you are probably being charged for the additional off-site storage in addition to inventory carrying costs.

Before you can suggest changes to this layout or resourcing, you need to know several things. For example, you don't know anything about defect rates, charges from our outsourced vendor, or the make-versus-buy economics of the hashed piece. However, the most important thing you should want to know is what is the customer demand rate.

Takt time is defined as the total available time divided by customer demand. Keeping calculations simple and using integers, let's set the days in the production table equivalent to the available time in a normal working day. If the demand number is in the 10 to 12 per day range, the strategy might be to reduce your efforts in the first and third production lines and consider redeploying those resources to cover the activities that are currently being outsourced.

If, on the other hand, customer demand for final product exceeded the constraint, then you should do everything you can to alleviate this constraint. Production line 2 should receive all your attention. Perhaps you could add shifts or duplicate machinery or buy the component with the additional machining step already completed.

You already know or can guess what happens once you've alleviated the constraint on line 2. The 15 per day machining step on line 3 becomes the new constraint, and you start over and concentrate on this constraint. Don't be disheartened. Playing whac-a-mole with constraints is far more efficient than lavishing time, budget, and energy across the factory when only one small part of it requires those investments to actually improve performance.

Seven Types of Lean Factory Waste

In addition to line balancing and improving product flow, you, of course, must consider reducing waste. Let's briefly review the seven types of wastes typically found in a factory environment.

1. Transportation—You saw this in the gray piece of the first production line. There isn't enough information in the process description to identify other areas.
2. Motion—Excess movement, which can be improved in the process or in the factory space layout.
3. Waiting—All the assembly steps were frequently idle while they waited for certain components to arrive.
4. Processing—The example does not contain enough information to judge if some of the steps were unnecessary.
5. Inventory—There clearly was more inventory than needed in both raw materials and finished gray and white parts.
6. Defects—There isn't enough information regarding defects in our example.
7. Overproduction—This is the worst waste. In addition to its direct wastes, overproduction tends to generate the other wastes, creating inventory, requiring additional motion, transportation, and so forth.

Paper Office Lean

Many offices require the physical movement of material, typically paper, which is a close analog to a factory assembly line. For example, an accounts payable process requires the assembly of three incoming parts: the purchase order, the receiving ticket, and the actual invoice. This "subassembly" then undergoes relatively independent processes, arithmetic check, duplicates check, tax and accounting code check, and finally approval and payment processing. This kind of office process, in which information is physically moved from desk to desk, is becoming obsolete. Today, workers are supplied with information devices that can speed up their jobs, sometimes uncontrollably and with unpredictable results. The computerized cousin of this same accounts payable department might, for example, receive an electronic invoice from the vendor before receiving any of the other documentation. In that case, the accounts payable clerk uses his or her computer to pull a copy of the purchase order from the company's knowledge management repository, and sends an e-mail to the supervisor, who might reply from her or his Blackberry that the item was received. If there are incentives for fast payment, the accounts payable clerk could trigger an EFT (electronic funds transfer) to the vendor. The total cycle time difference between a paper-based process and electronically supported process can be as much as months versus days or even hours.

Environmental Waste Enablers

It is not a giant leap to point to some of the many basic environmental office factors that can contribute to or enable waste.

Office Layout:
- Bad lighting or ventilation
- Poor office layout, which results in excess travel time between resources who work closely together
- Poor ergonomics for workstations and cubicles
- Poor office equipment, low-tech or outdated tools
- Slow elevators or awkward stairs, which impede vertical movement in the building
- Routine traffic bottlenecks such as slow office building security sign-in procedures or congested parking
- Delays in the kitchen or snack room
- Poor supplies management—over- or understocking, delays in accessing routine items
- Lack of conference rooms, teaming rooms, or collaboration space
- Inefficiencies in shared resource management such as magazine routing slips
- The degree to which informal information sharing is limited to a single site or group, such as the water cooler network
- Paper memos routed by hand to inboxes
- Poor communication between offices in different time zones, which can result in voicemail and e-mail replies being delayed to the next day

Most of these factors contribute to excess travel and delays or somehow contribute to increased error rates in daily work. We will not spend much time on these as they have been covered by many other treatments of Lean and waste and, although they are important, our emphasis here is on the information side of things.

"Prosaic" Information Wastes

Tip: Rearrange office space and layout to minimize such waste as common travel paths and to facilitate and encourage communication.

Poor office layout and environment often results in a failure to communicate. A common theme in office waste is distance, barriers, and poor visibility between suppliers and customers, both internal and external. Such things as collaborative Web spaces—simple and highly visual—are a key element in correcting these problems.

In addition, other simple opportunities—such as posters, visually clear spaces that help visitors understand the reporting structures and processes of the office, and clearly demarcated visitor space—facilitate communication in the physical office.

In the real world, however, most work groups are fully occupied territory: every desk is taken, cubicle walls block views of who is there and who is not, face-to-face communication is a scheduled meeting that requires aligning everyone's schedule with precious conference room availability. One simple trick to increase communication is to create visitor space. Just like the visitor parking space in front of the door to the building, visitor space must be prime real estate, clearly marked as "visitor's only." A consultant or a vendor should not be allowed to camp out there for extended periods; it isn't reserved space to handle resource peaks. It should be "short-term parking" to encourage members of the other links in the supply chain to spend some time in your shop.

Information Environment Waste

The following sources of waste are common to paper offices:

- Limited/insufficient bandwidth provided to users
- One or two generation lag in software deployment while IT "verifies" stability and security
- Failure to integrate workers' devices, such as iPhones, into the total system
- Overly restrictive IT security
- Slow IT hardware or Help Desk support
- Limited, outdated, or "overly standardized" computer software tools
- Restrictive Virtual Private Network (VPN) or other network features
- Lack of administrator rights to PCs (it's hard to be creative and adapt to new tools)
- Small personal e-mail folders or document storage
- Poor intracompany communication (for example, paper newsletter and posters instead of broadcast e-mail, text messages, forums, tweets, etc.)
- Restrictions against USB port usage, notably hard drives
- Restrictive templates and standards of presentation

- Paper-based manuals and documentation instead of corporate policies and work process steps.
- Lack of wikis or blogs
- Knowledge management is centralized hierarchical instead of communal, flexible, and searchable
- Local systems information sharing (such as posters or wall charts) that cannot be seen by remote or teleworkers

All of these contribute to an environment in which the company is trying to stop the tide of new and innovative software and the evolving processes that leverage them. And these are pretty strong tides.

Administrative Wastes

Lean administration is of vital importance to your company because workers have one foot in their customer-facing Lean processes and another in their housekeeping administrative processes. If the admin side is non-Lean, it tends to dampen the overall culture of continuous improvement. A company cannot successfully have two fundamental ways of thinking while at the same time requiring employees to switch hats: now I'm Lean, now I'm not. Therefore, for Lean to succeed, you must also win over the admin side to some degree.

Administrative support processes in the corporate world are usually made up of support processes to the core business such as finance, human relations, procurement, and customer services. The support process rationale is to enable the business processes to perform.

C. Northcote Parkinson, a professor of history at Raffles University, Singapore, articulated the logic of how administrative work tends to expand in what has become known as Parkinson's law. "It is a commonplace observation that work expands so as to fill the time available for its completion." Parkinson had studied British Admiralty statistics, which demonstrated that in 1914 the British Navy had about 2,000 administrators and by 1928 the number had grown to 3,600 although the Navy had shrunk by a third in men and two-thirds in ships. This reflects what usually happens to administrative support processes, which tend to grow in responsibility as well as size. The Lean challenge with administrators is that they are not customer-facing or market-facing. They are more insular, exposed to fewer examples of change from other companies, and tend to compare themselves with themselves of the past, adhering to their written procedures.

Therefore, compliance becomes the measure of performance rather than continuous improvements. Administrative work is actually geared more toward continuous expansion than continuous improvement. Consider financial reporting. Usually, the scope of reporting gets broader and broader as management's need for information changes over time. As new analyses and facts are added, very little of the old information is cut away. It is easy to add but difficult to let go. We advise the administrative managers of many of our clients to stop all reporting for a period to see what happens and who starts asking for what type of information. In this manner, drivers and sources of administrative waste are identified and can then easily be eliminated.

In addition to this mismatch between admin supply and demand, we typically see waste grow in the interfaces between admin subprocesses and between the functional borders of the organization. "Customer" is a powerful word in business nowadays, but the phrase "internal customer" is not nearly as powerful.

In admin, the internal customer is the true customer. However, often there is less respect for deadlines and timelines when the administrative work is between internal suppliers and internal customers. Often, this is accompanied by a low level of understanding of the internal customer's (the downstream subprocess) requirements and even less understanding of how the downstream customer uses the products or information supplied. (This lack of situational visibility is addressed in more detail in Chapter 3, and we demonstrate how to model its effects in Chapters 7 and 8.) This dysfunctional approach to production in administrative support processes is another strong driver of administrative waste.

Yet another is the combination of nonstandardized in/out data reporting templates. This typically leads to multiple collections of redundant information and overlapping reports.

Administrative Drivers of Waste

Poor understanding of the customer's demand for administrative support results in an imbalance between customer demand and the administrative services produced. Upon examination, it often becomes clear that a gap exists between what the core business views as important areas for support and on what the administrative support process is focusing its efforts.

Tip: Look out for:

■ Reports not being opened or read, or parts of reports not being used
■ Information in reports presented in an unclear or complex way, leading to unnecessary questions and necessary actions not being executed

---

Some groups have a single-minded approach to extend the scope of the administrative services without eliminating any parts of the service portfolio that are no longer in demand. This results in overproduction and increased complexity. Continuing to add data and information increases complexity in the administrative support process and causes capacity problems in data storage. Response times get slower and unnecessary investments are made to support this increase in capacity.

Tip: Look out for:

- Reports being reformatted and downscaled to meet requests
- Data and information not being used in the analysis and decision-making process
- Unrealistically complex or thick reporting packages

WARNING SIGNS OF ADMINISTRATIVE WASTE

- Complicated and massive how-to instructions and thick procedures manual as a point of pride. Both of these make work harder to do and require extended interpretations of how to apply the rules. In addition, creating and maintaining such an extensive manual creates waste.
- Too many key performance indicators. These blur the big picture and force unnecessary analysis before action can be taken.
- Too much data and information collected, processed, stored, and thrown at customers for analysis and comments. Most of the data and information originates with admin and is pushed to internal customers rather than pulled as a result of a customer request.
- No connection to strategic drivers.

Low focus on customer requirements of the downstream subprocess results in incomplete production, overproduction, or late delivery. Some of the classical sources of waste—overproduction, rework, double work, waiting and incorrect processing—are usually found here. All this affects quality, cost, and lead time negatively.

Tip: Look out for time spent correcting errors, nonvalidated data being processed, too many reverse loops backward in the process, and a low percentage of deadlines met.

Symptoms of administrative waste in customer workflow include:

- Unclear deliveries between supplying and receiving subprocesses
- Rework, double work, and unnecessary iterations
- Low respect for deadlines and time plans
- Correcting errors accepted as part of the process

Lack of standardized templates for in-data collection and out-data reports results in manual rework, overlapping data requests, and overlapping reports. Waste shows up as unnecessary searching for information and data, lots of manual data and information handling, and overproduction.

> **Tip:** Look out for illogical flow in the information data model, templates that don't seem to fit into the process and between the various business areas, and repeated requests for the exact same data.

Symptoms of administrative waste in internal processes and templates include:

■ Multiple data entry points
■ Illogical reporting templates in different layers in the organization
■ Unclear definitions of data
■ Overlapping reporting formats
■ Unharmonized reporting templates and reports

STEPS FOR LEAN ADMINISTRATION

Focus on the value that the customer requests. This is an important first step. It's aimed at challenging the administrative support processes to ensure they actually are fulfilling the demand of the internal customer. Ask your Lean team to start by:

1. Identifying all the services being produced by the administrative support function and group them into a service catalogue.
2. Then asking the customers, that is, the users in the core processes and their stakeholders, whether these services fulfill their needs.

The aim is to identify how much overproduction or underproduction is going on. This gap is seldom obvious and this information will set the team's direction for the types of services and processes to improve and or terminate. However, the Lean team needs to be careful when identifying the demand from the different layers of customers in the core processes. Since these customers usually don't pay for the services being provided, the demand can be endless. Provide a base level of services and then package the extended needs of different customers into additional service packages to be provided. This will help you challenge variations in content and service levels.

Define the administrative value and the process for each service. Once the Lean team has identified the administrative support processes that actually are in demand, this is the right time to challenge the administrative process through the lens of Lean philosophy. What in the process has value and what has no value? Here the Lean team typically uses a value stream map to identify where "Leanification" activities should be focused.

Let customer demand pull the production of administrative services. The universal rule for applying Lean is to produce only on demand. Make sure that the producers of the administrative support services talk to their customers on a regular basis to get a full understanding of what they actually need. The same is true for the stakeholders of the administrative processes. Questions to be asked include:

■ What legal changes are coming up that will affect us soon?
■ What additional information is required by management to explain performance and progress to the external stakeholders?

Don't forget to eliminate administrative outputs and activities that no longer are in demand.

Seek endless perfection in the value delivered to the customer. The knowledge workers in the administrative support process are usually a bit distant from the end users and tend to have a softer attitude toward the internal customers' demand. The role of the knowledge worker in administrative support processes is often geared to checking and securing compliance to corporate procedures and routines. This focus on compliance is often at odds with the idea of embedding continuous improvement in daily work. The Lean team has the important task of raising Lean philosophy awareness among the administrative support staff and helping them to translate customer needs and values into action that may vary from procedure.

Case Study: Applying Lean to Administrative Support Processes

During 2007, the global head of the finance and accounting organization in a global construction company decided to start practicing Lean in its Shared Services Center. The manager of the Shared Services Center had been to Japan and studied Lean at some well-known companies with strong Lean credentials.

The introduction to Lean began with the department head and his associates introducing their coworkers to Lean, the philosophy, its history, and its fundamental principles. How Lean works was illustrated with cases from typical administrative work environments. The session inspired their coworkers and generated curiosity about how it might work within the Shared Services Center.

A smaller group of "Lean Agents" was selected, and they went through a series of training sessions where they learned to apply Lean Administration tools to typical finance and accounting processes. Nonvalue-creating activities were identified, as were the typical areas of waste. The Lean Agents learned how to conduct whiteboard meetings in which they visualized the process by establishing a process control board where the essential operational data as well as the process flow were presented. These agents, who in time developed into Lean Administration specialists, learned to use Lean Administration tools to identify, analyze, and identify improvements.

After a few intense weeks of education and training, Lean Administration was introduced to the whole operation.

- A systematic continuous improvement approach to work had been developed.
- Managers and coworkers were now practicing the Lean Administration tools in different daily and weekly activities. *They begin to see waste.*
- Every day, they measured frequency volume, errors, and waste. *They begin to quantify waste.*
- Coworkers started to use small improvement cards or journals next to their workstations where they documented improvement ideas they identified in their daily work.
- Each week, one or several whiteboard meetings were conducted with a number of coworkers. These meetings focused on and analyzed the implications of all the yellow Post-It notes that had been attached to the production control board during the previous week and were based on workers' ideas.
- Problems were analyzed by identifying their symptoms and their root causes.
- Improvement areas and specific ideas were identified.
- Problems were reviewed and discussed multiple times. The 5 Whys technique* was repeatedly applied until the problem was deeply understood by all the whiteboard meeting attendees.
- The group then studied different options for solving the root problem.
- A tailored improvement solution was decided upon.
- Responsibility for carrying out the improvement activities and implementing the solution was determined.
- Each week, the manager of the Shared Service Center gathered the Lean Agents to go through the previous week's production data. Together, they reviewed the identified wastes and suggested improvements, and determined the priorities for the coming week.
- Published progress and action plans empowered the coworkers and reinforced their Lean efforts.

---

* The 5 Whys is a root-cause investigation technique that, as the name implies, keeps exploring the cause–effect explanations by digging deeper. The 5 Whys technique, developed by Toyota, is an effective technique but is heavily dependent on the skill of the questioner.

■ Lean Agents and managers spent time on the "floor" to understand and solve problems by going where the problems occurred.

Tip: Look out for:

- Too many signature levels
- Too many levels of review
- More analysis or work than necessary
- Reworking of assumptions (the waste of correction)
- Contradictory inputs
- Excess effort gathering routine status and progress data
- Reports no one reads
- Extra copies, filing and handling of documents
- Unclear job descriptions and long learning curve
- Obsolete databases, files, and folders
- Overuse of manuals and other paper information
- Purchase orders that do not match quotation
- Errors—typos, misspellings, incorrect data
- Excessive wait time for information, at meetings, and so forth
- Poor office layout
- Unnecessary e-mails
- Data and progress locked in individual PCs
- Out of sequence work

Communication and Transportation: Spaghetti Diagrams

We can trace the paperwork product through this type of office in exactly the same way that we tracked material moving through processing stages in a factory. Figure 2.4, called a communications circle, is a handy diagram providing a shorthand version of the voyage of the documents.

This diagram tracks the paperwork from a construction site through the payment process. At the top, the vendor delivers the material and the job superintendent receives a delivery ticket. Later, an invoice goes from the vendor to accounts payable. Purchasing also sends the purchase order to accounts payable. The subsequent steps trace the approval process—the physical transfer of the documents from the construction site to the back office in the headquarters, and the subsequent processing of payment until it is dropped in the mail. This diagram identifies and counts the number of steps, but it doesn't quantify the amount of time involved, performance, or distance or delays for any one step. It is quite abstract.

The diagram in Figure 2.5, often called a spaghetti diagram due to its tangled complexity, traces some of the same information, but places it in physical context of distance and office layout.

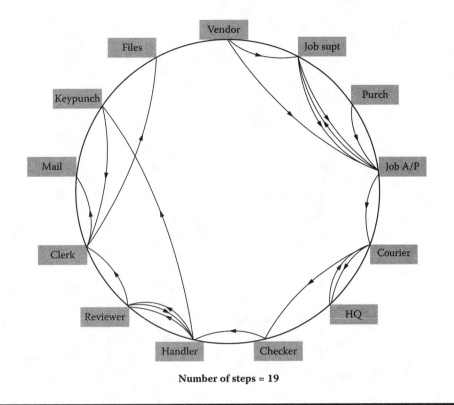

Number of steps = 19

Figure 2.4   A communication circle diagram highlights the number of handoffs in a process.

Here you can see the paper path and the amount of travel and number of hand-offs involved. Even though most of the workers are tightly located in one area, the need to travel to corner offices on other floors is the driver of excess travel. This is only one view, of course, and it doesn't include the travel time, wait time in all those inboxes, and so forth. The additional time for this process was in the 5 to 10 percent range. This would be particularly important to a check processing organization that has the chance to capture early payment discounts or incur late payment charges.

All of these observations are important dimensions of the process analysis and data gathering phase. They are relevant because the process was paper based and physically routed from one worker's inbox to another.

If this office had been using an automated payments systems, imaged documents in lieu of paper documents, received e-invoices, and paid via EFT, the spaghetti diagram would have looked very different. No routing of paper to inboxes, no back and forth to the fax machine, file cabinets, and mailroom. Nothing to keypunch. Later in this chapter, we will discuss how we would begin our Lean analysis of this type of information in an information age back office. We will analyze it in detail in subsequent chapters.

Tool Tip: Spaghetti diagrams can be created manually or with the aid of software tools. Figures 2.4 and 2.5 are representative. The communication circle was created using eVSM and the floor plan diagram was

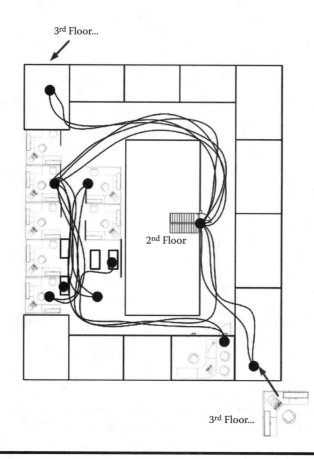

Figure 2.5   A spaghetti diagram overlays the process movement on a physical dimension to highlight travel.

done in Visio. We did use eVSM to quantify the travel, but the visual information was more than enough to get the point across.

To create a spaghetti diagram for a paper office, begin by drawing the office layout and noting the location of employee workplaces and office equipments. Note the location of storage, archives, stairwells, and coffee machines to help you trace and analyze unnecessary movements.

So, how do you create a spaghetti diagram for an information age (electronic) office that has relatively little paper to transport and relies on e-mail and the company intranet, and why do you need it? After all, if you accumulated all the time that your e-mailed files were actually in transit between routers and e-mail inboxes, the total would be a scant few seconds. The diagram is still powerful, but its spaghetti has a different flavor, one that emphasizes confusion rather than distance and implicit time away from your desk.

The traditional spaghetti diagram is still useful in the modern office to evaluate the locations of shared equipment such as fax machines (see later in this chapter) and printers or to analyze office layout and enabling physical interaction between resources whose work is tightly coupled. This seems a minor point, but it may not be.

Repeatedly, even in the most modern and high-tech organizations, we see a person promoted past the "cubicle level." The person gets a private office but since the only available office is all the way on the other side of the floor, the person packs up and dramatically increases her or his distance from the team she or he manages and constantly works with. Those six to ten people will now make three or four roundtrips to her or his office every day, forever. Half the time, they'll get distracted en route or find the boss isn't there or already has somebody there. Do the math. That private office is costing the company a lot.

In the same vein, many senior managers place their direct reports in the nearby offices, thus increasing these managers' distance from their respective teams. This is about not only the arithmetic of travel time but also the opportunity waste of missed chances to provide guidance or leadership, or failure to communicate priorities or status. Rank may have its privileges, but they should not extend to the wanton creation of waste. If they knew, customers and shareholders wouldn't be interested in paying for these extra costs.

The first line of defense against this argument is that location doesn't really matter. Wherever you can check e-mail and answer your phone is as good as any other place. At best we think this is only partly true and that electronic systems will have to be a generation better than they are now before they're enough, but more on this when we discuss what the Web 2.0 will bring in the future.

Tool Tip: The e-mail spaghetti diagram is easy to draw for a fixed process. You can create one for each use case or process description. Basically, you overlay the "who" part of the process description with the actual organization chart (see Figure 2.6).

Figure 2.6 is an information spaghetti diagram. It highlights information flow for the process against the resources receiving, sending, or handling that information. The black curved lines represent a core process for the organization,

The picture these spaghetti lines convey is one of many handoffs, several recursive iterations, and a great deal of implicit delay. Unlike factory spaghetti lines, these can have branching and dead ends; it is possible to send information to multiple locations simultaneously, but it is not possible to walk to several locations simultaneously. And the dead ends represent locations where the information is received but not subsequently processed. Sometimes this represents cc'd information and sometimes filing; usually it represents waste. It's important to recognize that these lines represent just one project in an organization that had about 300 in its active pipeline. You can imagine what a complete spaghetti diagram would look like.

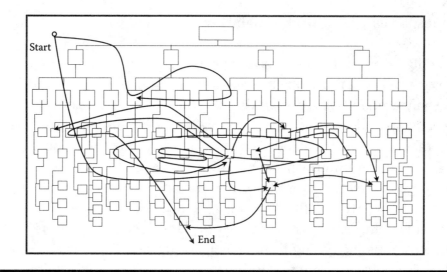

Figure 2.6   An information spaghetti diagram shows information flow overlaid onto the organization chart.

We have also left out all the metaprocesses associated with this. These include status reporting, resource requests, scheduling conference rooms, and a host of other adjunct activities that are usually ignored but increase in difficulty and cost as these core processes increase in complexity and cross multiple organizational boundaries.

This group, like most, is organized in vertical silos. Management directives and priorities tend to move north–south. Yet the process shows a great deal of east–west movement and the repeated crossing of organizational boundaries. Since senior management (the only resources that can coordinate across multiple silos) are hardly involved in this process at all, it seems likely that these boundary crossings and handoffs will generate a great deal of wasted time and effort.*

The information spaghetti diagram serves the same purpose as the traditional one. It creates "did you realize that" awareness. This group was highly computer-based and considered themselves accomplished multitaskers. Many of them had formal Project Management Institute (PMI) certification for project management. All top talent and well managed, but the invisible nature of information flow coupled with time pressure kept them from seeing all this transport and all these handoffs. There were no overflowing in-baskets of paper, no temporary stacks of work orders awaiting attention, and so forth. Any walk through the office would have shown smart people, fully utilized, and busy bustling around in a seemingly productive way.

---

* Naturally there will always be some form of escalation process to resolve disputes and deal with emergencies. Most processes do not include these in their description and the goal of the process designer is to minimize this rather than to rely on it.

The Sad Fax Facts

One of the themes of this book is the proper integration of emerging software and hardware tools into a Lean office environment. Often these tools initially "pave the cow path"; they use updated tools to accelerate, not necessarily improve, the existing process. These accelerated processes have not redefined the purpose of the process and driven out waste. In fact, they can create new, unanticipated wastes. For example, the ability to copy electronic files in one or two keystrokes has eliminated retyping documents but has made version control of evolving documents tougher for workgroups. Before tackling electronic work, let's look at the interim hybrid stage of paper and electronic transmission: the fax machine.

Few things in the modern office are as archetypal a generator of waste as the fax machine. They are easy to replace with modern-day equivalents such as e-fax services that deliver a PDF to your e-mail account or full-featured fax servers, yet many businesses continue to use faxes, perhaps because the physicality of the paper somehow seems more real or legally binding.

But consider all the wastes that your fax machine is responsible for, day in and day out:

- Direct waste of resources—The fax hardware itself and the opportunity waste of the capital tied up in it, the consumption of paper, toner, and electricity, and the use of a phone line.
- Waste of travel—Back and forth to the fax machine.
- Waste of time—Waiting for the fax to be scanned, waiting for the fax to finish printing, and waiting for the people ahead of you to finish.
- Extra processing waste—The document is probably already in electronic form, so to use a basic fax machine you must print it before faxing it. Then you may file it "just in case" along with your fax receipt. All this consumes time and space.
- Delayed processing waste—The overall communication cycle is much longer, on both ends, and the fax might be set aside or placed in a bin until the recipient arrives to collect it.
- Error waste—Faxes can be lost, smudged, or unreadable, and may be misplaced.
- Extra maintenance, materials inventory, and space set waste.
- Idleness waste—Even in a busy office, the fax machine has a low utilization throughout the day. If people walk to the fax and find it busy, they often leave and repeat the trip and wastes later.
- Inconvenience waste—Walking to shared fax machines leads to a proliferation of private faxes or, worse, a dedicated fax operator.
- Inconvenience to customers or colleagues—More people have e-mail accounts than personal fax machines, so why submit those on the other end of the fax to all these wastes?

Tool Tip: If you want to get a read on how your kaizen or Lean team is doing, nothing beats face-to-face meetings or discussion. Few approaches are worse than relying on e-mail communication. Even if you do have physical meetings, it's best to summarize and attribute the team's ideas, positions, and working hypotheses in an open way. We prefer a dedicated intranet site where the team's work, progress, and assignments can be tracked and accessible to all, especially "tourists," who just come by the site to look. This credible and tangible example is one of the best ways to spread Lean through the organization.

Although this community or social approach is great for the team, it will fail to capture the reactions and concerns of the extended stakeholder group—the silent majority that may review the site but are not likely to contribute to blogs or post questions. You need a combination of push and pull tools for this. An excellent device is to place a Google Moderator page on your site and actively push for and track contributions. For an extended group, an e-mail-based survey instrument such as those provided by SurveyMonkey.com is very simple and cost effective.

Another simple and useful tool is a Q&A polling tool such as Doodle.com. The link is pushed to your selected users and the results can either be open to all, which acts as a societal prod to respond, or only available to the moderator who can then summarize the poll results. Of course, as with all surveys and polls, a small number of carefully crafted questions are the key to success.

Information Age Lean

You can classify office wastes into four broad areas. This is a high-level taxonomy, not an enumeration of specific wastes. (We will go into more detail within these categories as needed, and the details will vary in importance depending on whether we are describing waste in the factory, the paper-based office, or the information age office.)

1. Information handling and processing—This is the group of wastes affecting the main work stream and process of getting work done. These products are key because they are customer facing (whether the customers are internal or external customers doesn't matter; whoever receives your work is your process customer). This is the area we are most interested in: the work process and supporting tools.
2. Administrative support process—These are the internal, non-customer-facing processes, such as developing internal budgets, performance reviews, expense account processing, accounting, and many more that keep the

office functioning. Often waste comes from a disconnect between the customer-facing (aka revenue-generating) processes, and the risk- and control-motivated support processes. How often have you heard people complain about the administrative hoops they have to jump through to get approval for a small-ticket item needed on the project?

3. Office layout and infrastructure—The office environment itself can contribute to or in some cases be directly responsible for waste. Factors such as a noisy environment, high cubicle walls, outdated software tools, and segregation of teams and work groups can all drive waste. As important as this is, it is slightly less important in the information age office than in the paper office. Knowledge workers need to collaborate with far-flung colleagues, vendors, and telecommuters. Too much emphasis on solutions in the physical office tends to devalue these other important resources. For us, the emphasis is on virtual layouts and work streams regardless of location.

4. Knowledge waste—The bright young and technologically savvy workforce is the key resource. Cultural or organizational factors that inhibit or dilute their contribution is arguably the greatest waste of all. A key factor for Lean success in the information age is team members who are aware of current technologies, can identify and analyze problems from a Lean perspective, and are motivated and encouraged/permitted to develop solutions accordingly.

Visible Waste: The Parts We Can See

For IT Lean there are certain wastes that are readily identifiable when you look at legacy operations from a Web 2.0 lens. These center on expensive legacy tools or enterprisewide software whose functionality is often exceeded by less expensive, if lesser known, competitors. These ideas imply visible changes such as switching software platforms and we examine some of these in the following sections. But then we move on to the indirect implications of some of these tools: the lack of visibility and collaboration, and the high error rate from miscommunication and poor coordination; in short, all the consequences of working with invisible information.

Software Waste

How many software tools does your work computer have? General office personnel may only use two or three applications. Some workers' computers are simply glorified e-mail terminals. On the other hand, scientists, researchers, engineers, designers, software developers, and many others use dozens of separate applications, although only a few of them are used regularly. Clearly, unused or underused software is an obvious waste.

For simple tools, one new Lean solution is to use Web-based or SAAS (Software as a Service) tools. Some of these tools are open sourced and are either free or have minimal cost. Others are on a monthly subscription or on a pay-as-you-go basis. This is an excellent solution for midscale software—a project management planning tool, for example—that is used frequently but nowhere near constantly. Why pay to have the box on the shelf? An added benefit of this approach is that it also solves the problem of maintenance and upgrades—whenever you log on, you have the latest and greatest by default.

Of course, one of the enablers of software waste is the implementation of a companywide software toolset policy. Many companies have a "standard," which they distribute to all employees. Experts, who may require specialty packages, often have to jump through hoops to obtain these needed packages, whereas many clerical personnel never touch most of their standard kit. If only we had a nickel for every shrink-wrapped office manual sitting in those cubicles!

Tool Tip: Many knowledge workers are married to their BlackBerries and iPhones. Most frequently check e-mail via VPN or work at home, on the weekends, or even on vacation. They are becoming used to modern tools provided by vendors outside their organizational IT but which interacts with it. This trend will continue. For example, many people use tools such as GOTOMYPC to access the files stored on their office computers from home or on the road. Another approach is to use a neat little tool such as Dropbox, which is actually a Web-based storage volume that functions just like the hard drive on your computer except that it is shared by all your computers or your group's computers. For example, you can file your document to Dropbox from your work PC, and open it from your Mac at home. There's no synching because there is only one file. Shared storage is far from new, but it is remarkably easy to do now, which makes sharing information between your work and home computers, or between work groups, commonplace.

The next evolutionary step is to have your applications and utilities—not just your files—on the Web. One of the advantages of Web-based document storage or Web-based applications is that it allows you to be extremely mobile. Use any computer anywhere, and have the exact same features, functionality, and document access as if you were using the one in your office. Computers become access ports similar to pay telephones (remember those?) ubiquitous and democratic, but just as pay telephone users largely switched to mobile phones, people will probably migrate computing to the next generation of handheld computers. It is too soon to tell whether these devices will look more like Netbooks or iPhones or something in between. They will, however, be designed around the key factors of size, battery life, and instant on. The latter is critical if they are to serve as a two-way communicator and is possible because these devices do not have an elaborate operating system—they just get you to the cloud. In any case, you will have a

pocket or at least pocketable computer that will have fast access to your
personal workspace and tools, not just the Web.

IT departments cannot easily control many of these tools and approaches;
indeed they are designed to be used by everyday consumers trying to address
a need and not by professional IT personnel. What will happen as IT departments bar more and more of these new powerful services? First, it will provide a
tremendous competitive advantage to the smaller competitors who do not labor
under these prohibitions. Second, it will create a backlash among workers who
finally get fed up with having better tools when they work from home than their
own corporation provides.

This change is inevitable. Just as mainframe IT finally allowed those pesky
personal computers to come into the company, LAN IT will have to allow these
modern features in. Trying to develop the equivalent functionality in-house
means competing against the entire innovative strength of the market, an uncom-
petitive strategy.

Specialty software is a big expense. Low demand means that all the expensive,
groundbreaking development costs must be spread over a relatively thin base
of users. You won't find this kind of software on the shelf at your local Staples.
Rather these are the kinds of tools that provide vital analyses or insight, yet are
not used 100 percent of the time. They are expensive occasional tools such as
high-end computer-aided design (CAD)/computer-aided engineering (CAE) systems, simulation software to study factory layouts or complex supply chains,
specialized medical or other vertical industry software, and so on.

One Lean approach to avoid wasted expense is to activate these licenses via a
USB dongle. In this way, several users can share the same occasional-use application simply by passing the dongle around. Only one copy is in use at any one
time and the vendor has only sold one license; essentially, they're getting paid for
the dongle. (There are also software-based flexible licensing approaches, favored
by IT because they are centrally controlled.)

The upside for the vendor is that many more customers become aware of their
tool and spread the word or take this tool preference with them to their next
employer. Their dongle licensing in no way cannibalizes their sales the way a lite
or student version does and, if the power of their tool is recognized, the team
will need more dongles to satisfy demand.

Some extremely sensitive security locations disable USB ports to impede data
loss through USB drives. Such companies would probably also balk at SAAS solutions. *Security can be more expensive in its side effects—process delay and limitations—than in its direct implementation costs.* Don't be hypersensitive. Make sure
you have the security you need and not one jot more.

Software Expense

With the exception of the operating system itself, the most common applications are the office suite tools. This field is dominated by Microsoft Office, which won the office wars long ago with its combination of product quality, bundling of useful applications, and tight interconnection of its products with its operating system. These tools and, more important, the file formats they generate are the de facto standard in business. As of this writing, the street price for MS Office is approximately $400 for the full-powered version. Large enterprises, of course, purchase site licenses and have their own IT people install the software on workers' laptops or desktop computers.

The problem with a one-size-fits-all suite of software is that it really only fits the needs of a very small percentage of the workforce. Most clerical staff use Excel very little and rarely, if ever, delve into its deeper powers. The majority of Word users still seem to format everything with hard tabs, hard carriage returns, and so on. Of course, in the aggregate, there are many power users, but how many individual Office application installations that are fully utilized? If you learned that you were incurring a major expense for something that was being used to only 10 or 20 percent of its capability, wouldn't you investigate further?

When companies evaluate this type of software, the dominant, if not the only criterion, seems to be the number of features, not ease of use, productivity, cost effectiveness, time to answer, or anything of the sort. A small percentage of the users dictate the purchase because they must have certain advanced features and everyone else gets the same tools so they can open each other's files. Doesn't seem very Lean.

Be warned that this topic tends to generate passion nothing short of a debate on the Second Amendment: "You can have my Excel when you pry my cold dead fingers from the macros ..." Still, there are cracks in the edifice of Office. There are a half-dozen capable competitors struggling to survive by offering very low prices, high feature count, OS transparency, and file compatibility. Some are the not-quite-dead desktop applications and some are the new breed of Web-based applications.

There are many word processors, spreadsheets, databases, and so forth in the software market, but we're discussing the bundled suites that you would expect to be delivered to knowledge workers as a standard toolset. In addition to Office (in its many forms: Student, Standard, Small Business, and Professional) and its lite cousin, Works, there are several players: OpenOffice, StarOffice, and IBM Lotus Symphony. These actually share much of the same DNA: StarOffice is the supported version of the free OpenOffice and backed by Sun Microsystems. It has many features beyond Office including, for example, a drawing package, database, PDF import/export, and support for Linux. It also has several collaboration and document sharing features—we're quite keen on this—such as workbook sharing and a built-in wiki tool, and it costs about one-tenth the price. It's an excellent choice for small and even large offices. (There are indications that MS Office will include online collaboration and such features in its next version.)

However, this is not the place to make the case for switching your desktop suite even though we would love to test the Lean point that anything the customer wouldn't want to pay for should be considered waste. (What would happen if you gave employees $400 and told them they could buy either MS Office or StarOffice, their choice, and keep the change?)

The real reason to talk about alternatives to Office is to discuss the new breed of Web-based tools. These offer not just a one-time savings at time of purchase but true and sustainable process improvements. The best known of these is Google Docs, but Thinkfree and Zoho are strong players. Thinkfree looks so much like MS Office that it might be easier to switch to it than to adapt to new versions of Office. In their current form, these tools have a lot of breadth but not quite as much depth and polish as their desktop cousins.

The ability to access your documents from anywhere or to easily link someone else to your documents is nice, but the real benefit is in work process streamlining. Anyone who has e-mailed evolving versions of large documents within a team has experienced this pain: the intrinsic waste of multiple copies of the same document, the rework waste that inevitably results when different members of the team make contradictory or negating edits, or build-on sections that will be discarded by others, and the far greater potential for error that comes from having so many separate-but-equal versions. As Google says on its Web site, rather than attaching a document to an e-mail, attach e-mails (invitations) to the central document.

The whole company needs file sharing, improved search capability, enhanced collaboration, and the use of a basic set of features. But only a small percentage of power users need the entire feature set offered by most office suites and packaged software (see Figure 2.7). So why does the corporation spend the money to give everyone the "evaluated winner" among software tools when most of that functionality is wasted? Is it because this small group of experts is involved in the evaluation? Why does the tail always wag the dog? Our point is that these experts alone would get the full package or the extra software and, because they

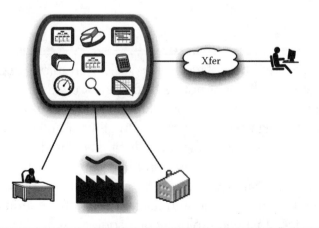

Figure 2.7 Most office, field, and telecommuting workers can share tools in the cloud. Power users can transfer data and results to these formats.

are experts, can easily convert their work to and from the universally compatible format. This happens every day when outside service providers transmit work to and from their customers.

This problem has been perpetuated in part by pundits and reviewers, who gravitate toward the high end of features and capability, despite the fact that the great majority of users do not share their criteria and would prefer something more intuitive and focused on the most common uses.

There are adoption challenges here as well. In seeking to lessen bloat, you not only encounter the natural resistance to change and fewer features argument, replacing the suite of tools increases the statistical likelihood that you are impacting somebody's favorite tool. To make such a change work, you need to build on existing successes such as shared calendars. Introduce one new tool, for example, a master scheduling or project management tool or a "special" presentation tool that makes multimedia slides but also supports online delivery, from which workers can reap immediate benefit. This is the *Lean corporate penetration strategy* in a nutshell: start simple, demonstrate success, spread to other areas.

Mapping software is a good example of the coming future developments. Until recently, these were desktop applications requiring subscriptions or the purchase of updates every year. Now, this segment is dominated by online maps that offer previously unimagined features. In addition to efficient routing between two points, you can add satellite views, hybrid views, bird's-eye views, plus a mass of up-to-the-minute local information. It's not that the roads are changing so quickly that software distribution by CD and so forth can't keep up; the real issue is that innovation from Web-based map producers is coming at such a fast pace that the whole concept of a version no longer really applies. It is truly a matter of continuous improvement and perpetual Beta. We suspect that questions like whether to upgrade to Office 2007 or stay with the 2003 version will become as archaic as synchronizing your watch to the city hall clock tower. Your online software will always be improving. You will notice some improvements immediately, others not.

Tool Tip: Perhaps the best place to start a slow, insidious migration to the collaborative Web might not be through an office suite, but through presentations. SlideRocket is a PowerPoint-like competitor that is purely Web-based allowing access and editing to all your collaborators without the constant e-mailing of massive, slightly changed slide decks. Not only is the act of collaboration simplified and wasteful e-mails and possible errors eliminated, but you have a far better workspace. All the assets are centrally maintained and tagged; no more scouring your hard drive for that deck that had the particular squiggly graphic you need.

If you haven't experienced this improvement, you're in for a treat. This is a real productivity game changer: like that magic moment in the first Visicalc demonstration when all the numbers just updated automatically and a hundred-year tradition of green pads and calculators instantly became obsolete.

Best of all, the product results are gorgeous. There's no feature or quality compromise like there is in using an online spreadsheet. SlideRocket produces multimedia decks as attractive as anything Steve Jobs wows his audience with in Apple's Keynote, and it's all done in the same process-efficient Lean way of Google docs. If you spend a significant percentage of your time creating decks—especially in looking for assets to add to your deck or with which to edit others' decks—you need this tool.

Invisible Waste: The Parts We Can't See

Early in Chapter 2 we looked at diagrams of a factory process to illustrate the concepts of waste and line balancing. When you look at this factory problem, it really has limited dimensions. Our example deliberately ignored many other important aspects such as quality and cost. But suspend disbelief for a moment longer. It's largely about balancing. We must balance the output to the customer demand and balance the various production lines so that one slow component doesn't dictate the performance of the entire operation. The unspoken underlying principle in this factory process diagram is that material and time flow left to right. This seemingly fundamental behavior is violated in information-intensive office processes.

Unlike a physical process, we're interested in more than just a mismatch of rates when we begin to review high tech information flows. The Gantt chart, Figure 2.8, represents the way things are supposed to flow in an R&D (research and development) organization—each activity following its predecessor in a clean, finish-to-start succession, but in reality other flows exist even if the official project stage seems to follow the Gantt chart.

The thin lines represent information flows. Those below the Gantt chart tasks represent parallel flows. This figure shows that a downstream activity is getting information about the results of an upstream activity in an "out-of-process" way. Typically, this is because the downstream resources want to get a head start on their tasks or because the official process is slow and they seek to circumvent the normal communication path. In the pre-electronic age this wasn't possible; a telephone conversation could not carry enough information to provide the basis for design work. But with e-mail, Web sites, and so forth, it's common for workers to ask to be cc'd on many such upstream tasks, even if they consider it only a "nice to have" piece of information.

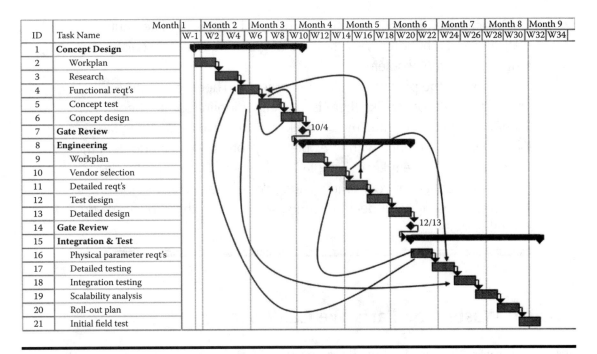

ID	Task Name	Month 1		Month 2		Month 3		Month 4		Month 5		Month 6		Month 7		Month 8	Month 9
		W-1	W2	W4	W6	W8	W10	W12	W14	W16	W18	W20	W22	W24	W26	W28 W30	W32 W34
1	**Concept Design**																
2	Workplan																
3	Research																
4	Functional reqt's																
5	Concept test																
6	Concept design																
7	**Gate Review**																
8	**Engineering**																
9	Workplan																
10	Vendor selection																
11	Detailed reqt's																
12	Test design																
13	Detailed design																
14	**Gate Review**																
15	**Integration & Test**																
16	Physical parameter reqt's																
17	Detailed testing																
18	Integration testing																
19	Scalability analysis																
20	Roll-out plan																
21	Initial field test																

Figure 2.8 A Gantt chart's dependencies do not typically include hidden out-of-sequence or recursive information flows.

People think they are doing a good thing by getting a jump-start as information becomes available. In product development, for example, the engineering department may release information early, which is picked up by purchasing to get pricing, industrial engineering to develop layouts, and many others, and they all believe they're creating value by starting early. What we repeatedly find is that all they're doing is generating the waste of correction. All this stuff will change, and it is very predictable that it will change, and it will maybe change several times before you have the information to do the job right. With GMS, staff is now identifying processes that they should not start until good data is in hand and they can perform their role right the first time.

**—Lou Farinola, director of the General Motors Global
Manufacturing System (GMS)**

What Farinola is describing, which we will expand upon and represent diagrammatically in the matrix section, is the information age error of mistaking continuous flow with speed. They are not the same. Getting a head start on your part of the continuous flow of information is about as effective as dancing faster than your partner simply because you can. Multitasking is also partly to blame here. The logic is "while I am waiting for X, I might as well get started on Y," which seems sensible on the surface but can create a greater unintended negative consequence than any potential benefit.

The thin lines above the Gantt chart activities (Figure 2.8) represent back-flowing information, which occurs whenever an information worker makes an assumption (or mistake) about a piece of information that hasn't been officially created. This piece of information is essentially traveling back in time. If we were designing the heat sink on an air conditioner, for example, we would need to know what the total heat load will be. We use a value—we assumed it, we infer it from the documentation, we took it off the vendor Web site, we used the value from the last similar air conditioner we designed, or it was given to us. Now we've done our bit and other designers will locate the compressor, route wiring, and so forth around our piece. As it happens however, marketing decides that air conditioners shouldn't look like shiny aluminum boxes; they should look greener and friendlier, like a boxy bush. Instead of a reflective coating, it's covered in a matte green finish. Poof! All the thermal assumptions we made are wrong and we have to resize our heat sink and all the work done by others based on our earlier design will have to be reviewed or redone. Sure, the requirements should have been frozen (from my perspective) and marketing should have developed their friendly bush plan much sooner, but the world is imperfect.

The other interesting type of out-of-process information flow is circuit flow. In Figure 2.8, the fourth and fifth steps in the Gantt chart seem to be mutually dependent—a chicken-and-egg relationship as shown by the communication lines. This is fine in this case because you want to have mutually dependent activities as close to each other as possible, and this is just another way to represent an iterative step. Sometimes, however, these information circuits are bigger, often much bigger, and sometimes they cross organizational boundaries, which impairs the tight communication necessary for truly iterative design, and occasions priorities that are at odds with one another (critical for one, but dependent on the iterations of another who thinks it low priority), and places all the intermediate steps at risk. This situation is one of the biggest causes of the waste of rework.

As communication paths increase with technology, this situation of parallel, backflow, and circuit flow information is getting worse. All the new branching and overlapping electronic means of communication act as accelerants to this information fire.

In subsequent chapters, we will expand on this concept of information flow versus process flow, and we will develop a concise diagram to represent it as well as a methodology to analyze and improve upon it.

Chapter 3

The Perfect Information Storm

People have enthusiastically adopted many modern tools and information devices only to feel overwhelmed by the volume of data and complexity they bring. As a result, we have largely been paving the cow paths—*accelerating processes rather than improving them*. We are approaching a tipping point that will drive us to adopt better tools.

The Evolution of Information Systems and the Impact on Lean

If we have learned one thing from the history of inventions and discoveries it is that, in the long run, and often in the short run, the most daring prophecies seem laughably conservative.

—Arthur C. Clarke, *The Exploration of Space*

Processes, people, and tools are interwoven into the complex systems of business. Some of these elements can be extracted to be worked on or improved independent of the others. An interim software upgrade is a good example of this.

Often, however, there is a natural feedback, sometimes delayed, among these three key elements. Give an organization that produces paper documents for clients a new tool or capability, overnight delivery for example, and you will see that its delivery process changes accordingly; the extra days afforded by this are too valuable to ignore and the deadline becomes the day before it is due. Evolve this to e-mail and PDFs and the company adapts to same-day delivery and eliminates all the steps and the time it takes to print and bind the documents.

The recent past, the present, and near future can be categorized as three distinct phases (see Figure 3.1) in the evolution of information systems, and this evolution has largely been driven by the available tools.

Before the Web, documents were produced on paper, either handwritten or typed. This dictated a sequential processing. There were some parallel

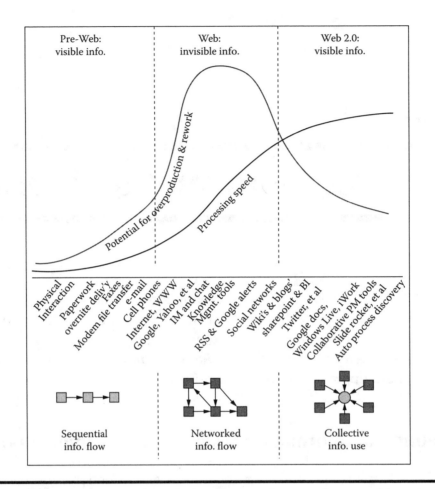

Figure 3.1   The first phase of Web evolution increased processing speed but also waste.

information flows: you could make a phone call to get a small piece of information, but, more likely, that phone call would be to request another document containing more information than could conveniently be verbally transmitted. Inventory was kept in the supply cabinet. Work-in-process was in your wooden or metal inbox. Completed product was mailed in an envelope to be delivered by the post office or messenger (inter- or intracompany) and filed in a multidrawer cabinet. All very visual and simple to understand.

Then the Web and a host of other tools exploded onto the work scene and dramatically accelerated everything. E-mails and electronic files replaced interoffice envelopes and file cabinets. We were able to get information in support of our work very quickly and from multiple sources in multiple places. Information flow became networked, and it became largely invisible. Colleagues can no longer tell if you are busy by glancing at the stack of papers on your desk. These invisible communication networks had their own problems: overloads and bottlenecks, out-of-sequence flows, version control, duplicate files, and so on.

It therefore seems logical that the next, inherently Lean step in the evolution will keep all the benefits of speed but will increase the situational visibility and effective collaboration of high-tech workers. Whether the technologies are called

Web 2.0, cloud computing, or something else, the basic functional requirements of high throughput, less waste and rework, will be met.

The Recent Past: The Dim Days before the Web

All our computers, cell phones, and gadgets have become so commonplace that it is almost difficult to imagine what an "information intensive" office environment was like just a short eyeblink ago.

The Early Days: Longhand–Wang–Printer–Fax

In the early days of the electronic office, small personal computers were starting to make their presence felt but they weren't as common as dedicated word processors made by Wang and others, and their software was limited. Modems (strictly low baud telephone lines) were around, but faxes were far more prevalent and came with a far simpler user interface. Overnight shipping was becoming commonplace. Xerox machines were the dominant piece of office equipment and every small office had an IBM Selectric typewriter and some form of binding machine, probably plastic comb spirals or thermal glue.

Once the final draft of a report was complete, the Wang operator printed a clean version and ran multiple copies off on the Xerox machine. These were carefully punched in lot sizes that would not jam the machine and laid out for assembly. Graphics were done separately, perhaps on that newfangled Macintosh in the graphics department, and were manually inserted in the appropriate place. These were called "facer" pages because they faced a numbered page and were not paginated by the word processor. Covers were preprinted card stock, and secretaries were adept at getting the document title to show through the die-cut window.

One by one the multiple copies were assembled, bound, placed in a box, and, if the document was late, a junior team member carried it over to the FedEx office for shipping. In our early consulting careers, we went through this process two or three times per week. This was state of the art 20 years ago.

Nowadays, of course, your report naturally is a text and graphics integrated PDF sent via e-mail in a few minutes or via File Transfer Protocol (FTP) or a similar service, such as YouSendIt if you are concerned about getting snagged in a spam folder or corporate IT screen. Today, your document might be a self-animated slideshow with your own recorded voiceover to ensure your recipient hears every nuance of your message or a video, or animation, or … You get the picture. We've come a long way in a short time.

Tool Tip: Although we rail about e-mail as a process that has gotten out of hand and compare it, unfavorably, to collaborative tools and shared workspaces, e-mail is the natural way to communicate with those who are not in your collaborative circle, such as vendors and clients. Today, due to spamming and virus worries, many corporations have significantly tightened their security. These portals routinely screen for executable files, zipped files, or even PDFs, and block large attachments or limit their user's e-mail folder size.

This poses a problem: Many modern work products have large embedded graphics or Java scripts or links, which look suspicious to the security rules. How, then, do you send your large final report or large marketing brochure to your customer or sales target? One great solution is a service such as Yousendit.com, or WeTransfer.com, or FileFactory, and their several competitors. You upload your large work product and the recipient gets an e-mail with a link to the file, which can be downloaded using a browser. There are many other good management features such as history, selectable duration of downloads, and the ability to customize the portal the customer sees with your company's logo and look. After getting a call from an angry customer who never received the final report you sent on time, you will learn to appreciate such a service.

It is painful to look back on the period between Xeroxes, fax machines, and e-mail through a Lean lens.

Case Study: Pre-Lean Communication

Some time ago, one of your authors worked in a small company with offices in Los Angeles (LA) and New York (NY). Cross-continent collaboration on a report, for example, looked like this:

1. LA author created text in longhand.
2. LA admin would word-process the text, print it out, and fax it to NY.
3. NY admin would retype the text from the fax (no file sharing, naturally), print it out, and give it to the NY author.
4. NY author edited and added text, longhand.
5. NY admin incorporated new text and edits, printed new version, and faxed it to LA.
6. LA admin would incorporate new changes into its filed version, print new version, and give to LA author.
7. LA author would make more longhand edits, and so on.

It was the unvarying incantation of work, in tetrameter: longhand–Wang–printer–fax … longhand–Wang–printer–fax … It went on all day.

The delays, extra processing, extra transport, waste of paper and toner, and rework was staggering. Yet, we thought this was pretty heady stuff. After all, we were coauthoring a report with somebody across the continent. And we could get a short document completed this way in a single day and have it delivered (FedEx again) to our client the next morning. Of course, there were multiple originals, and editing done at cross-purposes, but we learned to pay close attention to version control. Of course, mistakes happened: printing errors, missed FedEx closings, spelling errors and typos, text errors traceable to the committee process, and so on. But nothing's perfect, right? We were working hard and the workday was defined by the FedEx closing time—you had to leave the office to drop the stuff off on your way home.

How Information Circuits Create Waste

Case Study: The Travel Authorization Process

One of the most common tradeoffs any process development team ponders is security versus efficiency. You balance between the delays in a tool sign-out process and the cost of lost tools. The worst of both worlds exists when a process is slowed to gain a level of security that is illusory or irrelevant. Sadly this is all too common in the workplace. Workers learn to pay lip service to procedures or paperwork that are not actually providing any benefit because this is the path of least corporate resistance. The administrators want their forms completed because they will be audited based on the completeness of their forms in the files, not on any effect those procedures may have had on the overall process and the corporate bottom line.

In one such real-life corporate example, we will examine the relatively simple information requirements associated with a common administrative function to demonstrate how information circuits can create waste.

The company is a giant global leader in its industry, a modern company with far-flung offices and a staff well trained in computers. It is a company that recognizes that time is money. Its workers have a lot of face-to-face sales time requiring air travel. Naturally, like any other company, they want to control expenses, ensure that the travel is justified, the lead warrants the expense, the most cost-effective booking is being arranged, and the proper accounting is applied to the expense. The company has built its travel approval process, Trav-O, into a streamlined workflow using Microsoft Outlook forms. When salespeople wish to book travel they complete an Outlook form with the required information, cost, and accounting, then e-mail it to their line manager and the appropriate person in accounting. They review the form electronically and click on a button to add their electronic signatures to authorize the travel request. After the trip, salespeople submit their airline receipts along with a printout of the authorization for this travel expense and include it with their normal expense account documentation.

This system seems fine. At the first glance (see Figure 3.2), it looks like a smooth and efficient process built right into the everyday workflow using that most ubiquitous business process, e-mail. When you look at the process closer,

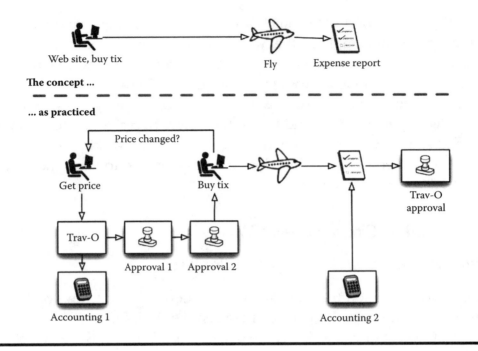

Figure 3.2 Waste in a simple corporate travel process.

more holistically, you will see that some significant areas need improvement. For example, this travel expense process requires a lot of explicit information like name of the airline, flight number, date and time, and exact cost. To complete the Trav-O accurately, the salesperson has already logged onto the airline Web site, or an aggregator such as Expedia.com, investigated the best routes and flights, and made a selection.

But rather than purchasing this flight through the Web site and generating an e-ticket, which is just one click away, the person has to comply with the Trav-O process: save the itinerary, copy out all the information, create and submit a travel expense form, and wait for two separate company replies. Then the person has to log back into the travel site, pull up the itinerary, and complete the purchase. This example is not unique to this company. It is more or less common practice for many blue chip corporations in America and Europe today.

This simple example, which comes from a smart modern company, illustrates a fundamental type of information waste: the *information circuit*, which is a closed-loop information transfer between two or more points that are dependent; often referred to as a circular reference, or more popularly, as a chicken and egg problem. In this example, the salesperson needs approval from accounting before giving credit card information to the airline to receive the flight information, and the accounting department needs the flight information before they can give the necessary approval information. What initially looks like a smooth process has in fact at least one iterative loop and two or three sources for the introduction of errors. For example, the last seat on the flight might be taken when the salesperson returns to book the preferred flight, or the price may have changed, or one of the reviewers may not respond in a timely fashion, or there is a misunderstanding about the accounting codes or the purpose of the trip, among a host of other reasons. As a result, the whole cycle must begin again. Another important type of waste is the *creation of unnecessary information*. For example, most of us do not memorize eight- or ten-digit accounting authorization codes; therefore, whenever one is needed we almost certainly have to look it up or, even more wasteful, we have to call or e-mail someone for it.

But the need for this accounting detail for the first part of the travel expense request is superfluous, since it is never entered into any accounting system. It's the expense report that is actually used in financial accounting. This makes sense because plans change, or the trip might be combined with other expenses, and so on. The final accounting codes are what matters, not the planned ones.

The salesperson has not yet incurred expenses and temporary or placeholder charges are not placed into an accounting system. This whole exercise is a wasteful data gathering control, a nonvalue-added activity that gathers no useful data and provides no control whatsoever. Anyone who has done design work, systems engineering, or requirements management is familiar with this concept, known as the orphaned requirement because it is required, but is never used again.

As bad as this example is, the reality is far worse because absent the ability to obtain preapproval by this method, most salespeople travel anyway, and then go through the ritual of obtaining preapproval trip authorizations even for trips that have already taken place.

No one checks to determine whether the travel is actually by the least expensive mode, only that all the appropriate forms received get a tick in the box. All of these forms are reviewed by the administrative personnel for the salesperson before they are submitted. Then they are reviewed by accounting. Next, they are handled a third time when scanned as PDFs for record management. Finally, some percentage is spot checked after the fact to verify that the accountants are doing proper accounting; that is, the watchers are watched.

Now, you might be an accountant and are jumping up to say that these are necessary controls—that without both preapproval to weed out unnecessary flights and careful review to make sure lowest-cost flights are purchased, expenses would skyrocket.

If there is a lot of face-to-face selling and a lot of air travel, those expenses are probably significant, and serious control is necessary to keep them in check. Wasting expense account money is, after all, a serious waste too, and it is necessary for companies to control their cost of goods sold and to ensure that single expense policies are being followed. However, there is more than one way to skin a cat. For example, rather than an exact cost, an approximate cost could be sufficient or verification that coach travel is booked. This is far simpler than getting and entering the exact amount. Instead of detailed accounting, a checkbox could be used to indicate whether the expense is chargeable to a client, is sales related, or is purely an administrative expense. The salesperson could fill out the form, send it off for approval, and then go to the airline's Web site to complete the transaction. Another approach would be to set dollar limits, either on a per-flight basis or per-month basis. Presumably, the company, with a large group of road warriors, is focusing on trends in general behavior and not one or two individuals' specific travel consumption. To get the right corporate behavior, you could simplify the travel guidelines instead of policing the expense report and adding a lot of resources to ensure compliance. If a company audits expense reports for procedural compliance, it might be a good idea to audit them for content and total cost. Anyone abusing the expense account principles would then receive a hearty fire-and-brimstone speech, which would be more salutary than low-level nagging from a junior accountant requesting additional paperwork

To err is human; to really foul things up requires a computer. In our fathers' day this process could not have existed. So much preauthorization via paper processes would add too much lead time to travel. Instead, they would have used preapproved spending limits with the occasional, gray area phone call. However, the ability to create fast workflow instruments such as Outlook forms enables this kind of behavior. You can't get much more anti-Lean than reviewing 10,000 or so forms, each requiring multiple approvals and handling, that add no value.

Our traveling salespeople had to take the following steps:

Step 1: Download reservation details.
Step 2: Pass the details and cost codes through the approver loop.
Step 3: After receiving approval, go back to the reservation system to finalize the purchase of a ticket.
Step 4: At the end of the month, complete an expense report.

Figure 3.3 is a simple matrix depicting this process. Here we have a row each for the reservation, approval, and expense report steps. The first column of the matrix is the same as the first row; the second column is the same as the second row, and so on, so the 45-degree slope is grayed out. A check in any box means that the work done by the task in that row number requires an input from the task in that column number. As illustrated in the figure, items 1 and 2 (cost and accounting) are raw inputs, that is, they are independent information generated by the airline (cost) and the salesperson (what shall I charge this to?). Item 3, the Trav-O, uses both cost and accounting as inputs and, therefore, an *x* appears in

		1	2	3	4	5
1	Cost	■				
2	Accounting		■			
3	Approval	X	X	■		
4	Expense report	X			■	
5	Client bill				X	■

Figure 3.3   Matrix analysis of a travel process.

columns 1 and 2. Item 4, the expense report only uses cost.* The salesperson adds the final charge codes when he or she completes the expense report without reference to the Trav-O form. Last, the client bill reflects only the final disposition: what the trip cost and to whom it was charged.

In this simple matrix, there are no entries in column 3 because no subsequent step actually uses any of the information created during this entire Trav-O process. In the terminology of requirements engineering, it is known as an orphaned requirement; and in Lean terminology, it is called waste.

To be fair, there is more than one way to diagram this process. It is possible to break the process up into (1) gather flight data from Web site, (2) gain approval for flight, and (3) finalize reservation. If the process were written in this way, our diagramming technique would show a clean progression with no recursion at all. On the other hand, you would have to turn a blind eye to the fact that this requires you go back to the same Web site twice to do a job that can easily be done in one visit.

If you believe that a valuable activity is one that your clients would be willing to pay for if it were itemized, then a value stream analysis of the process would look pretty bad. To test this assumption, we found that it took three minutes to book a basic flight on Expedia; whereas using the Trav-O process, it typically took 24 hours and the actual working time is more like 8 minutes even if there are no errors or missed e-mails, and the additional work and interruptions does not affect anything else anywhere. The extra 5 minutes doesn't sound critical but when you consider approximately 3,000 salespeople making two to three flights each week, this company's travel costs start to add up. Even assuming no mistakes and no impact on other work, it could amount to $3 million to $6 million per year, depending on whether you consider resource costs or lost opportunity cost (from billings and sales). If you include all the administrative, secretarial, accounting, and auditing costs necessary to support and document such a large volume process, this figure doubles. Using our favorite Lean test, would this company's customers appreciate paying an extra $12 million for this extra processing. The answer is clearly no.

The Present: The Dawn of the Web

Information used to be something you sought out: actively looking up a telephone number in the yellow pages or flipping through a card catalog file in the library. That relationship has changed, and information surrounds us, pressing in. We have only to turn on one of our info spigots: the Internet, e-mail, cell phones, instant messaging, and so forth to be swamped with more than we can easily handle.

* Actually, the expense report uses accounting information, but not this accounting information.

Information: The Dark Matter of Business Process Analysis

Astrophysicists in the 1930s could not reconcile their calculations of the apparent gravity of certain visible galaxies with their orbital speeds. The mass of the galaxies was far too small for such fast orbits so they concluded something else must be present, something that added mass but could not be observed. This is known as the missing mass problem. In astronomy and cosmology, dark matter is a hypothetical substance that does not interact with electromagnetic forces, therefore cannot be directly observed, but whose presence can be inferred from other effects.

As astrophysicists pursued this problem, it became evident that there was a lot of this missing mass. In fact, the bulk of the universe seems to be dark matter. Only about 5 to 10 percent of the stuff in the universe can be seen directly. The term *dark matter* reflects our ignorance and sense of wonder. Information flow is the dark matter of the modern high-tech office environment. The equivalent of visible matter is the "official" business process procedures and documentation, including operating manuals, standard operating procedures, business process flow diagrams, new employee instruction manuals and courses, document templates, delivery schedules and calendars, business meeting minutes and memoranda, and so on; all the codified representations of the way we are supposed to do business.

All the unofficial, back channel, and non–ex officio ways of getting things done are the dark matter. They can't be seen, that is, an audit of methods and procedures would not reveal them, but their effects can certainly be felt. Ask yourself if any of your coworkers have taken you aside and explained "how to really get things done around here."

Many of the symptoms explained by dark matter, dark information, are day-to-day occurrences in the complex high-tech office. These include wrong assumptions (that information came from somewhere), work performed out of sequence, steps in the official process skipped, cut-and-paste information errors, unsanctioned information that came from outside the process such as a vendor's Web site or a legacy project, among many others, all of which contribute to Lean information waste.

It is easier to understand projects failing or deviating from their official schedule and pro forma work plan when you realize that there is an alternate way to getting things done—a pathway just as real, though not as brightly lit.

Like another famous path, this information-intensive path is paved with good intentions. The currency of knowledge workers is *information*. One way or another they will find the information they need to do their work motivated by their perception of expediency and efficiency. If the upstream information provider was slow to fill this need by the official process, they will circumvent it. Unofficial e-mails, instant messages, hallway conversations, whichever will provide anxious information workers insight into what they need to get started. Something as simple as obtaining a rough indication of the results of some early testing in the project can happily set information workers to preparing their work in order to get a head start when the official information arrives. In fact, much of this preparatory work is at risk because it is predicated on unofficial information that is likely to change.

Another way downstream workers can get an early start on their information contribution is to manufacture the information. In its simplest form they assume the value (never was the adage about "assuming" more valid). Another approach is to get the information externally, perhaps from a vendor or partner Web site. Finally, information workers can use a value from a similar project that resides on their hard drives from the group's institutional knowledge. Under the guise of fast tracking, or getting good value out of slack time or downtime, the seeds for a lot of rework are sewn.

What's worse, this phenomenon is increasing. We have our own red shift or Doppler effect in place due to the increasing pace of point-to-point communications techniques and the very high penetration of these hardware appliances. Who doesn't have e-mail or Internet access? What about wireless phones and BlackBerries where you can get voice, text, or files any time of the day or night? Instant messaging? RSS feeds? And access to the large corporate files and knowledge management systems? The information infrastructure and tools to pass information along are multiplying at a dramatic pace, as is the quality and speed of search engines. People today, especially our up-to-date young engineers and knowledge workers, have far more access, at their fingertips, to information than has ever been dreamed.

For those who need to see evidence of this dark information, consider how many minutes (or even seconds) you go in an office environment without seeing someone on a cell phone, checking a BlackBerry, doing e-mail, or surfing the Web. BlackBerries and iPhones have replaced flipping through the newspaper as the idle pastime while in the men's room. Possibly the only time you won't see electronic data creation or consumption is at a business meeting with strict cell phone and laptop rules. Of course, people are in that meeting in the first place to, well, exchange information.

Of course, the existence and proliferation of communication tools does not mean that they *are* being used outside of the official business process, only that they *could* be. In the old days of the paper-only office work, these methods practically did not exist. Even if we expand the "paper-only era" to include FedEx and fax machines, before e-mail and the Internet became ubiquitous office tools, we were firmly in the dark information era. As long as information workers believe that they are fast tracking or multitasking, they will use these tools as enablers and accelerants.

Dark information is not only created and enabled by tools such as instant messaging and e-mail, it also has an insidious feedback loop that spawns other generations of e-mail in a rippling effect. Hasn't it become a near constant complaint in the high-tech office today that there is so much e-mail we are drowning in it, that it is preventing us from getting our normal job done? Many people rely on evenings and weekends to catch up on e-mail in an attempt to free some hours during the day to do actual work with actual people.

This dark information phenomenon is part of the problem. Because our information work is largely invisible, we have to keep pointing it out to each other. Bricklayers don't need to do that. They can all see the wall going up before them. In the absence of a visual progress system, constant status updating takes the form of a broad e-mail string with multiple ccs and bccs. Because our organizations are hierarchical and since there is no clearer central and visible way to assess the status of a project or evolving design, the only way for workers to keep their managers informed (and to provide often needed CYA is via the use of the cc and bcc fields.

And, irony of ironies, people often use the "requested read receipt" to learn if their e-mail managed to swim through the ocean of competing e-mails and was actually read by the recipient. These receipts, of course, just add to the e-mail traffic.

Tool Tip: Don't replace the version control nightmare with elaborate process and document management solutions. They are too cumbersome and require too much sacrifice in speed and ease-of-use for the safeguards they provide. They either fall into disuse or serve as an unvarying time tax imposed on all the workers—a terrible form of waste. Think of the KISS principle, adopt fast simple Lean tools, and learn from them. Tell yourself that you expect to have it right on or about the third iteration; that is, after your suspected requirements have been modified by user experience and feedback.

A couple of the other information wastes that have become everyday occurrences since e-mail came to dominate our work experience are the broadcast e-mail and the asset grabbing e-mail. The broadcast e-mail is very common in large organizations. It goes something like this: "I'm working on a project for a secret customer and I need to know if anyone has any experience developing financial metrics for insurance companies. Please let me know and send me your materials right away." Of course this e-mail goes out to, say, 300 people, and enough of those hit the deadly reply-to-all button to keep this conversation evolving in your in-basket for the rest of the day. If you are a procrastinator, or merely someone who actually reads all your mail, this chain will freeze you up like a deer in the headlights. Until you get the final five or six e-mails from some of these recipients begging that everyone please stop using the reply-to-all button.

One of the implications of this broadcast mail is that the company in question has very poor knowledge management. The requester cannot find the relevant information in the corporate knowledge base and has to resort to this broadcast appeal. However, this is only partly true. Knowledge management in the sense of a large organized database is probably, and we say only probably, a declining factor in high-tech business. These systems are too hard to create, too hard to maintain, and too hard to design with elegant and efficient interfaces. As soon as they start to slip, people resort to the broadcast. Even if they don't slip, frustrated researchers will assume that their failed search is more likely due to a poor knowledge management system than anything else. Surely we must have this somewhere. The result: the broadcast e-mail. The heightened capabilities of modern search engines and their ability to search within documents, PDFs, and databases directly, will drive a migration to what we call "dumb knowledge management," where material is gathered but little effort is spent in organizing or indexing it since the search engine will do a superior job on an ad hoc basis.

In today's world, you know that you've made a good presentation, or at least an attractive and professional one, when you receive the asset grabbing e-mail. "Great job yesterday, George. Can I get a copy of your slides please?" This is sometimes flattering and fulfilling in a professional way, but sometimes it's just laziness and greed. It all depends upon whether the requester wants your conclusions or your assets: the diagrams, charts, photographs, and so forth that you used to polish up your PowerPoint deck.

There is an easy way to determine the real intent of the requester that has become quite common. When you receive the asset-grabbing e-mail, you gleefully respond by sending the person a PDF version of the slides. If he thanks you or says nothing, you'll know he wanted to keep your story and conclusions intact for later reference. If he immediately replies asking for a native, editable .ppt file, you'll know he's an asset grabber. It's quite understandable. Generating these assets is time consuming and information workers are always looking for shortcuts to be efficient and save time. The ability to reuse some of the assets created by a colleague is naturally attractive. The point is that this is just another example of Web 1.0 behavior: Communication is accelerated by technology but is still fundamentally point-to-point and noncollaborative, which generates a lot of waste.

Alternatives exist and they are both good and growing in popularity. SlideRocket is an excellent example of one alternative. This tool/Web site provides all the collaboration and shared asset support you need without compromising features or power.

Modern communication technology is so fast that it has made what was once an awkward end run into the standard mode of information sharing. In the physical world, workers might gather around the work, the clay model of the prototype car for example, and discuss its merits. In a paper process world, workers might pass around the case file or folder so that everyone can look at the same thing. In the information age, workers sent bits of information flying around to each other in various ways, all very fast, but still they each saw only a piece, or a subset of workers were the only ones sharing information. Communication was still point-to-point, albeit networked together it's true, but imperfectly, as anyone who went on vacation and tried to catch up on the status of a fast-moving project can attest.

In the high-tech world today, you can do one of two things: have an all-hands meeting where you share a snapshot of the project or some critical piece of information, or conduct detailed, evolving communication between two or three workers who dive deep into a problem or issue to resolve it. In other words, you can share some of the information with all of the people, or all the information with some of the people, but you can't share all the information with all the people. This is the real challenge for Lean in the information age. Certain Web 2.0 and cloud computing tools may contain the answer.

The Future: What Will Web 2.0 Bring?

The term *collaboration* is practically synonymous with Web 2.0 since so many of the tools and Web sites springing up today are seeking to improve workflow and synergy between knowledge workers. You might think that most of the thrust is around innovation or new product development, but actually the most common application of these collaborative tools is around business process improvement (BPI) for company operations.

This is essential for Lean. A knowledge of possible alternatives, especially those that have been successfully adopted elsewhere and are not just a conceptual sketch, is a key input into kaizen or brainstorming sessions.

The trend started years ago with the proliferation of Virtual Private Networks (VPNs) that allow remote workers to act as if they had access to the company's tools and assets. This is like extending the company fence around its remote workers, but there are still limitations to what's inside that fence. While some of the custom tools will no doubt be mission critical, today's young knowledge workers are looking wistfully beyond the fence and noting what else is available and what is being denied them. We will examine a few categories of these modern tools focusing on those that may provide insight into continuous process improvement.

There are many examples of aggressive consumer-focused companies that are leveraging social media such as Twitter, Facebook, and YouTube. Ignoring them right now would be a mistake because the volume of possible touches and the potential to kick off that highly desired viral adoption is just too good to ignore. Recently we read how a startup e-book site was drawing 20 times the site visits of any of the established publishing houses.

We use the word *established* to highlight part of the problem. Web 2.0 sites embrace change and constant evolution. They have to; competition to gain the attention of what is probably the demographic with the shortest attention span seen to date is tough. Established means boring. Web 2.0 is filled with "new" and "improved" and "free"—the three magic words of marketing. And they back that up with new features and tie-ins (how many iPhone apps have been rushed to market in order to appeal to that segment?) as well as dramatically low prices on certain services because their revenue model, in part, is based on advertising and links.

We will discuss IT's role in all of this in more detail in Chapter 5. For now, it is important to remember that IT is usually a gatekeeper. They block access to certain services, with the rationalization that they have already satisfied the requested functionality through one of their in-house tools (forgetting who the internal customer is), and they deny admin rights to install new software on the basis of support costs and security. (Blocking admin privileges for knowledge workers seems as logical, to us, as blocking lumberjacks from using any of those fancy new chainsaws. Axes, after all, have been thoroughly tested and are the approved tool.)

Rather than being a gatekeeper, IT's role should be spirit guide. By assigning a few IT resources to the spirit guide role, the organization can efficiently leverage all the massive creative output of the marketplace, and help operations groups design and adapt their processes based on these emerging tools. The company will be a more modern and exciting place to work, it will help attract smart young Web workers, and IT can lay claim to a portion of all the delivered Lean improvements.

There is an existing model for this spirit guide role: the social sites aggregator. Dozens of services are springing up that help coordinate and customize the use of the multiple big social networking sites. IT can create process-specific portals that mash up existing sites and features sets along a redesigned workflow: a process home page and control panel on steroids.

Tool Tip: If you despair that your IT department will step up to this plate, there are some alternatives in the form of two hard-to-categorize products that do much of this Web 2.0 spirit guide job for you.

Bantam Live is part microblogging, part social CRM (customer relationship management), and part networked collaboration. This is an online service where business teams can collaborate in a workspace and build business relationships across the Web.

Jive Social Business Software (SBS) has all the features of collaboration and work community and networking software in an enterprise platform that may satisfy IT. Your knowledge worker teams may be able to stop stringing together workarounds using popular social networking software. Both these products are beating corporate IT to the punch in the aggregator role because they understand that work doesn't have to be this hard and that this message will resonate with today's knowledge worker.

Day-to-Day Collaboration Tools

The two largest categories of collaboration tools are the basic office suite tools supporting word processing, spreadsheets, presentations, and the collaborative project management tools. We discussed the office suite tools in the previous chapter. We dive into the vast field of team collaboration and task management in Chapter 4 in our discussion of the wastes of project management. We won't repeat those discussions here, but if you are at all doubtful about the crying need for collaboration and avoiding the issues of e-mailing documents back and forth or the issues that stem from poor situational visibility and feedback in project management, you only have to glance at that segment of the Web development marketplace. It is churning with creative activity. These areas are ripe for improvement, and change, with so many forces pushing in this space, it is inevitable.

Lean Communication Tools: Video and Desktop Conferencing

The topic of long-distance communication, for example, videoconferencing, showcases a very clear example of the differences between the big-company, capital-intensive solution and the Lean solution. This user application touches upon some of the key strengths of Lean and weaknesses of the big-company solution.

The big-company solution requires not only the capital expense of purchasing and installing dedicated videoconferencing facilities but also all the delays associated with running this as a big project including detailed requirements definition, IT security concerns, requests for information (RFIs), technical review and selection, contracting, and deployment (alpha test, beta test, and rollout), capped off with rounds of training.

On the Lean side, workers simply start using Skype, GoToMeeting, WebEx, Glance, Fuze, or any other of the many technologically advanced entrants into the space. Their power and obvious value drive viral adoption throughout the organization. Their value proposition of excellent results with zero time, zero cost, and zero help to install is hard to argue with.

Figure 3.4 illustrates the difference. In the "big company" case, the person calling the videoconference begins by scheduling the special conference room with the video equipment to ensure access to the shared resource. With a date and time, he or she then schedules the actual video conference with his or her colleagues (assuming they could get the video facilities on their end at this same time). Not every building has video capability; therefore, some conferees will have to travel to one that does on the day of the conference. The time and support of a video technician, or perhaps a designated admin, will be needed to help with the unfamiliar equipment. Only then is everyone ready for the video meeting where participants can see and hear one another on the screen.

In the small company use case, the person initiating the videoconference doesn't have to schedule anything or travel anywhere. Presence indication tells you your colleague is online and you can initiate a video conference with one click. Even better, since you are at your computer, you have access to all your materials, files, and other assets, and can transfer them immediately, share screens and desktops, and review them simultaneously, or even pass control over to your colleague.

Video quality is a function of bandwidth and, in a shared office environment, this might be an issue when comparing desktop video to a dedicated video

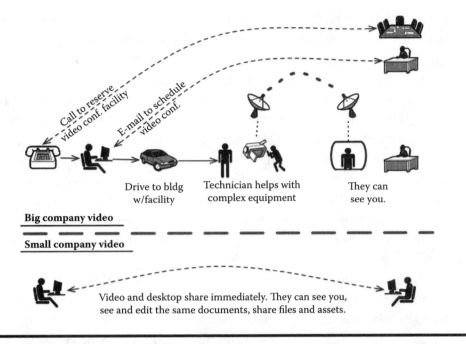

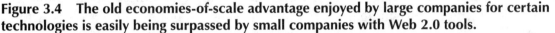

Figure 3.4 The old economies-of-scale advantage enjoyed by large companies for certain technologies is easily being surpassed by small companies with Web 2.0 tools.

system. A dedicated video system has a long installed life to amortize the capital purchase; however, in the marketplace, technologies move fast enough that the low-cost solution surpasses the high-cost solution within the latter's lifetime. Expensive tools, especially in these areas of rapid development and evolution, encumbered with several years' amortization, are essentially a financial waste. They also limit their workers to years' of inefficiency as the asset is paid off.

Both approaches intend to reduce travel time and cost and improve on the voice-only aspect of a phone call. Some of the new expensive systems are naturally growing in sophistication and picture quality. When you compare the immediacy of desktop videoconferencing, its ease of use and cost, the elimination of travel time and hassles (including leaving your desk to use the special conference facility), and the increased functionality of file and desktop sharing, there doesn't seem to be much of a comparison.

Microblogging

Twitter, the phenomenally successful microblogging application, allows individuals to follow the 140 character tweets of others. It is very good for disseminating short bits of information and is popular among journalists, political activists, and teenagers everywhere. There are three obvious business applications for services like this in business:

1. External mass marketing, viral marketing
2. Replacements for official newsletters, broadcast internal communications
3. Tool for managing projects, particularly lean projects

We leave the details of the first idea to the marketing mavens. Internal broadcast communications offers several advantages. It can replace official newsletters effectively. Short messages appear to be very informal, casual, and friendly. They are also very fast. Corporations finally have a tool that has some chance of moving as fast as the rumor mill. Winston Churchill said that a good lie could go halfway around the world before the truth could get its pants on. If we wanted to put people at ease about the latest gossip about the merger, this would be the tool to use.

Companies that have adopted microblogging internally have discovered that there is a very positive benefit in transferring information across departments. The engineering team, for example, might hear of some project concepts that marketing is considering long before they otherwise would. The added situational visibility will produce many benefits in avoided rework, better scheduling and handoffs, and improved collaboration.

Another bonus of microblogging is the additional social connections made by employees in different buildings, cities, or working from home. These employees do not get to bump into each other in the elevator or at the water cooler; therefore, microblogging can help fill the inherent social gaps. Simple updates like "the color printer is down again" or "I've heard there's going to be a party after softball practice tonight" can help coworkers feel connected, even if they're too far away to be affected by either the printer or the party.

There are several Twitter clones that bring the benefits of microblogging to the enterprise: Yammer, Present.ly, SocialText, OfficeMedium, and HipChat among others. These can add vital functionality to business-related microblogging. They are simple to use, but, unlike Twitter, they are secure. You can share information among easy-to-configure teams and groups within the company, but your messages are invisible to everyone else. These business microblogs also allow the sharing of media (images, documents, video, and audio clips). They have question-and-answer functionality built into them so they are excellent communication devices between boss and employee, employee and technical expert, and for fielding questions between presenters and their audience. They are available in all browsers and smart phones, which contributes to their portability and immediacy. And while this microblogging trend may look frivolous to those who think e-mail is already "all that needs to be invented," just look at how comfortable your younger resources are with it. And recognize how naturally (and efficiently) your next generation of recruits will take to it.

From our point of view, one of microblogging's best uses is by the Lean team in both doing and promoting the Lean work itself.

> Doing—As a replacement for yellow sticky notes. Most Lean methodologies involve something like the process we describe in the Lean admin section in Chapter 2. Teams gathered around a central process description and annotating it with notes (the ubiquitous Post-It, or yellow sticky) to document their data discoveries or suggested areas of improvement. Microblogs can serve as this data and idea documentation vehicle. They are always available via

users' handheld devices and they can be sent automatically to a team member designated to update the whiteboard prior to the meeting. The other team members will have had the opportunity to review them prior to the whiteboard meeting, which saves time.

Promoting—Also known as communicating or evangelizing. Lean contributors can follow (in the micro-blogging sense of the word) the Lean team leaders. Members and other interested parties can keep abreast of the Lean team's developments, and whiteboard session results can be broadcast to all interested stakeholders. Outside the team, other process owners thinking about bringing Lean to their own workgroups can use microblogging to closely follow the evolution of a similar project in detail prior to taking the leap themselves.

Screencasting and Recording

We live in the video age. Cable TV and MTV have grown up into YouTube and citizen reporters armed with a video camera in their phones. Although video demos and tutorials are a common Web site sales tool, they haven't quite penetrated the enterprise space. But they will. The drivers are too powerful to ignore. It's easier, faster, and therefore cheaper to create on the frontend, and it is far more powerful, and more likely to be used, on the backend. Assume you need to train a new hire in a task that takes about five minutes to do. Would you write a lengthy procedural document, get it reviewed, stamped official, and incorporated into the company manual, or would you just have the trainee look over your shoulder while you demonstrated it?

Nowadays it's remarkably simple to create a screencast of your computer desktop, and you don't have to worry about lighting, sets, sound levels, or if the camera is adding ten pounds. You just turn on your recorder, demonstrate the task with or without voiced commentary, and save the video file. Have your top expert create the demo if you like, then all new hires can be trained by the best, and they can watch it as many times as necessary without fear of bothering you.

Take it a step further. How many service, sales, or consulting companies keep their PowerPoint decks for reuse? Probably, most do. Yet half (at least) of the information and value of these presentations is in the delivery, but almost no one saves detailed speaker's notes or advice on what points to emphasize. Wouldn't it be better to have your star salesperson's pitch available for your entire team to review? Your sales efforts would be better and more consistent, and your salespeople would come up to speed much faster.

Next time, rather than ask for a copy of the deck, ask for the video or the screencast. Collect these and encourage others to make them. Never mind the elaborate knowledge management system. Just tag them, give them a reasonable title, and let your people find them. Some manuals and procedures may still be better served in print format, but that number will dwindle over time. Soon your team will be watching the pitch on their video phones on the way to their sales meeting, where they will deliver the same pitch and build on it.

The screencast tools segment is large and growing larger. They range from fancy and feature filled to good and free; there is sure to be something that fits your needs. Among those to consider are Breeze, Camtasia, Camstudio, Jing, ScreenToaster, Screenflow, OnAirRecorder, Flowgram, and Wondershare.

This is classic Knowledge Worker Lean: It uses Web 2.0 tools, it fits in with the young Web worker culture, and it will save the company a ton of money while delivering a far better product than those outdated printed manuals no one reads. While you are at it, record some video for your Lean Web site too. Make a before and after screencast walkthrough of the process and deliver the message you want people to hear rather than expecting them to analyze flowcharts and reach the conclusion on their own.

Brainstorming and Design Collaboration

There is a lot of "drawing" in Lean. Process maps are represented as line drawings or flowcharts, and they are heavily annotated in kaizen sessions, alternate designs are sketched, and so forth. Whether this is done casually, in PowerPoint for example, or with more professional tools such as Visio, it often doesn't matter. Sharing and commenting on the diagram is usually a common experience, but creating it is usually the role of an individual who ends up "owning" the diagram, and edits are channeled through that person. The group gets together to review the diagram once it is ready, and incorporates changes and edits from the last session.

Drawing and markup collaboration is an ideal Web 2.0 application. It enables remote workers, it allows markups and ideas to happen when they happen rather than at scheduled meetings, and, more important, it makes the document a shared design rather than one owned by a single team member who may be biased against some of the suggested edits or changes.

There are two classes of drawing collaboration tools: process design and brainstorming/whiteboarding collaboration tools. In the former category are tools such as Flowchart.com, Lucidchart, and Gliffy, which will allow multiple members of your Lean team to contribute both to the initial process discovery and mapping stage as well as the suggested process change stage. The process design tools sacrifice a little power compared to tools like Visio but make up for it in collaboration, team building, and especially solution buy-in. It's much better to watch a design evolve, even if you only commented marginally, than to have it sprung on you fully formed as a final design.

The whiteboarding and brainstorming collaborative applications are also extremely useful. You can literally schedule a shared kaizen brainstorming session online with workers or consultants in different cities, which makes them easier to schedule and more cost effective. In addition, since you can record or share them, it is more open and egalitarian as well as useful in training and evangelizing Lean. No closed-door brainstorming session will ever motivate the people who were not in the room.

It's interesting to note how little exposure this entire class of tools has received. "You can actually do this?" is the most typical reaction. Yet there are many powerful tools for this virtual simultaneous sketching and marking up. Among them are Scribblar, Groupboard, Dabbleboard, Depicto, Twiddla, Scriblink, Showdocument, Vyew, and, one of the earliest entries, GE's Imagination Cubed. If you have trouble scheduling your kaizen sessions or wish to include remote workers, try these. The ability to include contributors from different cities and time zones, plus the ability to record the session for review (no more "Who erased the whiteboard!") can make a huge difference to your kaizen efforts. It can be particularly useful at documenting the Lean journey for both management and new Lean team members.

Kaizen Sessions of the Future

In Chapter 2, we briefly outlined how an admin Lean project in a paper-based company worked. We described the whiteboard sessions where the team comes together to annotate the existing process with performance data, questions, ideas, and so forth. Here, we've just described some tools to help bring part of that experience online and to a potentially wider audience.

However, a kaizen session is more than just scribbling on the whiteboard. All the data gathering (performance, observations, and ideas) has to be mapped to the process and the rest of the group has to be brought up to speed about what it means.

There are many ways to do this, but by far the most common is to have these ideas on small cards (index cards, yellow sticky notes, etc.) and place them on the visual depiction of the process. This immediately locates the idea in both time and space (sequence and location) relative to the process. It is a simple visual system that facilitates shared understanding and discussion—a classic Lean approach.

Once again, this entire approach is based on the assumption that we're all in the same place— something that is implicit in a physical process environment such as a factory. The *information* age office is different. The information flow is not confined to any one physical space; indeed, it likely spans multiple locations, teleworkers, and so forth. In the same way that Web sites are better than posters for disseminating Lean information across a dispersed process team, a new type of collaborative application will emerge to enable continuous process improvement.

Although this new application doesn't exist yet (we hope that developers will take note of this opportunity), the good news is that many of its features and characteristics such as tagging, collaboration, and mobile phone clients, are well developed and being used in other ways and in other tools. What's needed is to put the pieces together. The goal is for this tool to be more powerful as well as accessible and visual in the virtual sense. It also needs to be as easy to use as a regular whiteboard.

For now, the basic interface is still a process diagram, typically broadcast on the wall for the team members in the room and visible online for those joining by Web conference. We can take advantage of mobility apps so that team members can capture and send ideas directly whenever they have them and be received, parsed, and incorporated in the whiteboard session as a markup. We can leverage the improved what-if capability inherent in computerizing our process. In addition, we can improve recordkeeping and playback so that team members can revisit sessions or catch up if they missed one. Let's call it the Kaizen Killer App. for Teams (KKAT).

KKAT high-level functional requirements should be able to:

- Replicate the pen-and-paper process brainstorming experience.
- Translate that experience to an always-on Web page.
- Receive and parse annotations directly via microblogging, e-mail, SMS, or Web site. These annotations should be placed automatically where they are relevant on the process map.
- Allow ideas and suggestions to be commented upon, voted upon, and ranked by the team members.
- Allow remote users to contribute and see edits being discussed in the room through a Web-enabled drawing, typing, and highlighting brainstorming tool.
- Allow team leaders to easily create multiple baselines and variants, including combinations of these ideas and suggestions. There can be planned Lean process evolutions as well as hypothetical ones, which are merely being evaluated. In some cases, two or three alternate and mutually exclusive ideas could each generate a possible future process map.
- Offer simulation and analytical capability that will allow team leaders to test the performance of suggested alternatives. They may tie into a value stream mapping VSM representation that automatically updates value and speed calculations, or they may support a discrete event simulation. Software allows the team to consider many more alternatives in more quantified detail than they previously could.
- Provide recorded brainstorming and discussion sessions where ideas and design evolutions can be recorded for playback and review. This can be done in detail for Web meetings, so that team members can catch up or teams can backtrack, if needed, to review previous baselines.
- Provide a process evolution playback function that will show a slide show summarizing the change-by-change progression of the process diagram complete with high-level performance indicators. This not only documents the improvements, but serves as an excellent so-what evangelist tool for Lean adoption.

All of these components exist! Alternate baselines are a well-understood hallmark of requirements management tools. Capturing and parsing e-mails to annotate collaborative project management tools is being used by Wrike and others (described in the next chapter). Incorporating Yammer or Present.ly into the annotations process of process brainstorming seems a natural evolution. Social sites already exist, thanks to open innovation and other trends, whereby colleagues rank ideas being discussed, and those ranked are weighted based on the reputations and skill set of those providing feedback. Video meeting participation and recording webinars are commonplace. Moving from a process diagram to a simulation is well understood and straightforward. Add a good scenario management capability and your team will be intensely powerful.

Based on this, a future process improvement session might go something like this:

1. The team gathers, partly in the room and partly online. The process board interface is shown, prepopulated with the observations, questions, and suggestions of the team.
2. The polling/ranking function is already highlighting the ideas based on collective perceived value (this can be impact, timeliness, whatever the group values).
3. The high-ranking ideas cluster around two main themes. Two variants from the current baseline are created.
4. Parameter values are discussed and agreed upon, and both theoretical process variants are run in simulation. Results are discussed and reviewed. A set of changes is agreed upon and implementation assignments are developed.
5. The baseline is updated. Microblog broadcasts inform the broader stakeholder community of the planned improvements, including the simulation results quantifying the benefits. Feedback is invited.
6. The next improvement cycle begins.

It sounds fast moving and exciting. But, then again, legend has it that all those accountants and Wall Street types who saw the first demos of VisiCalc were amazed at how entire rows of numbers would just magically update when the user changed an input variable. We think the KKAT is right around the corner.

Chapter 4

The Great Modern Office Wasteland

E-mail, excess complexity, reporting, multitasking, high utilization, and parallel project management. These are just some of the large-scale wastes common throughout modern business organizations, which may surprise you.

We write about waste everywhere in this book. Lean, after all, could easily be described as the "art and science of waste removal." We have bullet lists of different kinds of wastes, tables showing examples of wastes, lists describing enablers, and conditions that may hide waste. Most of them are self-evident once they are called to your attention. For example, a poor office layout leads to excess travel time.

The wastes discussed in this chapter are a little different. Most people don't consider them wastes because they are powerful tools such as e-mail. Some people define their personal proficiency by their ability to multitask, so how could that be a waste? Many service organizations consider high worker utilization analogous to success—and revenue. How could that be a waste? Because of attitudes like this, we take our time discussing these forms of waste. Their impact, after all is tremendous.

The Waste of E-Mail

We touched on the problem with e-mail as a process when we introduced the diagram of the collaboration flower in Chapter 1, and in Figure 4.1 we use part of it to highlight some of the more obvious direct wastes inherent in this process. But e-mail has other problems and indirect wastes, one of which is its imprecision and potential for miscommunication. Some people write very clearly and elegantly, and reread their e-mails to ensure they are making the point they wish to make unambiguously. Most do not. There is simply too much e-mail to write to

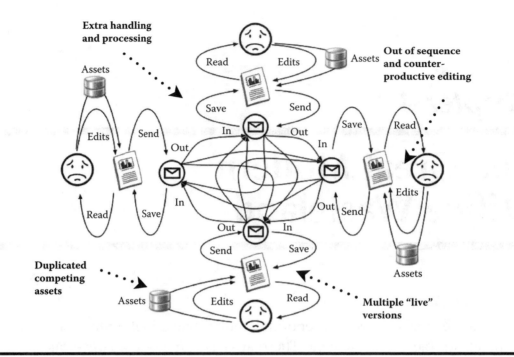

Figure 4.1   These direct process inefficiencies are only some of e-mail's wastes.

craft all of them carefully. Making matters worse, e-mail is often a string of connected messages, and you may be joining in the middle of an evolving discussion and the points being discussed may mean different things to different participants.

Tool Tip: It seems that everyone knows e-mail is a problem. Many specific tools—wikis or other cloud/Web-based approaches to collaboration — are being used to try to avoid it. Personal behavior and self-help systems, like the Getting Things Done (GTD) technique and the "inbox zero" approach, are fine, but they are not the solution. The Lean principle of poka yoke suggests that the real solution is reducing the amount of incoming e-mail in the first place rather than improving our e-mail habits. In other words, don't become really good at fly swatting; put up a screen. As long as e-mail is used for person-to-person communication, it will affect our workflow habits. Google is one of the very few organizations doing something about this. Their Wave product will bring collaboration and shared assets, as well as other benefits, to e-mail itself. If it is adopted in sufficient numbers, it will certainly reinforce the kind of Lean/Web 2.0 solutions we envision here.

Even Microsoft, cognizant of the e-mail toll on productivity, has built coauthoring and real-time connectivity directly into the workflow of Office 2010. This should mean no more e-mail collaboration flower. Let's see. One of the advantages of collaborative techniques is to downplay reliance on e-mail.

There is an often-quoted study by Mehrabian at UCLA* that concluded that the words only carried about 7 percent of the content of the message. Thirty-eight percent was carried by the tone and inflection and 55 percent was conveyed by body language. As others have noted, these percentages should not be casually applied to an analysis of e-mail. They were done before e-mail became so ubiquitous and they were intended to evaluate simple emotions such as like/dislike and not the types of complex messages that may be contained in an e-mail.

We have seen and heard of enough e-mail faux pas to feel that this is directionally correct if not precisely accurate. A lot of communication errors lurk in the simple e-mail. Pick up any modern human resources manual and there's bound to be a lot of advice on e-mail do's and don'ts. (A Google search of that phrase has over 3 million hits.)

There is a nonverbal dimension to e-mail that should be studied further, and we're not just talking about emoticons. (We used to think emoticons were teenage silliness until a few witty e-mails caused offense and blew up in our faces. Now we feel they're more like insurance; they provide deniability and contemporaneous evidence that you were just joking :-)

And there are many other nonverbal inferences. What if you write a long and detailed e-mail and receive a very short and incomplete reply? Is the issue being dismissed as unimportant? What if you ask three specific questions and only the first and last are answered? Is someone hiding something? What if you write a delicate e-mail to a colleague to resolve an issue on the down low and he cc's your boss in reply? Is he deliberately escalating?

Case Study: When Words Are Not Enough

Let's look at a classic Mehrabian words-are-not-enough example. Let's say that as the leader of the Lean team you try to touch base with all the stakeholders who are coming to your team's presentation pitching a new improvement idea. You receive the following e-mail from one of the important stakeholders: "I don't have a problem with your idea."

Depending on whether the emphasis is placed on *I*, *problem*, *your*, or *idea*, it might mean any of the following:

■ "I'm not the one who has a problem with your idea."
■ "I don't have a problem with your idea, just the supporting data."
■ "I don't have a problem with your idea, but with how others will interpret it."
■ "I don't have a problem with your idea, per se, but it's not right for us."

Placing this respondent in the "supporters" column for your idea may be premature. What we should have done was gather more dimensions of feedback:

* Albert Mehrabian, *"Silent Messages"—A Wealth of Information about Nonverbal Communication* (1981).

- What does *he* think of the idea?
- Does he see adoption challenges for others?
- What are the technical/process implementation challenges?
- What is the timetable for implementation and what are the enabling steps?
- Does he have the time or resources to support it?

Covering all these points, and the *nuance* of meaning that may exist in each component answer, is very difficult to achieve in an e-mail with someone on the periphery of your project.

You have to recognize that some percentage of your process workers or stakeholders is going to start from a philosophical position of opposition to Web 2.0 ideas. Let's call them the Luddites 2.0 and recognize that they are a real challenge. Many office workers scoff at using internal wikis and blogs to improve productivity. To them, these are silly-sounding, made-up words. They forget that not too long ago, they (or those like them) weren't even using e-mail. And not too long ago, the idea of cut and paste to assemble documents literally meant that, and it was a task performed by low-level clerical staff prior to retyping the clean final draft. The argument that "e-mail is all right and all we need" is a remarkable position to take. Is it really the zenith of process design and the final product of office evolution? The patent office needn't worry. Many new inventions are coming.

The Waste of Excess Complexity and Process

The effects of poorly understood dependencies can be devastating. They can cause projects to fail because the project manager did not consider conflicts with other projects such as shared resources or vendor contributions.

They can cause multiproject portfolios to fail through lack of coordination. For example, a design group with dozens of projects and project managers may not have thought to group them into dependent families. Therefore, the individual project managers do not know that the delay in another project will directly affect them because they are using an output or interim deliverable on their project.

We worked for a large electronics firm that was trimming its portfolio of approximately 200 projects in development. But because the interproject dependencies were not fully understood, the effects of canceling some projects dramatically increased the cost or difficulty of other projects that had been relying on work or deliverables from the canceled projects. This involved more than just transferring the work from the canceled projects to the new projects because the project manager failed to understand that the scope of the surviving projects had just increased and resulted in late-arriving scope changes, which were very disruptive and expensive. In the end, the department canceled about 30 percent of its projects but spent roughly the same in budget and schedule with more haggard and frustrated project resources.

Case Study: Complexity and Process

One could argue that at least in one instance the effect of hidden dependencies caused an entire industry to fail. Not too long ago the nuclear power industry enjoyed a fantastically attractive financial driver. There were strategic challenges, such as ultimate waste disposal and really bad public relations issues, but the business plan was just too good to ignore. A coal-fired power plant has a 100-car train arriving every day to deliver fuel. A tremendous amount of equipment and effort is necessary to handle the coal, store it in vast black heaps, crush it, move it by conveyor, pulverize it, burn it, scrub the flue gases, collect and remove the remaining ash, and then repeat endlessly.

In contrast, a nuclear power plant has a small truck drive up to it once every couple of years to deliver fuel. Moreover, once built, it runs continuously as base loaded units. What went wrong were the spiraling construction costs, which were 20 and 30 times above the original budgets. There were many audits and regulatory hearings to explain these vast cost increases and, if we had to use one word to summarize the reasons, it would be *dependencies*. The true impacts of regulatory changes were always far, far greater than realized. There were hearings where one expert witness after the other took the stand and tried to explain escalating costs with metaphors like "ripple effects" and "unintended consequences" in an attempt to convey how seemingly innocuous design or regulatory conditions can generate wave after wave of major design changes.

One simple example is what came to be called the II/I (two-over-one) program. Certain systems were designated as safety Category I critical systems that required heightened safety factors and the inspection and documentation necessary to prove it. Every piece of equipment, pipe weld, and pipe hanger (the metal brackets that pipes hang from) belonging to a Category I system was tracked, radiographed, inspected, and documented. Subsequently, it became obvious that this wasn't enough, because there were many Category II and III systems snaking for miles in the reactor, turbine, and auxiliary buildings that did not have the same stringent controls and yet were physically located above or near to Category I systems. The failure of one of the Category II systems could cause it to fall on the Category I system, which could fail and have a domino effect.

Consider the sheer number of these systems and components, the space limitations and constrictions that would make rerouting them very difficult, and the fact that many of them were already built and even encased in very dense and heavily rebarred nuclear-grade concrete, and you begin to see the unfolding costs. What's more, all these new inspections, redesign, and replacements happened in those same constricted spaces while construction tried to maintain schedule.

The amount of rework was staggering. Project costs skyrocketed and threatened the financial stability of what had been the most stable entity imaginable, the regulated utility monopoly. The escalating construction costs of all this rework negated the financial advantage of the nuclear industry and changed the whole discussion. It was not a catastrophic event like Three Mile Island that killed the nuclear industry; it was innocuous little bits of hardware, the metal straps that Category II pipes hung on, that did it.

The important lesson is to understand the systems view of the work. You cannot always apply a Pareto view (the 80/20 rule) and concentrate on the big-ticket items because minor items, through dependency and complexity, can have an impact far greater than previously thought possible.

Defining the Process in Information-Intensive Work

In most Lean or process reengineering activities you begin with some form of diagnostic or as-is process evaluation to understand the process, baseline cost and performance, and establish a jumping-off point for suggested changes or improvements. In a physical process, such as a warehouse or manufacturing line, you would use a process diagram to describe the sequence of activities and flow or materials. A more complete description would include a depiction of the controlling flow of signals, typically in the opposite direction to the material, that govern and pace the process steps. Visio flowcharts with swim lanes, Integration Definition for Function Modeling "zero" (IDEF0 models, a common flowchart approach), and value stream maps are all good examples of this. But information-intensive work, without the physical dimension of manufacturing or assembly, is not as easily depicted this way. The product is information, and each activity can add or change the information, but it can be hard for most of the stakeholders to see the effects of those changes as they happen.

One of the fundamental things needed to understand Lean improvement for information activities is a new way to represent information flow and to distinguish between information that is product, such as a design spec value, and information that is process control signaling, such as project scheduling data. Developing and using this technique is one of the key elements discussed in this book, but before we can introduce it, we need to put the problem in context.

Large and complex information-intensive work—the kind that spans more than one department or group, and takes weeks or months to complete—suffers from three fundamental challenges:

1. Complexity
2. Psychology
3. Multitasking as a process design (see Figure 4.2)

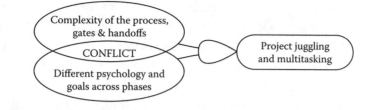

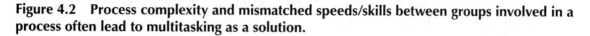

Figure 4.2 Process complexity and mismatched speeds/skills between groups involved in a process often lead to multitasking as a solution.

These are not wastes in themselves but are conditions contributing to and enabling the Lean information wastes. We will address the first two in the following and leave multitasking for its own section later in this chapter.

Complexity

Knowledge workers, as we define them here, perform information-intensive, white-collar work that may use standard tools or procedures, but the result, of necessity, is a relatively unique or creative product. Researchers might use a similar process: search the same Web sites, refer to the same reference materials, subject their results to the same analysis, and package results in a standardized manner, but those results would be unique to the specific problem being researched. Establishing the market price of a piece of real estate, determining the merits of a particular insurance application, establishing the chemical composition of a particular compound, and so forth, are all examples of standard procedures with unique information and explicit case-by-case results. The steps that a real estate agent, insurance underwriter, or lab technician would follow in the aforementioned analyses could easily be written in a procedures manual or graphical flowchart.

The range of practical process documentation varies widely depending on the complexity of the process and variability of results for the individual steps. The individuals developing these process diagrams usually strike a compromise between the true level of detail implicit in the process and the need to represent the logic behind the process graphically. The process steps for assembling a child's bicycle, to start with a simple example, can be very explicit and mechanistic. They can lead you from the beginning to the end of the process with no variation: do step 1, do step 2, do step 3, and so forth. Yet even in this trivial example, we can find room for comment. Who hasn't come across a set of instructions that seemed to make no sense and that practically begged for you to set them aside and rely rather on common sense and native understanding of what a child's bicycle should look like? And even if the instructions are crystal clear, there's probably plenty of opportunity to interpret them by, for example, attaching the pedals prior to attaching the seat or customizing the handlebar with a horn or bell.

At the other end of the spectrum, we have highly creative processes such as developing a new technology or consumer product, or preparing a marketing plan or legal brief. These activities, too, can be described as a series of steps, but the problem is that many of these steps involve branches; the subsequent path is dependent on the results of the current step.

If you are developing a marketing plan, some of these paths might be dictated for you based on your experience and understanding of the product pricing, target demographics, and market needs, and some of them may not be made clear until you have conducted some customer surveys, focus groups, or reviewed your competitor's marketing strategy. Without this information, you simply could not proceed.

If, for example, you had three steps in sequence and each of them had two possible outcomes (admittedly a simple scenario), your project would have eight possible paths. If you were to develop truly detailed maps diagramming the creative process, you would find that it becomes very bushy indeed. So bushy that it becomes impractical. In certain companies or organizations, the office process can be categorized somewhere along the spectrum between the noncreative "cookbook" process and the highly creative "artistic" process. That doesn't mean cooking can't be creative or artistic, but some office processes are more deterministic than others. Processes such as reviewing an insurance claim, for example, are going to follow a more predictable path than a project to sketch out a concept car design.

Of course, many types of projects or processes, such as new product development, run the gamut from highly conceptual or abstract activities early in the process to very pragmatic and specific details toward its conclusion. In the beginning, the team in the proof of concept stage is asking questions such as, "Has anyone ever done this?" "Would anyone buy this?" "Is it possible to do this at this price point/form factor?"; whereas at the end of the project the questions (if all has gone well) are more like, "What is the rack size in inches?" "How many inches of foam do we pack it in?" "What are the pin-outs on this connector?"

This head-in-the-clouds–feet-of-clay dichotomy is one of the causes of dysfunction. The early part of the process is generally referred to as "the fuzzy front end of design." Depending on your perspective, this is either an accurate characterization of the highly variable, semichaotic process we have been describing or a convenient canard that scapegoats the scientist types from ever hitting their schedules and deliverables.

In our experience, adherence to the official process is typically pretty strong toward the later systems integration phases of product development. It is somewhat consistent during the engineering phase, and it's quite inconsistent if not largely lacking in the early proof of concept stage. A review of some 300 projects that we performed for a client showed that only about 40 percent of the projects handed off from design to engineering in the formal stage gate review meeting actually followed the official company development process. Part of the explanation for this is the variability in complexity of design activities. At any point, surprising results can cause the project to take a sharp unanticipated turn or add delays.

Other factors are at play besides complexity, including psychology and poor process design.

Psychology

The broad stages of design are fundamentally different, in perspective, level of detail, left/right brain considerations, and so forth from most other corporate roles as to actually attract and nurture totally different types of people. The creative but absent-minded professor types will be clustered near the front stages of a development process, and the detail-obsessed implementation types will be at the back end. At first glance, this seems not only natural but also desirable, an efficient match of resource skills to job descriptions. Horses for courses, as the British would say.

If these horses would each stay on their respective courses, all would be fine. The creative types are perfectly happy to brainstorm endlessly with each other in the concept group, and the implementers getting ready to deliver the product are each drawing up detailed schedules and plans and routinely meeting to update them. The problem is intergroup coordination. Sequential waterfall or stage gate design processes require handoffs between these disparate psychologies, which means you have two problems: (1) the Lean problem of continuous flow or line balancing between two groups in series, and (2) the strong personalities/cultural barrier between the groups that is so often cast as a problem of personalities and individual shortcomings rather than a systems problem.

The continuous flow side of the problem is simple but daunting. Imagine you had two machines performing two manufacturing operations sequentially just before you ship the product. The second machine performs a polishing function with a very predictable cycle time and throughput of, let's say, eight units per day. The first machine, however, is a sealed oven that pops out its product anywhere from one hour to a month with no advance warning and no status information. The volumes are too low to deal with this problem statistically and with line balancing based on an average throughput. To make matters worse, the polishing machines are specialized and work much better when matched with the product of specific ovens. It's a frustrating balancing act.

Many companies use testing instruments such as the Myers-Briggs Type Indicator (MBTI) or the Belbin Team Inventory to understand and categorize personality types of their employees. There is a large body of work both pro and con regarding the effectiveness of these techniques in selecting team members. Fortunately, we don't have to go into that level of detail. We can be satisfied by just making the simple observation that there is a higher than normal percentage of Myers-Briggs INTPs (Introversion, Intuition, Thinking, Perception) or Belbin Plants in the front end, and they have to communicate with a population of ISTJs (Introversion, Sensing, Thinking, Judgment) or Completer-Finishers as the internal customer. This does not lend itself to easy or satisfying communication. They see things differently, they have different values, and they use information in different ways.

The scientists at the front of the process tend to continuously expand the investigation; if left alone they would pursue many different avenues of experiment and analysis. However, they are not particularly good at providing content information because, after all, this content could easily change with the very next experiment. So most of the information stays in their desks or on their laptops or in their heads until shortly before the handoff meeting where they deliver the project to the downstream group. At this point, their hands are tied and they have to write everything down. By now, of course, they are in a hurry, because this handoff meeting is approaching, and so several of the documents or analyses that are deemed less important are never done at all. This is fine with the downstream group. They are so happy to have anything at all pop out of the creative oven that they will take the project and profess themselves happy even though some of the deliverables are missing. They would rather complete those deliverables themselves than stick it back in the unpredictable oven.

It may seem like we are belaboring this point, but it is an important issue. This handoff between groups is very tricky. We have the personality differences and we have the potential for organizational rivalries. Together they feed back on themselves exacerbating the problem. Since the groups use different types of information for different things (design versus control), any information design has got to handle the translation between them.

The Waste of Reporting

Departmentwide performance or true multiproject status can often be impossible to assess accurately. This is because of the mistaken belief that individual projects are independent whereas they are highly dependent on shared resources, on external vendors, on requirements and change management, on poorly understood progress reporting, all of which hangs on a project schedule that all parties know was at best an estimate.

Individual project managers are loathe to draw excess management attention by reporting progress or status that is less than the level anticipated in the original project schedule or implicit in the due date. At the next level down, individual contributors, who are working on parts of the project plan, are loathe to tell the project manager that they will miss dates or performance targets. After all, they are used to heroic last-ditch efforts to make these dates; therefore, they tell themselves that even if they are behind right now, they'll move some other things onto the back burner and meet the deadline.

Case Study: The Kremlin Effect

The result of all this "professional optimism" is not unlike the situation the Central Intelligence Agency (CIA) faced during the Cold War. During this period, the massive Red Army was scattered across an immense geographical area, which posed a daunting data gathering challenge for the American spies. But since the Soviets had such strict hierarchical central control over every facet of the military, the obvious solution was to bug only the Kremlin where all the different threads came together to form a comprehensive accounting of operational readiness. The problem, however, was not one of real-time data collection and comprehensive reporting (what we in the corporate West now call "business intelligence") but rather one of psychology. Imagine that you are in charge of a remote Siberian outpost and your inadequately trained and supplied, and underpaid conscript troops are in something less than, shall we say, battlefield readiness. Are you likely to report the bald facts or dress them up a little? Especially when, in your experience, all the other remote outpost commanders inflate their readiness and no one's honesty has ever been praised for having the worst but most credible readiness report.

Now imagine what the regional commander does when he receives his half-dozen or so mediocre readiness reports from his outpost commanders. No regional commander has ever been promoted to sector command by having lackluster readiness reports. So, he dresses them up a little before passing them on. And so on by the sector commanders and the theater commanders, all the way up to the Kremlin. And if you are only monitoring an electronic bug picking up the final stage of these reports, you would come away with the impression that the Soviet Army was in peak condition, bristling with well-oiled armaments, and every bit as good as its hockey team from top to bottom. Of course, you would have been wrong, as history has shown.

The "Green ... Green ... Red" Phenomenon

More than just psychological factors contribute to project managers inflating their projects' status. Often they truly believe that the project team can still pull this off and hit its schedule milestones. This is especially true in companies that have poor requirements management and inadequate upfront planning, that is to say most companies. There is an old adage in product development that 1 hour of requirements management is worth 10 hours of design, which, in turn, is worth 100 hours of testing. This is an empirical truism and another manifestation of what we call the *waste of rework* (we mentioned rework in Chapter 1 but in Chapter 7 we will provide a more formal treatment) . For now let's just say that most projects have a very busy final phase, and, when the team is successful, they will all walk around and use metaphors like "the goal line stance," "pulled a rabbit out of the hat," "the project from hell," and other colorful descriptions. If you've worked around project teams, you're familiar with this dark humor celebration.

The culture implicit in this behavior is one that has come to accept that these last-ditch efforts are common or unavoidable and, frankly, has learned to celebrate them by rewarding the late nights and heroic efforts necessary to meet schedule. Of course the irony here is that all the team's resources focusing on the last stages of project 5 are ignoring projects 6, 7, and 8 that are in earlier stages.

The lack of attention that these projects receive practically guarantees that they, too, will require heroic efforts in their final phases to close them out. If you were to do a postmortem on one of these projects (we have done many), you would conclude that the earned value curve throughout the project's duration has a hockey stick shape. Very little seems to get done throughout the first half of the project; as schedule pressure increases, more and more attention is paid to the project; and finally there is the hectic flurry of activity to close the project out. Yet each of these projects probably has a formal project plan and a dusty Gantt chart somewhere with the more or less clear expectation of linear progress throughout the schedule. But since much of the actual work happens in the final stage, and everyone involved knows this, how can the project manager accurately report status?

What actually happens is what we call the "Green … Green … Red" (GGR) phenomenon. Project status is always reported as green—ubiquitous high level status representing on budget and on schedule—until the project is so close to the deadline, and so far from complete, that hitting these targets can no longer be sustained even as a hope. Suddenly, and seemingly out of nowhere, the status turns red just before a major project review or milestone. This does not happen because of brinksmanship on the part of the project manager or the project team; it happens because of a lack of true status visibility.

Perhaps the project could have been saved with the typical Herculean sprint to the finish, but the resources weren't available because some other project started its sprint just before yours did, or some uncontrollable dependency, such as the inability of a vendor to deliver, became the problem.

As we've seen, complexity of the project is a large problem. Psychological and cultural issues can greatly affect handoffs and working relationships between groups as well as influence status reporting, all of which help to perpetuate firefighting and finger pointing. But the factor most directly linked to waste in the Lean sense of the start-and-stop nature of project work is brought about by a lack of situational visibility and multitasking.

The Waste of Multitasking

Multitasking is a relatively modern phenomenon, which increased with paperwork and dramatically increased again with the assistance of electronics. Modern communications and information appliances both create and enable multitasking. Creation happens from the speed at which a new task can intrude on the one currently worked on—the phone rings, the e-mail pings, the BlackBerry vibrates, and so on. Conversely, things like application switching or tabbed browsing mean that a knowledge worker can shift attention and work in a split second. Who among us hasn't thought something like, "While that's printing, I'll check CNN.com"?

A backlash is starting within the core demographic of the knowledge worker: software developers and Web workers. They live in the full midstream of information flow and not along the banks or the mild eddies where you find occasional surfers. You can see hints that multitasking is taking its toll in the proliferation of countermeasures. Tools built along the Getting Things Done (GTD) principles—a hugely popular personal productivity method similar to 5S at the individual level (but that's our Lean perspective on the world) or the Pomodoro Technique™ (a time management technique where you shut everything out and focus on a single item for 25-minute blocks of time)—are common among developers. The Agile Manifesto and many other principles of modern software development also work along these lines; that is, short, uninterrupted tasks, and new services like Kukoo e-mail and Web page blockers act as self-imposed watchdogs to keep you from straying into multitasking. This is no odder than selecting a loud alarm clock to prevent your bad habit of falling back asleep.

Multitasking is a fascinating topic and, as card-carrying iconoclasts, one that we enjoy debunking. Despite the beginnings of a single-tasking revolution, multitasking today is talked about as a badge of honor, proof of one's ability to cope with the fast pace of the modern lifestyle. People will tell you that they are good at multitasking or that they are the kings or queens of multitasking. The idea of multitasking as a positive thing has become deeply entrenched in popular culture, and it is viewed, in part, as a social issue; for example, it is thought to be a key trait for women who need to juggle family and careers. Just because we can do several things simultaneously, such as watching TV while doing the dishes or speaking on the phone while checking our stock portfolio on the Internet, doesn't mean that multitasking should be an important approach to resource or project management in companies. We hate to say it—it'll sound bizarre to many readers—but *multitasking is bad*.

Let's be sure of our terminology. We can do things simultaneously, parallel tasking, such as listening to a book on tape while walking on a treadmill or eating dinner while watching a football game on TV. These are not multitasking since none of these activities, and certainly none that we are doing at the same time, require a great deal of attention. The "attention density" of the activities we are discussing is important. Certain complex or creative tasks, such as playing a difficult piece on the piano or playing a game of chess against a strong opponent, require all of your attention. Chewing gum while walking does not. So to say that we are multitasking because the washing machine is running while we speak on the phone is not really the kind of multitasking we are talking about. Our definition of multitasking requires two or more activities having enough attention density requirements that you have to switch between them.

We are also not talking about fast tracking, where you plan activities based on the long lead-time of one of them. For example, you call the pizza delivery first, and while waiting for it, you vacuum the living room. The pizza arrives once you have finished vacuuming and then you have dinner. Similarly, you might reserve some laboratory space for your experiment next month even though you have not yet fully designed it because, if you were to wait until the experiment was fully designed before requesting lab space, it might result in additional delay.

The multitasking we're talking about is more like trying to research and write three books at the same time or working on six design projects in various stages. There is research indicating that some people are better at multitasking than others are; some people can perform seemingly remarkable feats of multitasking naturally (for example, the chess grandmaster who can play 20 or 30 games simultaneously). But none of these are at their optimum. A grandmaster plays "exhibitions" against 20 weaker players simultaneously, but he doesn't play critical matches this way.

The impact of multitasking in the project oriented high-tech office is immense, and the startling thing is that most companies see it as anything from a core competency at best to a necessary evil at worst. Have you noticed how many employment ads clearly state that one of the required skills is the ability to juggle many things at the same time? Most engineers, programmers, and other project-oriented personnel are skeptical that management will stop using multitasking as a primary resourcing approach. They see multitasking as the only real way to cope with the resource requirements involving multiple projects. The dominant theme in many companies is the overreliance on certain key experts, who are often assigned to a large number of projects either as primary contributors or as reviewers. As we shall see, this leads to deliberately overloading, constraining, and lowering the efficiency of their most valuable resources.

Another fundamental business driver for multitasking is employee performance metrics and reward systems. Evaluating employees on a high utilization, hours billed, or timecard revenue is a guaranteed driver of multitasking. Different project managers will approach some of the "star" personnel and ask them to contribute to their project. As long as these resources can charge their time or otherwise gain credit or recognition for the effort, they will do it. It is not uncommon to find outstanding young consultants, financial analysts, or attorneys billing 150 percent of their available hours (over a 40-hour week). Tracking time and effort is one of the few ways corporations have to ensure that their people are not idle. This ultimately leads to delays and the underutilization of resources and costs far more than the slack time they were trying to prevent.

And let's not forget the final driver of multitasking: resource management. Like the resources themselves, midlevel managers are motivated to have their people charge as much time as possible to drive revenue for their group. They know they are making money directly off multitasking and are typically surprised to find out how much more they are losing indirectly. This problem is commonplace. When we installed one of our first white-collar Lean visual management systems, the data seemed to indicate that several key resources were 400 percent allocated against the company's projects. Since this was clearly a logical fallacy, our tool tried to fix it. It did some resource balancing and projected delivery dates far beyond the existing plan of record for those projects. After much discussion with the client, we had to turn that feature off. The client insisted that these resources must be involved in those projects, and they could not countenance delaying those projects, so they opted to ignore this contradiction.

Case Study: Theory of Constraints

Let's look at this from a theory of constraints perspective. Suppose you have three machines—A, B, and C—feeding each other in series. Machine A can produce 10 widgets an hour, Machine B can process 6 widgets each hour, and machine C can process 12. How many widgets can your operation produce? The answer is six; the additional capacity that machines A and C have cannot be utilized. Allocating your performance improvement budget "fairly" across all three machines would be a mistake. Whatever improvements you made to machines A and C would be wasted since they are already overcapacity. All of your attention should be on the constraint, machine B. In a multitasking environment, your resources are the constraint, and all the other project and portfolio considerations such as project priority, project schedule dates should all be subordinated to the job of maximizing the output of your resources, especially the key, overburdened ones.

Ironically, multitasking impedes performance in several ways simultaneously (multibad?). The sins of multitasking, which we explain in the next section, are:

- Lowered productivity of individual contributors
- Lowered productivity of the entire group or project
- Masked performance issues and hindrance of our efforts to make Lean improvements
- Increased difficulty measuring performance

Finally, multitasking means that you accept more projects than you can handle—you are trying to cope by multitasking. This means that your production efforts start looking like a stakeholder competition with project managers trying to get your people to work on their project and executive sponsors calling to escalate issues of schedule and project priority.

Tool Tip: Instead of multitasking, try standard work, which is a systematic way of allowing the knowledge worker to document standards for performing tasks. This provides a foundation for continuous improvement through the elimination of waste. Everyone involved can see at a glance what should be, compare it to what is, and thereby see waste.
The benefits are:

- Key skills required to perform the standard work are captured.
- Specific tools, quality, and safety points are identified.
- Training and skill assessment are standardized.

■ A tool for cross-training and new knowledge worker training is provided.
■ "Tribal knowledge" problems are eliminated.
■ It identifies how to do the standard work.

Multitasking: The Switching Penalty

In the last decade there have been several psychological studies evaluating multitasking in attempts to determine what its impact on overall productivity might be. Most conclude that multitasking significantly diminishes productivity, especially, as in our case of information-intensive or creative projects, when the tasks involved are complex or new to the workers.

In the mid-1990s, Rogers and Monsell[*] studied the impact of switching tasks on a predictable schedule every two or four hours. They found that people were slower after switching tasks even though the switch was scheduled and they had had time to prepare and mentally adjust to the change.

In the late 1990s, Meuter and Allport[†] experimented with simple tasks among bilingual subjects. The people in the study switched back and forth between their primary and secondary languages performing simple tasks such as identifying numbers and shapes. They were faster in their primary language and slower in their secondary language, but interestingly, they slowed even further when switching back to their primary language. The switching penalty closed the performance gap that originally existed as a result of familiarity with the language.

In 2001, Rubinstein, Evans, and Meyer[‡] conducted experiments with young adults in task switching using activities such as math problems and object classification. For all the tasks evaluated, the participants lost time when switching from one task to another. This productivity impact increased as the complexity of the task or the unfamiliarity of the task increased.

In 2003, Yeung and Monsell[§] studied simulated real-life multitasking situations. Here, subjects switched between long and complex activities, similar to the kinds of projects we are interested in, rather than just short experimental tasks. Because the tasks were ongoing, the subjects had an additional challenge; they needed to remember where they were in the ongoing task. Since they were switching among multiple projects autonomously, they also had to decide when and to which project to switch. All these additional complexities increase the cognitive load of multitaskers and impede productivity, thereby increasing overhead.

---

[*] Rogers, R. D., and Monsell, S. (1995). Costs of a predictable switch between simple cognitive tasks. *Journal of Experimental Psychology*: General, 124, 207–231.

[†] Renata Meuter and Alan Allport, "Bilingual Language Switching in Naming: Asymmetrical Costs of Language Selection," *Journal of Memory and Language* 40 (1999): 25–40.

[‡] Rubinstein, J. S., Meyer, D. E., Evans, J. E. (August, 2001). Executive Control of Cognitive Processes in Task Switching. *Journal of Experimental Psychology*: Human Perception and Performance. Vol. 27, No. 4, pp. 763–797.

[§] Yeung, N. P., and Monsell S., *Journal of Experimental Psychology* (2003) 455–469.

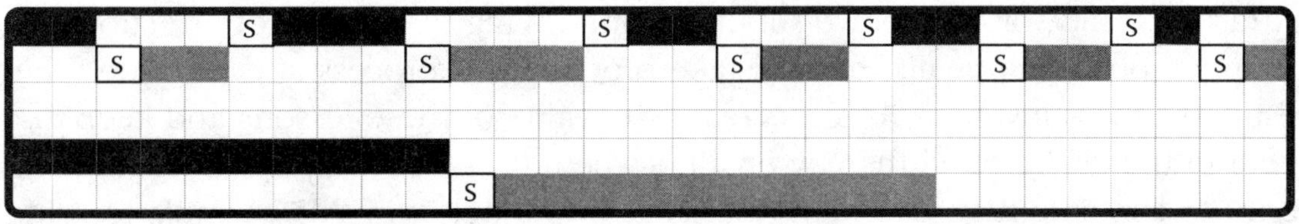

Figure 4.3 Multitasking creates a time penalty, S, for every switch. Even the lower priority gray project finishes sooner without multitasking.

The basic idea here is similar to all the Lean Factory examples of batch production versus continuous flow. Even the low-priority job is finished slightly sooner in the nonmultitasked environment and the high-priority job is finished far sooner. If your metrics include average project duration, then multitasking projects are killing you. The only advantage of multitasking is the positive social contract to project sponsors of low-priority projects, who believe they are getting as much attention as the next person even if they would be better off without it.

Researchers generally conclude that there is a significant overhead associated with task switching that imposes a productivity penalty at the very lowest level of the system, the efficiency of the individual contributor (see Figure 4.3, which illustrates this problem). Individually, these remembering, refocusing, and decision-making switches might be small, but their cumulative effects can be very significant. Meyer quantified the effects of these brief, though frequent mental blocks as resulting in a 40-percent reduction in productive time. (As many telecommuters have learned: "A dozen interruptions of five minutes each means that I have lost the entire afternoon, not just an hour.")

Multitasking: The Lean Waste Penalty

One of the seminal points about Lean and its introduction to American and European business was the concept of learning to see waste. This important mind shift allowed people to reevaluate their usefulness and the benefits of certain existing practices. One of the most obvious was inventory level. Just a decade or so ago, it would be common to stockpile excess inventory just in case. Perhaps this entire inventory was purchased in bulk at a lower unit price, or perhaps it was thought to be a safeguard against the vagaries of an inefficient supply chain, or perhaps it was just comforting to know that we had lots of material on hand lowering the risk that the operation would slowly stop for want of feedstock.

Lean teaches us to see this entire extra inventory, whether feedstock or in-process inventory, as waste, and not just financial waste. Excess inventory ties up money that we will not consume for a long time. Excess inventory masks the true performance of the system. For example, if we have ordered an excess of parts for a particular operation, and we find that there is a high reject rate among those parts, we are relatively unaffected (we think) because of the presence of the extras. We might even congratulate ourselves, "Good thing I thought to order extra." In reality, of course, we should be improving the quality of our supply chain, emphasizing quality and mistake proofing our process at every step. The result of excess inventory is to decrease the value of these lessons and keep them in the background thereby enabling them (to borrow a pop psychology term) to continue their bad behavior. It would be better in this example to bring the factory to a halt once, learn our lesson, and fix the supply problem. The worst lesson we can learn from this is to always order more of everything.

In the information office environment, multitasking has exactly the same insidious effect as excess inventory has in the factory. It hides a host of sins and keeps us from learning where the true problems lie and on what we should be spending our time and effort on. Have you ever had a coworker say something like "Don't worry, I have plenty of other things I can do right now." Juggling multiple projects creates a very busy worker but that certainly does not mean there is no waste. You may have eliminated the waste of idle time but created waste elsewhere. A busy worker or a busy team creates the illusion of efficiency in the same way that factory workers used to think that keeping their large, capital-intensive machinery running 100 percent of the time must be the most efficient use of resources. In addition, it plays to the ego of a worker or team: "I'm the lead programmer on eight major projects. If I left, all hell would break loose!"

In general, multitasking workers are trying to do the right thing for their projects and their company. The basic idea is that some projects naturally have downtime or delays, outside workers' direct control, and it would make no sense for workers to pay attention to a nonmoving project—like cats watching an empty mouse hole. Therefore, workers will naturally switch attention to an active project. Which project gets attention is also a product of conflicting priority or competition between project managers, and not just a practical assessment of where attention will make the most difference. What is in fact happening, from a Lean perspective, is that every time multitasking workers try to be efficient by switching work from one slowed, delayed, or inactive project to one that is "ready," it masks the effects of whatever caused the first project's delay and ultimately perpetuates a system that tolerates significant amounts of waste in its projects.

Figure 4.4 adapts a common Lean cartoon showing the effects of excess inventory. The high water level keeps the boat above the rocks in the same way that excess inventory insulates the process from the effects of supply chain issues and masks the problem. Typically the cartoon is accompanied by a second diagram in which the water level has been lowered to where the keel is scraping the rocks. At this point, the contributing wastes can no longer be ignored. Reducing multitasking will eliminate this false cushion of security and highlight the information waste in the system, which is the first step toward resolving the problem.

Multitasking: The Project Penalty

What is probably the best-known experiment to illustrate the effects of multitasking in a real-life multiproject environment was developed by Tony Rizzo while

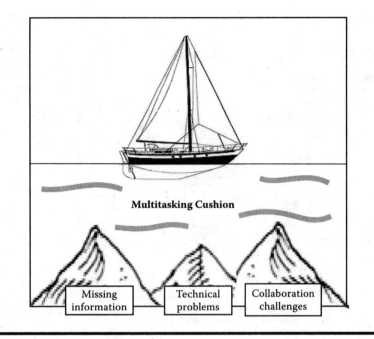

Multitasking Cushion

Missing information

Technical problems

Collaboration challenges

Figure 4.4 Because there's always another project to switch to, multitasking can hide, not mitigate, the wastes inherent in the process.

at Lucent Technologies. It is called the bead game and it is both highly illustrative and fun because its results are so dramatic and surprising. Essentially, it demonstrates that the same resources, doing exactly the same amount of work get far better results without multitasking than with it. We have run this game several times, participated in it ourselves, and seen it run or reviewed countless others. The results are always consistent and yet so counterintuitive to some of the participants that they have a very hard time accepting the evidence they just witnessed. It's not infrequent for some of the participants to raise claims of fraud or even magic.

The game is very simple in concept (see Figure 4.5). Three people perform simple, if somewhat contrived operations, to sort, process, and re-sort groups of beads. The first resource starts with a mixed bowl of beads and, using only one hand and a spoon, sorts them by color, placing each group on a plate. In the second phase, the two other resources process the beads by turning them all face down and, once that is accomplished, turning them all face up again. The mechanics are made somewhat more complicated, and the attention density increased, by forcing these resources to use just one hand and a spoon to do the processing. One of the resources processes two of the colors while the third resource processes the remaining color. They can't begin processing until the first resource has completed the sorting process and filled the plates with beads of one color. When this processing step is completed, they return the three plates to the first resource who, again with just one spoon, shovels all the beads back into one common bowl. Thus, there are three phases: sorting, processing, and integration.

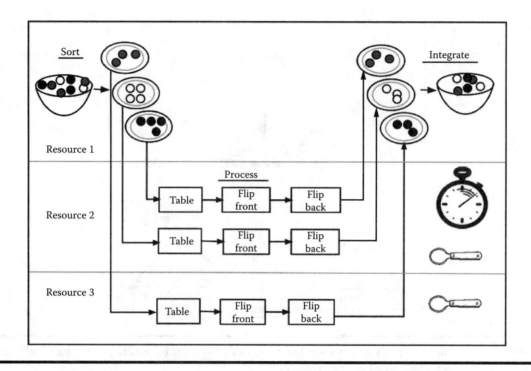

Figure 4.5 The bead game demonstrates the waste inherent in a multitasking, multiproject environment.

Although this is not very challenging intellectually, the multitasking wrinkle is that they need to do this for two projects, not just one. Shortly after the first project begins (let's call it the red project), the blue project is launched. It is the same in every step as the red project, sorting and integrating feeds in exactly the same way, but because we are experimenting with multitasking, each worker has to switch from one project to the other after three steps, so three spoonfuls for the red project, three spoonfuls for the blue project, and so on. To add some realism, we introduce two new characters: the red project manager and the blue project manager. Each of these acts as a watchdog to make sure the resource is attentive to the needs of their particular projects. These project managers are partisan (have you ever met one that wasn't?) and will typically ignore it if one of the resources makes a mistake and fails to switch away from his or her project. The project managers add a lot of motivation, not to mention decibels, and ensure that frequent switching happens.

The final character is the timekeeper who notes the start and stop times for the red and blue projects. There is a wide variance depending on the youth and competitive nature of the participants, but typical times for this experiment are between 6 and 12 minutes to complete both the red and blue projects.

Now we run the experiment again but remove multitasking and the constant "motivation" of the project managers. The blue project is introduced, accepted is more the word, just as phase one is completed for the red project and the first worker delivers three sorted plates to the other two. Everything proceeds exactly as before except the workers at each stage concentrate on completing the red project before the blue one. Typical times to complete both red and blue projects without multitasking are between 2 and 3 minutes. That's a 75-percent reduction in cycle time for the identical projects with absolutely no change in capacity or cost! (This is where the naysayers start looking for a trick.)

The secret to the performance difference is partially due to the attention switching described earlier, but it is also due to Lean concepts of *continuous flow*, which lead to a far more efficient use of resources. In the experimental run using multitasking, resources 2 and 3 were idle for a far longer time because resource 1 was trying to fill six plates simultaneously rather than three. Similarly, resources 2 and 3 took much longer to do their processing. This was especially true for resource 2, who was juggling two sets of beads for two projects, thereby delaying phase 3 and, this time, idling resource 1.

Despite its dramatic results, this multitasking experiment was comprised of just two projects. In our experience, today's information workers juggle between six and eight projects. Furthermore, the beads on plates are highly visible, the start and stop signals could not be clearer. As we have described, this is one of the problems with Lean in the information age: Information flow is very much harder to see and that adds to the effect of information project multitasking.

Multitasking: The Performance Measurement Penalty

> If you cannot measure it, you cannot improve it.
>
> **—Lord Kelvin**

One of the most frustrating aspects of multitasking is its effect on process measurement. It should be evident that fundamental process improvement methodologies, such as define, measure, analyze, improve, and control (DMAIC), aren't going to be very beneficial if we can't accurately measure process steps, and heavy use of multitasking makes this next to impossible.

Case Study: Measuring a Process

Let's say you are developing a pro forma "typical schedule" for a process or doing a value stream analysis for a process that has 20 or 30 tasks scattered among a few different organizational groups. Each task produces a piece of information or an interim document. If you line up these constituent tasks in order and sum their component durations, you should have a hypothetical baseline to inform and kick off your analysis.

Assume that you use the appropriate interim deliverable as an example and you ask the worker responsible for developing it how long it takes. In most cases, you will get an answer that has something to do with multitasking. The interviewee can do a primitive value stream map in his or her head, and will anticipate the following question: If the deliverable seems to represent five hours actual work, why does it usually take a month to produce?

Multitasking information workers tend to resist this kind of value stream analysis. Multitasking becomes the go-to excuse. They have many other things on their plate (attention and switching). They had bigger fish to fry (frequent project reprioritization). There were external factors delaying this project (why had this project been accepted?). The implicit understanding is, since the workers were busy 100 percent of the time, the result could not have been better than it was. In this type of company, the attempt to quantify these steps will receive only limited acceptance. It is quite difficult to build process improvement platforms on such shaky measurement foundations.

Multitasking: The Command and Control Penalty

The final indictment that we shall lay at the feet of multitasking is what we call the command and control penalty. Sometimes multitasking is a deliberate design. We once had a customer describe his proposed consulting engagement as a way to increase multitasking measured by his "projects per engineer" performance metric. More typically, multitasking is grudgingly accepted as a suboptimal but necessary solution to the problem of too much work with too few people.

The too much work aspect of this imbalance is often due to a misperception on the part of management as to how to load and plan their work. Sometimes the R&D (research and development) managers or the factory managers have to learn to just say no, or at least real soon now. The problem arises when this strategic resource allocation problem morphs into a corporate relations problem. We know a design manager who called all his overworked engineers into a conference room and explained that there was a lot of work coming ahead and that this would require even greater Herculean efforts on their part. Although there were just too many projects coming in from all parts of the organization, they weren't going to let the company down by turning some of them away.

This senior division manager was very conscious of his role in product development. The future of the company depended on sales revenue coming from the projects on his drawing board. They were going to deliver whatever the cost. The problem is that by taking all these projects on simultaneously, by meeting the priority demands of so many project sponsors from different parts of the organizations, and by trying to be as responsive as possible to shifting market demands and priorities of ongoing projects, they were in fact slowing the output of the organization rather than increasing it. Not to mention the wear and tear it caused on the morale and efficiency of these critical design engineers.

A few years ago, we created a classroom simulation covering the design and production parts of a manufacturing company as part of a consultant-training course. In this exercise, the consultants would read interview notes from fictional characters (the chief marketing officer, plant managers, R&D managers, and so forth) scattered around the manufacturing company. The interview notes from the two plant managers were markedly different. Without using the specific Lean and Six Sigma terms that might tip the reader to what was behind the approach, one plant manager described an efficient operation where theory of constraints ideas were understood and applied, multitasking was minimized, pull scheduling was in place, and several other modern Lean initiatives were described. The other plant manager talked incessantly about being responsive to its customers, open to escalation and changes to the delivery dates and scopes of the projects, shifting projects in production to keep up with the fast-changing market strategy, and heavy use of expediters to ensure that all this happened.

When the trainees read the simulated interviews with project sponsors throughout the organization, the second plant manager was universally liked. He was a responsive team player who kept his customers' interests uppermost. The disguised Lean plant manager was disliked for being stubborn and hard to work with (these opinions were the reverse of those of their respective factory workers). The trainees admitted, however, that the first manager had a better on-time delivery record than the popular plant manager. Had the consultant trainees received a proper analysis of the financial and performance spreadsheets, they would also realize that the unpopular plant manager was contributing practically all of the manufacturing division's profit.

Many of the students in the course were swayed by the good customer service intentions of the accommodating plant manager and, therefore, thought his performance was superior. If only the Lean plant manager had done a better job of communication. His factory was more profitable, his on-time delivery was far better, his overtime was much less, and worker morale was far higher. Armed, as you now are, with a thorough understanding of the penalties behind multitasking, he could have explained all this to his internal clients. They would have seen that both the company and each of them individually were better served by a nonmultitasking approach.

In recent years, there has been much analysis of multitasking because of the many thin (low attention density) types of communication technologies that have sprung up. You will either consider text messaging a supplementary tool or an all-encompassing passion (depending on whether you have teenage children). Kids text while in class, watching TV, on the playground, or even speaking on another phone. There is also much analysis, especially around attention switching, in connection with the use of cell phones or BlackBerries while driving. More and more of our economy is becoming a service economy, and much of that is dramatically increasing the creation and consumption of information.

Tip: We have discussed parallel and sequential information flow elsewhere, but want to reemphasize that just because you can switch tasks very quickly using high-tech appliances doesn't mean that you should.

The Waste of Time

We like to watch woodworking shows on TV. Within a brief span of minutes, the craftsperson converts a pile of lumber into an attractive and functional piece of furniture. Order from chaos, and there's finality to it. The last step is to apply the finish (even the word makes us happy). Note that the person on TV doesn't speak in wood theory ("Select the right wood and somehow get 30 pieces of it into these shapes"); he very practically walks you through all the steps and demonstrates the right tool for each one.

We admit to a deep fascination with the tools themselves. Humans are primarily tool users and all of our evolution demonstrates that tools provide competitive advantages: production accelerators in the factory, yield enhancers on the farm, and force multipliers on the battlefield. Tools, both hardware and software, are at the heart of the modern office. They provide fantastic utility and process information faster and faster with each new product cycle. They also are the greatest time wasters in the modern office.

In this section, we discuss both theory and specific tools. The topic of measurement is simply too intertwined with the measurement techniques to separate them. All companies seek utility from their employees. They hire the best people they can and provide training and tools to maximize their yield. They also have very practical considerations that drive time measurement and management: how much do we pay the employees, how much do we charge our clients, how much is it costing us to perform a certain task or create a certain product.

In the physical world, the factory or assembly operation we often refer to, time measurement is straightforward. Some device, a timekeeper or a time clock, captures the boundaries: the times when employees punch the clock, and direct-line supervision ensures they are productive within these boundaries. The latter is straightforward because it is obvious when an assembly line worker is not assembling, there are many visual cues such as a series of items coming down the line with one component suspiciously absent. In a large nonlinear operation such as an outside construction or harvesting operation, you need enough direct-line supervision to more or less constantly monitor utilization.

In an office of the 1970s or earlier, it was also quite easy. Perhaps a self-reported timecard was used in lieu of a time clock, but the type of equipment provided—typewriters, adding machines, and telephones—were difficult to use for anything other than work. You could try to write a novel instead of your market report on your typewriter, we suppose, but good luck hiding it quickly when the boss strolled by. It's interesting to note that "boss buttons" were an early piece of utility software for computers. With one click, these replaced whatever was on your screen with a legitimate-looking spreadsheet. They were an immediate success for all the obvious reasons.

This is one area where Information Lean has an advantage over Factory or Paper Lean: The electronic footprints of activity on a computer can be captured and reported upon to a degree that far surpasses anything available to workers or consultants gathering data with stopwatches, counters, and clipboards.

The Lean waste of time can be broken into three contributors: productivity, time management, and activity visibility.

Direct Productivity

Workers and managers are looking for tools to help them stay productive and resist the urge to deviate from what they need to do. In the office, this became an issue when Internet connections became widely available. The Internet is incredibly powerful and a great source of information, but when YouTube, news, sports scores, and so much more is at your fingertips, it's hard to stay focused on the job. How can people stay productive?

Time Management

Keeping track of what one does on the computer is a perfect task for the computer itself to do. People are not good at this, and most people hate to fill out timesheets and punch the clock. Yet, it's something that millions of people around the world have to do, and automation can help them. Converting this information into information that needs to be critically precise, such as a client invoice, is not easy and, with today's technology it should be used as an input to the worker completing a timecard rather than an alternative. However, when you consider that most timecards are hurriedly filled in with guesses or the occasional reference to a notebook or journal, there seems to be a significant opportunity for improvement.

Activity Visibility

In an environment in which information workers get work done sitting in front of their computers all day long, unless you probe the digital bits that are flying back and forth from one computer to another (or watch what people do from behind their backs), there's very little visibility of what's actually going on. Are people communicating? Are they getting work done? Are there any hurdles blocking progress? Which resources are being used? How much time is spent on resources? What type of knowledge and expertise is developing in the organization? In the knowledge economy, work gets done with little physical manifestation; so unless there's some instrumentation in place, it's incredibly hard to measure progress, address issues, and fix what's broken.

Nowadays application switching, widgets, and the Internet elevate time wasting to an art form (sometimes unknowingly or inadvertently). Have you ever wondered, "Where did the day go? I was here working all the time." The Web can be a real culprit here. Often a legitimate search will spawn a host of interesting and hitherto unimagined lines of inquiry. And investigating them is just a click away. You started by trying to get a train schedule for your business trip and, before you know it, you are fascinated by the promise of Maglev trains or reminiscing about that great summer when you memorized every lyric that Grand Funk Railroad ever wrote. This is like candy to a procrastinator. Many of these side trips are quite legitimate and business related with some future application, but trying to scan them and file them away for future reference slows the task. One approach to deal with the Web's many enticements is to try to bookmark everything. But you soon have a knowledge management problem: You can't remember what all those URLs were for and they are organized in a long, meaningless list. Another approach is to use one of a fast-growing category of tools to capture and categorize information quickly on the fly.

Tool Tip: Two such examples are Evernote and OneNote, both excellent products that allow you to paste a snapshot of the screen, copy the URL, and add a few simple tags so you can find the information later. Of course, you can type in text notes or even make visual notes with your webcam. Evernote can also search for text, even handwritten text, within these screenshots. You can search for items you remember only vaguely or you can flip through the screenshots to jog your memory. This tool also works with your phone, so you can add ideas and photos to your searchable shoebox while you are away from your desk. Personally, we find this class of tool (and there are dozens of applications with varying features) an extremely helpful way to serve the competing masters of curiosity and productivity. You know you have captured it so you can easily find it when the time spent to review it will not negatively affect some other activity.

Microsoft is working hard to avoid the innovator's dilemma in this category, and SharePoint and Windows Live are good examples as is Dynamics for enterprise business intelligence applications. Similar collaboration and documents-in-the-cloud solutions from the biggest players such as GoogleDocs and iWork join a host of very good collaboration tools for workgroups who are learning that e-mail just isn't the answer to all their networked communication problems. Knowledge workers should enjoy this time!

The introduction of the computer as a commonplace item on most desktops has changed productivity monitoring dramatically. Computers make a lot of things simpler, but they also make it very easy to waste precious time. Clearly, it is no longer possible to assess productivity by simply walking around the office and checking whether the employees are still sitting at their workstation. For all you know they are playing 3D Space Invaders in massive multiplayer mode on the Web and are totally unobserved, which would be like the office worker of the 1970s having several friends at his desk playing Monopoly and nobody noticing.

This failure to grasp that computers are far more versatile tools than their limited business application, coupled with antiquated productivity monitoring techniques, is costing businesses billions of dollars annually in lost productivity.

Some businesses try to limit time-wasting activities by blocking certain sites or software applications, but this is not always possible and most of the time is counterproductive. For instance, a business can use instant messaging to communicate quickly and easily between offices, but instant messaging can also be used to chat unproductively with friends. In this scenario, blocking the instant messaging application does not make sense.

There are keystroke logging applications that might serve to dissuade deliberately unproductive behavior, but we think these are a bad idea. They are highly intrusive and violate worker privacy, they require significant postprocessing to learn anything, and they only catch egregious transgressions since who can tell whether Maglev train research was a justifiable business inquiry or not?

The emerging class of solutions are time and activity analytics applications for computers that automatically keep track of where users spend time—by application, by Web site, by file—represented in a timeline, bar chart, and several other standard reports. The applications unobtrusively observe as users interact with programs, documents, e-mail, and Web sites, and then display detailed statistics of their computer usage in a set of intuitive and easy to use visualizations. Thousands of designers, architects, consultants, and developers among others are learning to use these tools to keep track of time and manage their productivity.

These are not spying tools; they may report how many minutes the word-processing application was in use but will not indicate the content. You can turn them off should you wish to invoke privacy or you can block certain applications or sites from data capture. The idea is to capture useful data, not people.

In our experience, most results about value versus nonvalue time coming from value stream mapping are usually surprising. The same is true at the individual level when using these automatic task discovery tools. It is easier to understand a work group having a high nonvalue percentage when the individuals in the group have spent a significant percentage of their time off process.

One of the most powerful features of these tools is tagging. To make the task of evaluating productivity a quick process, you can tag a group of applications or Web sites as "productive." The tool will then use the tags you create to display results. You will know at a glance whether the majority of the users' time was spent in productive applications or not. Tags can be customized to provide reports in categories that you find useful. As we write this, we have word processing, graphics, and note-taking applications tagged to "writing book." We get instant reporting on time spent against this activity. The fact that we are often surprised at what those reports tell us really drives home the notion that your perception of how you spend your time and how you actually spend your time can be significantly different. We could tag files or applications or Web sites

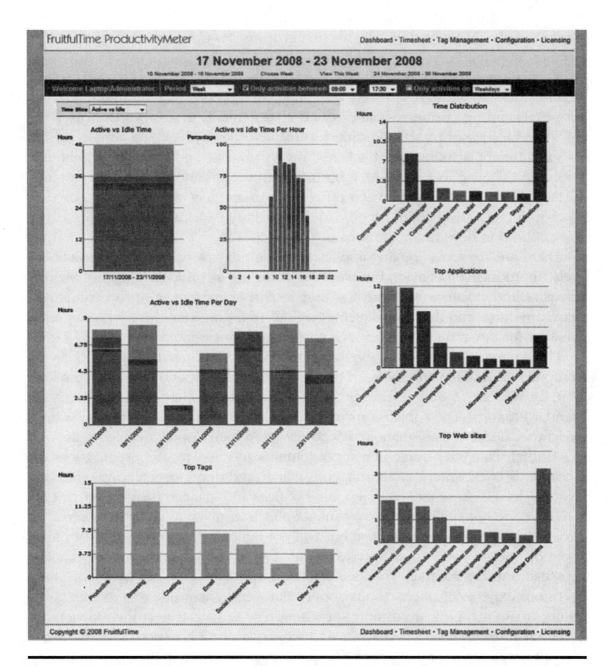

Figure 4.6   Modern tools can assess worker productivity and gather process performance data with far more detail than estimates or consultants' interviews.

against a client account, or an internal project, or in any way we would like to capture information.

Tool Tip: Some new tools that show tremendous promise in this area are Slife, ProductivityMeter, and Rescue Time.

FruitfulTime's ProductivityMeter (see Figure 4.6) is a lightweight client/server application that automatically monitors the activities of each employee on his or her computer rather than blocking individual applications or Web sites. The employee activity data can then be viewed as visual reports by designated users, such as team managers or supervisors, through a dashboard. The managers can assess quickly and easily the productivity of their team from their computers. The visual reports displayed on the dashboard of ProductivityMeter break down the time of each individual employee into active time, inactive time, or time away from the computer. Other graphs also show the top applications used, the top Web sites visited, and the overall time distribution.

In addition to powerful and flexible tagging, ProductivityMeter also has built-in timecard reporting. It can be used by an individual to gauge his or her productivity for analysis and improvement reasons, as a small business to capture billing-related data, or as a one-time project to assess how time is spent on a process to help establish the as-is baseline. When used as a group performance or collaboration tool, team managers are only a click away from knowing precisely how productive each team member was during a day, week, month, or custom date range. This is not all. A manager can click on any graph to drill down on a specific application, which makes it possible to identify the very detailed level of process performance that would never come to light during interview-based process discovery.

Slife Labs develops productivity, collaboration, and analytics software (see Figure 4.7) for individuals and businesses that center on the real-time observation and understanding of context and activities. The company currently develops two products, Slife and Slife Teams. The

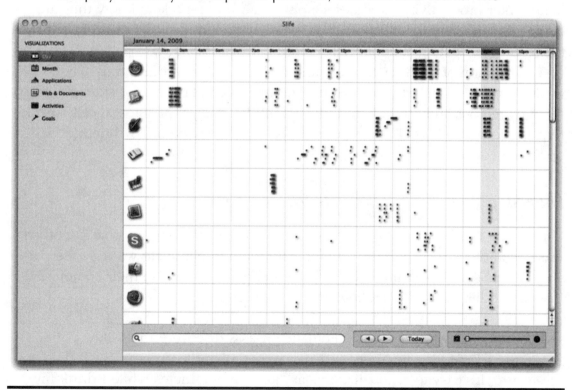

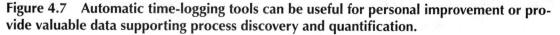

Figure 4.7 **Automatic time-logging tools can be useful for personal improvement or provide valuable data supporting process discovery and quantification.**

team product extends Slife to multiple users and is referred to as the "Google Analytics" of company activities. It provides detailed insights into the digital activities of organizations, such as how much time teams and workgroups spend on projects, and which applications and Web sites are used in the office. Slife Teams can be used for workforce planning, time management, software compliance, and in a myriad of other ways.

These tools deliver what they promise, but we see challenges. Many workers may balk at this passive observation and the "spy" word will likely be used. Lean practitioners, consultants, or the intellectually curious may install and use these low-cost tools because they promise interesting results with very little time investment. As a process discovery tool, they hold huge promise. They can be used to automatically log activities. Then those activities can be tagged to anything, including process definitions that are under review. These reports will quantify time spent in a process, with undreamed of detail and accuracy compared to staff interview data, and provide valuable input to process discovery and analysis automatically. Granted, they don't produce a flowchart of time-sequenced steps, but they are far better than interviewing workers to learn how much time they spend on "sales and marketing," and they are better than direct observation because there should be much less of a Hawthorne effect (the theory that worker productivity increases simply because the workers know they are being studied). Perhaps business process improvement projects could install such tools during a "data-gathering trial" period early in the study.

The creation of such an accurate and highly detailed process trail may be great for process analysts, but we suspect that others, lawyers for example, may see a dangerous audit trail. Future document discovery will automatically include requests for these logs. Their wealth of detail will provide happy hunting for opposing counsel.

Four-Step Program to Eliminate Wasted Time

Eliminating time waste in a process is one thing, eliminating information office waste is another. It helps to encourage your team to eliminate waste at the personal level. This program can help those seeking to minimize their compulsive Internet fiddling, social e-mailing, and twittering:

1. *Identify and quantify.* Use automatic process discovery tools like FruitfulTime, Rescue Time, and Slife to get a handle on how much time you waste. It's easy to rationalize this as "just a few minutes while I drink my coffee and get ready for the day," and it's quite another thing to look at a report in black and white showing just how much time you could get back.

2. *Get help.* We mean software help—the kind you can get privately and the kind that's sort of fun for knowledge workers to use anyway. Web blocking sites like Leechblock and e-mail tools like Kukoo can help you with both external interruptions and your self-induced interruptions. Simple desktop tools along the Pomodoro method will help you focus for half-hours at a time. If you do a few Pomodoro's each day, without accepting interruptions, you'll see your automated process discovery (APD) statistics rise in a very satisfying way. Xobni is another terrific tool that, while not reducing e-mail, will save you wasted time in finding old strings and files buried within your e-mail.

3. *Know why.* Are you trying to get more done at work? Or trying to leave work on time more often to spend time with the family? As you start to rationalize pushing back against these steps, you will need to refocus by referring to your underlying motivation.

4. *Goals and rewards.* We believe in the power of feedback. Track your performance against a goal, lowering "waste time" for example. Reward yourself when you get there. Do it again. Your waste reduction muscles will get stronger and your Lean contribution will be noticeable.

The Waste of High Utilization

In some organizations, high utilization is the very definition of productivity and success. Not only are the resources fully busy (as we know, idle hands are the devil's playmates, but in this context they are also hands that we're paying whether or not they are idle), high utilization implies that management is doing a good job of organizing and directing its resources and that the theater organizations, perhaps sales, are doing their jobs properly by providing enough work to keep these resources busy.

In service organizations such as the legal profession or consulting, the firm's revenue is tied to billable hours and therefore high utilization is even more critical. All these resources know that their financial worth to the organization is directly related to their hours billed. The highly utilized resource is the most prized one.

However, high utilization can also go hand-in-hand with other limitations to the system; which can be physical like travel, process related, or based on managerial policy. For example, if you ask most senior managers in a consulting firm, they will tell you that a big project is better than the equivalent revenue in small projects because it is more efficient. There are two contributors: the time spent by senior personnel on the sales cycle (small projects can easily take as long to close as large projects, therefore the more projects the more sales time, which means less time billing) and the time spent moving and allocating resources between projects.

SMED and SMEW for the Information Age Office

This is equivalent to single minute exchange of die (SMED) in Factory Lean. The reason non-Lean factories use batch-based production runs is the time spent in retooling for each run. Since retooling was obviously unproductive, the idea became to do as little of it as possible. So production runs, and subsequent batch sizes, grew in order to achieve this perceived efficiency.

Service organizations try to do exactly the same thing. If you send a consultant to the Cleveland Project on Monday and have him report to the Chicago Project on Thursday, you either have to bill for the travel time between the two projects (something that customers may not value and may be unwilling to pay for) or you lose billable time, and hence utilization. If you have a series of small projects in a row, the downtime between projects, since they will never have perfect end-to-start timing, will have a serious impact on your utilization if you are a consultant and on project revenues if you are the manager. Everyone quickly learns that you are much better off on a nice long project (long production run) than you are switching back and forth between smaller projects. (As we discussed when we talked about multitasking, switching back and forth between a large number of projects creates a very high percentage of nonvalue time between projects as well as low value time getting back up to speed on each new project after the switch.)

Curiously, this is exactly opposite to what these very same consultants tell their clients about factory operations. This is not merely ironic; it is a fundamental driver of the service industry, which favors longer and more expensive projects over nimbler, leaner ones. The ramifications of this to the economy when you consider the size of the project-based service industry are enormous.

The single minute exchange of worker (SMEW) equivalent for the service industry is to do exactly the same thing the factory has done—increase the percentage of value by minimizing these two "edge effects":

1. The physical transition between projects, especially travel time
2. The nonvalue-added administrative portion, especially the upfront sales cycle.

Minimizing travel time or converting travel time or downtime into useful billable time has always been the most common approach. Technology is aiding in this area but also creating whole new problems.

Three approaches to minimizing travel or downtime are:

1. *Get there faster.* There is no question that airplanes are faster than trains and in large countries like the United States that can make a difference, but this is probably not going to help much. Airports nowadays can add significant time to a journey. Almost as important are travel-enabling tools, such as Expedia, and mobile tools that provide updated status information direct to your pocket. The tools can cut down on travel planning and make it easier to switch plans en route.

2. *Mobile productivity.* Working on your laptop on the plane or in a terminal, getting your schedule direct to your BlackBerry or iPhone, and of course making cellular calls while out of the office are all ways to improve productivity. Most traveling service providers opt for this approach and most communications companies, airports, and airlines do their best to cater to this class of customer. Constant Internet connectivity, whether by Wi-Fi or cellular network, is standard now.

3. *Virtual presence.* A simple solution to avoid the waste of travel time is to not travel. In the kind of work systems we describe, most work products, including project status and visual management tools, are available online and physical presence should not be required. Indeed, given teleworking, distributed physical buildings of large companies, globalization, and the ever-tighter connection with your vendors and suppliers in your integrated supply chain, any system that requires physical presence is probably suboptimal. Some concepts, for example Second Life, take virtual presence to an extreme. We think there is interesting potential to electronic avatars and the technology is quite ready, but we are also certain most company cultures are not.

There are two fundamental approaches to reducing the administrative and sales components of nonbillable time:

1. *Electronic versus face-to-face selling.* There is no question that for some activities face-to-face selling is best, that is to say, the most effective; but it is also the most time-consuming and expensive. We expect that we have just seen the tip of the iceberg regarding e-mail marketing and especially social network–based marketing. There are many bright people out there making their living on commission, and if they can't figure out how to reach more customers more quickly via Linked In, Twitter, Facebook, and YouTube, we will all be very surprised.

2. *Always on service portal.* Although improved selling can save managers downtime, improved operations tools will provide SMEW for the rest of the service organization. The idea here is *micro*consulting, the service level agreement (SLA), hourly rates, and other contractual parameters are established once and "left open." Workers in the client company can essentially post the task they need completed (scope) and receive bids from their always-on consultant. This can be a point-to-point relationship between a client and service provider organization (Pfizer has something like this now) or it can be open—any of several service provider organizations can react quickly and bid on the piece of microconsulting. We wager that the competitive nature of this would provide tremendous speed and value to the client. Essentially this would be a day-to-day operations version of open innovation. Call it "open operations." We believe that this new model for consulting or "knowledge service" can be extremely effective in the years ahead.

Overly High Utilization

If there is a corollary to the waste of time caused by direct idleness and unproductive behavior, it is the waste of time caused by attempting too much productive behavior. Most organizations naturally feel that keeping their workers productive is a key to success. And surely productivity is a function of time worked (hours) multiplied by rate of work (efficiency). The latter is a function of many factors: quality of the resources, their training, their having been staffed on appropriate assignments that align with their skills, their tools and the ready availability of the raw materials (information) that they need to do the job, and their morale and motivation. We know this implicitly even if we sometimes don't do a good job of managing toward it.

On the other hand, most managers don't see the need to study the time component of this productivity equation. Their belief is that hours are hours; the more you work the more you get. Ever since the software industry, for one, became characterized by excessive overtime, people have noticed that the expected straight-line correlation between time and output for the same resource does not hold true elsewhere.

Famous works such as *Nailing Jelly to a Tree**[*] and *The Mythical Man-Month*[†] documented the phenomenon that no amount of additional resources seems to progress a project forward. Managers are aware of this too, at least the good ones are, but it's usually considered a special case. However, a great deal of overtime over an extended period will lead to burn out, and, beyond overtime burnout, is the day-to-day waste of trying to keep employees at close to full-time utilization.

There are two components to this: (1) the waste of inactivity (opportunity cost waste) and (2) the waste of excessive utilization (see Figure 4.8). The curve depicting inactivity labeled "Excess Capacity" shows what happens when there are too many expensive resources sitting around idle; time or cost go up (similar to saying resource costs are high). And as our excess capacity moves to zero with fully utilized workers, the cost of this excess capacity also moves toward zero, and, therefore this line slopes down from left to right.

If we think of the work coming into our department or group as a queue, we can apply some of the well-established mathematical techniques to understand this problem.[‡] Basically, the timing queue has a nonlinear relationship with capacity. The simplest example is what happens when you close one lane of a four-lane highway in the dead of night when traffic is low. The average speed of cars on that highway will not change at all. However, if you close that same lane during rush hour when capacity is very high, traffic will crawl to a halt.

---

[*] Jerry Willis and William Danley, *Nailing Jelly to a Tree* (Blue Ridge Summit, PA: Tab Books, 1982).

[†] Fred Brooks, *The Mythical Man-Month* (Reading, MA: Addison-Wesley Professional, 1975).

[‡] Interested readers should review *Managing the Design Factory* by Donald Reinertsen (New York: Free Press, 1997) or any solid work on Markov chains for deeper background.

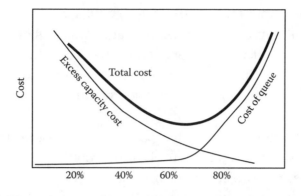

Figure 4.8 Total cost is the sum of unused (wasted) capacity and inefficiently used (over-burdened) resources.

This is critical to our understanding: queuing theory proves that with statistically variable external inputs, the system will experience delays even when it is below, perhaps significantly below, its fully utilized design point. In a system such as a group of knowledge workers, we would expect to see some delays and inefficiencies creeping into product design or development work when utilization levels reach about 70 percent and a very high degree of delay when utilization is above 90 percent. When teams are operating at very high capacity, every variation becomes a delay or an impact to another project since there is no buffer.

We have defined a system with two costs: (1) the cost of letting our resources sit idle and (2) the cost of decreasing their productivity by making them be too busy. The total cost of our system is the sum of these two curves (the heavy top line in Figure 4.8). This curve is saddle-shaped, indicating that the optimum operating point for a system is approximately in the 60- to 80-percent range. The precise location of this optimum loading point varies with complexity and scale. The larger and more interrelated the "surprises," the greater impact they will have on the other projects to which our high-utilization knowledge worker is assigned. Very low utilization drives up cost through direct effects (idle resources), but very high utilization also drives up cost through indirect effects (dependencies, hand-offs, etc.).

This will strike the service industry, lawyers, and consultants, for example, as dangerous nonsense. These businesses make their living by selling man-hours, especially the somewhat commoditized man-hours of their junior and middle ranks. To suggest that anything other than maximum utilization is the right answer will be discarded out of hand. But stop for a minute and think of any system running at full capacity. If there is any external dependency or any statistical variability, then every single instance will affect the system causing defects or delays, and, if there are multiple multitasked projects, then those impacts will inevitably be felt in another part of the organization. The accounting systems are good enough to catch the arithmetic of man-hour times billing rate, but they will not catch the off-the-books negative impacts.

The wrinkle here is that the service industry bills by time more often than delivered quality. Remember the key Lean adage: Waste is anything your customer would not pay for if it were itemized on the bill. Therefore, the service industry is not penalized for multitasking and waste; they are rewarded for it. The extra time wasted appears on the invoice with the same billing rate as value-added time.

Google, we are heartened to say, has a good idea about this. Employees have a maximum assignable utilization of 80 percent. The other 20 percent are reserved for personal pet projects and innovation. Young knowledge workers with their noses to the grindstone lugging 100-percent utilization or even overtime (plus fire drills) have no slack time to sit and think in a green field's way and contribute innovative solutions for the future. This waste, the waste of your best workers not thinking about innovation or improvement, is harder to quantify than a utilization number or a project delay but is far more important.

It may be that in strong hierarchical cultures this kind of worker independence is unachievable. However, we think that the appearance of being busy and overloaded is simply a management proxy for effort and productivity. If they had superior situational visibility, and they were getting great process output as reported by their metrics, they would learn to adopt this approach however counterintuitive. But in the absence of meaningful measurements we settle for the Plato's Cave version of productivity—a cluttered desktop, an overloaded calendar, and workers running from meeting to meeting.

The Waste of Parallel Project Management

A few aspects of business today demonstrate as wide a disparity between theory and practice as that which exists in day-to-day project management. In academia, business schools, and in special areas of expertise like the Project Management Institute or consulting companies, project management is a technically rich and analytically complex function. More than scheduling sequencing and organization, it deals with dynamic resource loading, risk management, detailed work breakdown structures, probabilistic analyses, and Monte Carlo simulations. But in many businesses, this evolving field takes on a cat herding aspect, an adversarial one at that.

To begin, look at some of the drivers behind formal project management:

■ The rationale for formal project management in large projects is scale; there are too many activities, too complex dependencies, too many resources, and so forth to be managed in a casual list-based manner.
■ The rationale for project management in small projects is the desire to relieve the working team members of the need to do administrative tasks such as data gathering, updating, and reporting.

■ The rationale for a formal project management office is standardization. In a multiproject environment, teams of workers will be formed and reformed under various project managers who should be, but don't always, do things in a consistent manner. To avoid confusion and multiple learning curves, a project management office appears to be the solution.

In the case of big projects, you sometimes have a central schedule, or master planner, that brings advanced analytics and expertise to guide the project management function. Most large projects, and all well-run ones, have sophisticated project management, but one of two scenarios tends to evolve:

1. If the project is very large, or comprised of several constituent projects perhaps from each of several vendors or subcontractors, the schedule/milestone view becomes dominant. There are simply too many variables around dependencies, risks, and resources hidden within each of these constituent schedules for the master planner to easily integrate into his or her analysis. The result of this scenario is a detailed though static Gantt chart that is difficult to keep up to date because the full network of project logic has not translated into the integrated schedule. The graphical representation of milestones and fates, the Gantt chart, becomes the lingua franca of the consolidated master schedule.
2. The rise of highly sophisticated master planning that is constantly evaluating shifts inputs and risks on a probabilistic basis or even running complex simulations. This highly advanced approach is quite useful in very large projects that warrant this effort, but these sophisticated extractions tend to increasingly isolate the master planning group from the day-to-day workers and even the management layer. It can be quite difficult for them to explain their analyses, and if there are acceptance issues, this group tends to get less accurate input data as the project progresses, which makes their job harder.

At the other end of the spectrum is a small project management approach. Because of their small scale and seeming simplicity, many of the features of project management are simply ignored. Most schedules do not have accurate resource loading not to mention probabilistic risks or critical chain analyses. Once again, the Gantt chart becomes the dominant view.

The Gantt chart is a rich picture, but this representation is approaching its hundredth birthday. Implicit in it is the legacy paper-based approach of having a scheduler or project manager gather information from direct contributors, collate and represent that in a plan, and update the plan.

If we were inventing project management reporting today, given our electronic toolset, we doubt it would still look like this. We suspect that it would be more collaborative and integrated into workflow, and that updating and notifications would be automatic and directly relevant to each user—probably pinging your mobile device if you select that option. That status would be on an intranet site and continuously updated reflecting changes in parameters such as risks, events, conflicts, resource updates, and so forth. In addition, users would have drill down similar to business intelligence and investigative tools. The high-level representation could be customized as a timeline, or something else, at the user's choice.

"Alleviating" the workers of the administrative burden by the addition of a project manager seems a reasonable approach. The direct result is to shift work from the core project resources and to place it with the appropriate expert. Unfortunately, the indirect consequence of this shift can actually be worse. The expert's project managers are now working in parallel with their teams rather than directly integrated with them. This can lead to competition for resources, the propagation of short-cycle multitasking, and the creation of a culture of "microfraud" where estimates and time durations are routinely inflated to provide a safety buffer against the project manager's desire to adhere strictly to schedule.

Figure 4.9 graphically represents an all-too-common project experience under parallel project management. Our diagram tracing the steps of such a project is a simplification but not an exaggeration. One of the causal drivers is that the project managers and workers have two different main goals: (1) the quality of the deliverables and (2) keeping to schedule. Because there are multiple projects-sharing resources, project managers often find themselves in competition with one another. Yet most project plans are written without any interconnections to any other project plans. Project managers with immediate delivery dates tend to win the resourcing arguments with those who seem to have plenty of time in their schedules. Therefore, almost all projects are locked in a cycle of slow starts and frantic dashes to the finish.

Project management becomes a fluid, intermediate layer between the management layer and the work team layer. See Figure 4.10. Is it possible to diminish or even eliminate this intermediate project management layer? For many projects, it certainly is not. Their scale and complexity justifies dedicated project management. On the other hand, the project management function, especially in an environment of many small projects, can be incorporated into the work team and management layers. The sophistication of project management software and tools today has reached the tipping point where ease of use has overcome the complexity previously driven by a rich feature set.

There is nothing odd about this idea. It wasn't too long ago that everybody wrote longhand and required a specialty resource, they were called secretaries, to convert that into a typed document using a special tool not available to all workers called typewriters or word processors. If you were interviewing a software engineer today, wouldn't you be a little surprised if he required a secretary to type his e-mails for him? Or if he needed an accountant to create simple spreadsheets for him? Doesn't this imply waste in the form of a hidden costs associated with this resource? A team of three engineers that requires a fourth resource to coordinate the work amongst them and report to management are each costing 33 percent more than we thought.

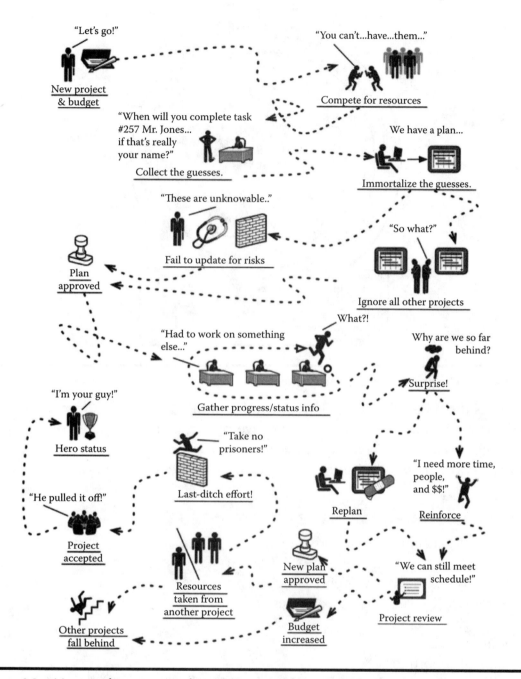

Figure 4.9 Most projects are run in a vacuum, without considering impacts on other projects' resources, budgets, and schedules. They can devolve into competitions.

We can see analogues of this in Factory Lean. The tendency to try to maximize the productivity and utilization of key resources (in the factory, these might be expensive welding robots; in the office environment, they might be product designers) is what led to overemphasis on expensive capital equipment and large batches, which in turn drove overproduction, excess inventory, and many other wastes brought to light by Lean and the theory of constraints.

Today, the combination of empowered resources and improved tools drive the collection and updating of project information. Similarly, improved tools enable the management layer to handle the reporting aspect of project management. What

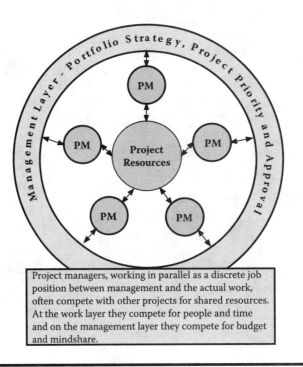

Project managers, working in parallel as a discrete job position between management and the actual work, often compete with other projects for shared resources. At the work layer they compete for people and time and on the management layer they compete for budget and mindshare.

Figure 4.10   The project management wheel.

remains is the "objective motivation" task—the cat herding. It is no wonder that when many organizations talk about effective project managers, they are mostly describing this aspect. *Good project managers are not necessarily technically proficient or analytical, but they can get their teams to deliver on schedule.*

COMMON PROJECT MANAGEMENT WASTES

Difficulty meeting scheduled dates
Lack of visibility and status
Inability to understand dependencies and effects
Too many e-mails and spreadsheets
Resource bottlenecks
Scattered data
Manual reporting
Lack of alignment between projects and strategy
Inability to measure causes of success or failure
Failure to realize potential of the workforce
Negative impacts to dependent projects/resources

Many of the modern techniques in project management, reflected in the features that are incorporated into the newer software tools addressing the subject, are focused on improving the timeliness and accuracy of project status as well as integrating project management activities directly into the workflow. These can be seen as a reaction to the "master planner syndrome" where a very few people gather input and conduct analyses while everyone else waits for their report. The future lies in a simpler, more participative project management approach.

The more people use something, the more valuable it becomes.

—Robert Metcalfe

On-demand collaborative software will allow you to select staff and manage projects across teams, departments, and divisions. Employees and team leaders can effectively collaborate on a day-to-day task via intuitive Web interfaces. Those removed from the project activities, such as senior managers, executives, or support services, gain visibility into the project's progress, its overall place in the portfolio, and its connection to departmental goals or strategies. Table 4.1 contrasts parallel project management and collaborative project management.

Basically, the collaborative approach addresses the same goal articulated by traditional project management, which is to relieve the administrative burden. In this case, the data-gathering burden is integrated into the workflow of the project's resources, and the status and reporting burden migrates to the dashboard

Table 4.1   Parallel Project Management with a Dedicated Project Management Resource Pool Compared with Self-Directed Collaborative Project Management

Parallel Project Management	Collaborative Project Management
Dedicated project managers	Distributed responsibility for updating and tracking
A few master planners	Collective planning
Adversarial relationship between project managers and work teams	Self-managed teams
Many projects in competition, high use of multitasking	Focus on a few projects at a time in continuous flow
Predictive planning, focus on hitting rigid end dates	Adaptive planning, focus on fast delivery
Projects start as early as possible	Projects start as late as possible
Projects have long cycle time	Projects have short cycle time
Many projects in progress	Thinner pipeline, projects in buffers
High work-in-progress	High output
Periodic updates and surprises	Accurate status in real time
Ever-increasing deviation from original plan, formal resetting of milestones	Active participation and execution, plan in perpetual beta
Manual reporting, presentation style	Auto notification, custom status dashboards with drill-down query

and executive query. The coordinating and motivational role of today's project manager still exists but is the charter of the project team leader. The team leader can now make tactical decisions based on accurate status at portfolio view since this takes much less time and does not require a dedicated resource.

Tool Tip: In this section, we largely discussed day-to-day project management activities and how they create waste at all three layers: worker, project manager, and executive. However, Lean is also concerned with defects, and in the realm of project management, the effect would be described as a "bad plan." In addition to bad input data on durations and resources, these defects in the plan can come from the failure to recognize the impact of individual risks, poor sequencing, or the combination of several small variations from the plan.

One way to analyze schedules is probabilistically, recognizing that task durations are only estimates and dealing with them as probability functions rather than discrete values. This capability is built into several tools or as an add-on such as Palisades software's @Risk For Project. One of the best tools for redesigning project sequence, especially in a dual phase design–build project such as construction is Adept Management's ADePT Design tools. These are based on dependency structure matrix (DSM) algorithms and read/write to the larger industry standard project management tools so that the analyst can work behind the scenes to create a better plan.

Even more detailed or custom analyses and simulations can be created. Discrete event tools such as Simul8 or Promodel's Process Simulator can represent simple project flows and evaluate a host of parametric what-ifs. System dynamics software such as Vensim can model more abstract parameters such as worker fatigue or the different error rates of new versus experienced resources. Agent-based tools, or a combination of agent and system dynamics tools such as AnyLogic,* can be used to develop very detailed models of individual behavior yielding aggregate results.

The Web 2.0 marketplace is generating many competitive entrants in this software category and forcing the large incumbents to adopt many of the features as well. Collaborating on a project involves a combination of project management, task management, document management, brainstorming or whiteboarding, scheduling, reporting, and workflow integration. One or more of these may very well be part of your kaizen sessions about bringing Lean

---

* Full disclosure: Although the authors have used or reviewed all the tools mentioned in this book, Gonzalez-Rivas developed a commercial arrangement with AnyLogic subsequent to the writing of this section. No tool reference was changed because of, or even since, that arrangement.

practices to your company's project management. The following is a sample of these tools:*

- One of the best known is Basecamp from 37signals, which boasts over one million users.
- In the small project, task-list oriented genre JuggleMyStuff from Jugglesoft is an interesting tool and Web service. It adds depth and increased flexibility.
- If you are a service organization and billing for your time, then Intervals layers in excellent time tracking and superior workflow integration to a good set of project management and reporting functions. Intervals independently created many of the features that we have designed for bespoke Lean project management systems.
- Another Web-based approach is 5pm, which bills itself as project management on time. In addition to project/task management, file sharing, and time tracking, it has a drag and drop interactive timeline for those who really enjoy the Gantt style view.
- Wrike is another midrange tool that emphasizes all the up-to-the-minute reporting and collaboration features, but is very tightly integrated into your existing e-mail workflow. Simply cc the Wrike software on e-mails with tasks and updates to your team and it automatically parses your e-mail and updates the project plan: schedule, tasks, assignment, and so forth. There is minimal administrative updating.
- On the more robust side is daptiv PPM. This feature-rich tool also boasts fast adoption and a minimal learning curve. It can be used by itself with customized dashboards and reports, or it can be used in conjunction with MS Project by importing and consolidating plans. This smoothes adoption because it does not require your expert project managers to give up the tool they are most likely already using.
- Another robust tool suitable for a large-scale installation is @Task. This tool really understands and emphasizes the benefits of project visibility and access to a large organization. The dashboard and reports are excellent (see Figure 4.11 comprised of selected screenshots), and their value increases with company size due to their greater need for visibility and assessment of strategic relevance. Individual views are customizable and the feature set is extremely rich: personal tasks lists, project risks, dynamic Gantts, portfolio and project dependency views, and so forth.

It is apparent that project management activities parallel to, and not sufficiently integrated with, the actual work can drive unintended consequences more severe than their intended benefit. These parallel systems are wasteful since they are based largely on meetings, the sneaker network (people with discs), and cutting and pasting into PowerPoint, which then leads to further meetings to present

---

* This category shows explosive growth. We were tracking a dozen collaborative project management tools when we started writing this book. By final edit, that list holds 96 entries.

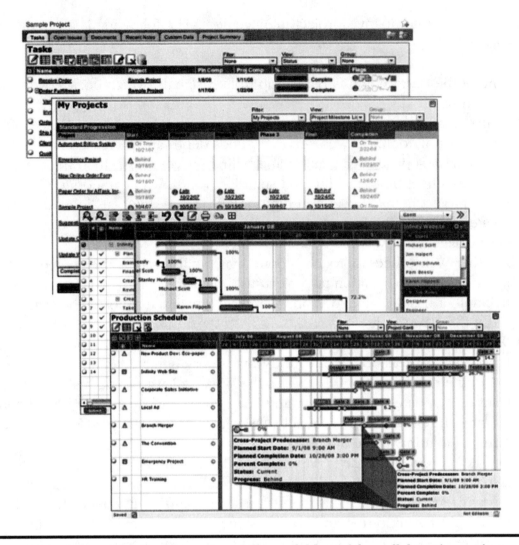

Figure 4.11   Screenshots from a commercially available tool for collaborative project management.

results. Status updates take time and effort; they happen infrequently but they frequently lead to surprises and subsequent reprioritization of work. Workers know that their future is uncertain but cannot estimate the number of hurry up and wait cycles, and so their best tool to meet the schedule is to create a conservative schedule in the first place. Sometimes even deliberate sandbagging is used where the original schedule is padded enough to survive later cutbacks and still leave plenty of margin.

The executive mantra has always been get more done in less time and the project teams are always trying to balance features versus schedule. What we envision with Lean project management is an organization where the team leaders and workers are the ones telling management that more can be done with less time and resources. Who wouldn't want that?

Chapter 5

The *I* in CIO: Information Transformation

Lean and IT seem to be enemies in many organizations. Lean emphasizes simple visual tools selected by the direct contributors, whereas IT gravitates to systemwide solutions selected and controlled by a central authority. However, in the knowledge worker space, information isn't metadata such as project status or scheduling—it *is* the process—and IT needs to be a critical part of it.

Information is knowledge, which is power. One way to think about information is as a flow of messages, which, once embedded in a person's mind, is knowledge. There are, however, two types of knowledge: (1) *explicit knowledge* that can be expressed, formalized, and shared through manuals or specifications; and (2) *tacit knowledge* that is not easily expressible and cannot be formalized, such as insights, feelings, morale, or working atmosphere. When information has been processed in someone's mind in the form of explicit knowledge, it can be translated into action.

One important implication of this is that once explicit knowledge is articulated or visualized, through models or graphs, it again becomes information, and for others to gain the same understanding from that information requires a shared knowledge base.

IT Tool Selection and Approval

Tool Tip: IT tool selection is an ongoing struggle between the compromises of customized off-the-shelf software versus in-house wheel reinvention. There are pros and cons to both approaches. From the perspective of IT management and maintenance, it might be preferable to control the proliferation of many little-known or specialty tools. From the business process perspective, it is wasteful to suffer the delays and compromises associated with modifying the process to fit a standard tool and wait for a lengthy installation process.

In the knowledge worker's environment, it is important to identify and emphasize knowledge, develop or emphasize a knowledge-intensive culture within the organization, and build infrastructure for knowledge sharing including both IT and personal connections. This means that a systematic approach for creating, storing and retrieving, transferring, and applying knowledge is needed.

Knowledge creation occurs when new knowledge is developed or when existing knowledge is replaced by tacit or explicit knowledge originating from the organization. An organization is a learning organism that creates new knowledge, but sometimes it can forget existing knowledge. Furthermore, there is a distinction between an individual's memory and organizational memory. Individual memory is based on observations and experience, and organizational memory can include culture, processes, and structure as well as information archives.

For this reason, it is important that the knowledge worker, through different storage and retrieval techniques, download and upload knowledge. In the West today, corporate organizations tend to have a data and informatics view of what IT shall support in the way of various groupware applications in order to expand the organizational memory. A good example is the virtual space containing information gained from past projects, which is accessible online by all employees, independent of place and time. Usually, you find a lot of data and information, but you really need to look hard to find knowledge.

To achieve useful knowledge transfer, where knowledge is transferred and shared among individuals, groups, explicit sources, and the organization itself, the company needs to: (1) perceive the value of the source's knowledge, (2) promote and secure the source's willingness to share knowledge, (3) build a set of rich transmission channels, and (4) promote and secure the receiving unit's willingness to acquire and use the source's knowledge. There is an old saying that goes something like "If the organization only knew what the organization already knows."

The chief information officer (CIO) is a job title for a manager responsible for information technology within an organization. He or she is the most senior executive responsible for identifying information and technology needs and then delivering services to meet those needs. The job description of a CIO differs in focus depending on the organization, the structure of the company, the size of the organization, and the business function of the company.

Depending on the organization, the CIO performs many functions: some manage an IT department, others work in headquarters, others manage the gap between information technology and information systems, and others focus on strategic issues. Although all of these tasks functions can be mixed and shared among many people in the IT department, it is common that all of them are the responsibility of the CIO. The key point is that the CIO has the major responsibility for IT throughout the enterprise. Broadbent and Kitzis* set out some priorities a CIO should focus on, which include to:

- Lead
- Know the enterprise and the competitive surroundings
- Have a vision on what it can support for business value
- Identify business needs and strategies
- Unite business and its strategy
- Develop a high-quality team
- Manage the risks throughout the organization

Many of these priorities describe the value of aligning IT and business to get the most profitability out of investments in IT.

What really does the *I* in CIO stand for? It seems to stand for IT to most people claiming the CIO position. The main responsibility is to secure the right infrastructure and application set up for the company so that it can share information. We believe the focus should be shifted to *transforming information into knowledge that the representatives of the organization can use to execute better decisions.* In a world where more and more CEOs demand that IT be like two plugs in the wall for electricity, the CIO who aspires to be part of the general executive team must rethink his role. He needs to change the perception of the *I* in CIO from information technology to information, and by that we mean information to fuel knowledge transfer.

For knowledge workers practicing Lean, it is essential to have accurate and actual information accessible in a simple, fast, and correct way so that they can visualize, analyze, and continuously improve performance; in other words they needed information that can be translated into knowledge on which to base executable decisions. Only in this way can the information technology in use play a valuable role in the creation of customer value. For CIOs who want to extend their influence to include true responsibility for how information is used in the organization, it is necessary to understand that Lean and IT are not enemies. They also must learn how to increase their knowledge of the current state of the information intense processes and develop their understanding of how Lean principles can be used to enable the efficient flow and use of information and knowledge in the organization.

---

* Marianne Broadbent and Ellen Kitzis, *The New CIO Leader: Setting the Agenda and Delivering Results* (Boston: Harvard Business School Press, 2005).

Automatic Process Discovery

It should be clear by now that most Lean initiatives emphasize simplicity and situational visibility, in particular the use of visual management systems. Where does that leave IT? Clearly, you don't need a large IT project to install a typical kanban system. Lean consultants are often small groups and industry experts who share their knowledge in part because they love doing Lean improvement work. Large IT projects, because of their risk, size, and resource requirements, are usually the domain of IT consultants and systems integrators. They are very different animals and yet they often find themselves competing for work at the same client.

This dichotomy exists within the companies themselves. Many business process owners balk at the need to bring in their corporate IT, with all the procedures, controls, and delays that entails, and instead just roll up their sleeves, launch some kaizen events, and take powerful steps—steps they control within their own group—along their journey.

However, suddenly, now that we've entered the area of information Lean, we have an opportunity to reach rapprochement between Lean and the IT department. This is their kind of Lean: information is at the heart of IT; after all, it's their first name. All of the Lean tools, both analytical and visual management, can incorporate IT as a strong player at the table. This is particularly true in the area of large enterprise applications of Lean where IT is indispensable. One of the best of these, and we consider this to be an area of tremendous potential and growth for the next few years, is automatic process discovery (APD).

SIGNS OF WASTE IN THE IT ORGANIZATION

Lack of guidance for business users about how to articulate their requests

Fulfilling requests that won't be used within the next two months

Addition of unnecessary functionality

Last-minute changes in business requirements during development

Application bugs

Requests that are not tied to business objectives and priorities

Frequent changes in priorities of projects due to guiding principles and rules that are unclear

Failure to bundle similar requests

Ineffective prioritization of maintenance requests

Unplanned task switching among developers

Limited cross-training of developers across different applications

Poor use of offshore resources

Key resources not available for planned work

Developers not fully utilized due to incomplete requests

Maintenance backlogs
Many partly finished requests
Lack of coordinated testing due to unbundled requests
Poor quality specifications
Uncoordinated releases

The As-Is Phase That Never Was: Why the Process Often Fails

It is estimated that almost 70 percent of all business process improvement projects fail.* In our experience, the figure is even higher for IT-enabled projects. The most common contributor to this terrible statistic is the poor quality of the as-is model. The methodology for this model is usually direct observation, interviews, and some data gathering from published reports. After all, industry reports say that while 75 percent of companies in the United States have done some form of process mapping, only 10 percent of them have large, consistent, programmatic efforts in place. Chances are you will be creating your own process map at the beginning of a project.

Though we have spent our careers doing this, we have to admit that there are many problems with this approach. The more invisible, that is, the more information intensive the process, the harder it is for consultants or Lean team leaders to find the underlying cause of problems.

There are several reasons for this. First—the literature hardly ever mentions this—the as-is model is boring especially to the process owners who already know all about it. Second, it is threatening; it's not that easy to open up to a stranger taking notes about your problems and shortcomings knowing that the report is going to your boss. Finally, and most important, the interviewees almost certainly don't understand the root-cause drivers of their problem because if they did, they would have been addressing them. The odds of discovering the full truth in your first pass through this process are slim, although they are not impossible.

Expert practitioners know to repeat interviews; to revisit hypotheses obtained in the first interview that subsequent discussions or fact finding had proven to be correct or incorrect. They know to juxtapose opposite sides of an issue in interviews. They know to build tests to evaluate some of the information given to them in their interviews. They know to take the official published information with a grain of salt. In short, they know to go to *gemba* (the Japanese term for "where the work happens") and take a good hard look. Some organizations routinely conduct interviews and physical inspections with a team of two or more, which increases the chance of catching nuggets of valuable information dropped

---

* "A full 66 percent of large-scale projects fail to achieve their stated business objectives, are delivered late, or are substantially over budget." Gartner Group, 2007.

during the interviews and brainstorming sessions. Sounds resource intensive, doesn't it?

This traditional means of investigating a process can be quite expensive. It is even more expensive when you are examining an information-intensive process because the consultants or Lean practitioners cannot gather the data directly but must ask for information. And, if the consultants are good, they will probably ask for data or reports that the organization never thought to do, which means it will take some time to get results from the busy data gatherers. Meanwhile, the hourly rate clock is ticking and the cost of the job is climbing.

Good service providers will keep an eye on their budgets and schedules, trying to conclude their phase on time and on budget. In other words, with all the unknown difficulties associated with the process redesign and implementation phases, the as-is phase usually gets short shrift. No wonder it so often fails.

How Automatic Process Discovery Can Increase the Success Rate

Automatic process discovery (APD) can change this. All this information work is done using information appliances with human interface and data entry, and a great deal of data logging and recordkeeping at the application and enterprise level (very fertile hunting ground to capture vast amounts of useful data real-time). Even better, the data comes unfiltered. Almost all interviews, corporate reports, and even direct observation by consultants tend to throw out the outliers. The natural tendency of almost all data gatherers is to ignore the exceptions and focus on the "main body of data." But it's a mistake to treat exception or outlier data as noise or spurious data (for a fascinating take on this see Taleb's excellent book *The Black Swan**) because it is so often critically important. The exception data, though a smaller population of events, might be far more expensive in operation (not to mention in a regulatory or legal sense) and could become a major cost driver. All this tantalizing accurate data, gathered in sophisticated applications, allows the Lean practitioner to construct what-if games.

Business process analysts until now have been operating more or less as doctors in the Victorian age did. Their diagnosis was based on experience, observable symptoms that the patient presented, and a case history provided by interview. APD brings us to the modern era and allows us to look deep, in real time, into our corporate patient. To extend the medical diagnostic metaphor, APD is like an MRI for business process improvement.

We can't speak for all practitioners and consultants, but we're not worried that APD may put us out of business. In accordance with the principles of Lean, we relish the thought of spending our time doing high-value activity and analyzing reams of accurate data, rather than the low-value activity of begging for inherently inaccurate data and waiting for it to arrive.

---

* Nassim Nicholas Taleb, *The Black Swan: The Impact of the Highly Improbable* (New York: Random House, 2007).

That being said, we freely admit to a bias for small-scale tools, because they are so much easier to get your hands on and test. This means that they are easier for those medium-risk Lean ideas we've been talking about. It may be possible that the team and workgroup versions of Slife and ProductivityMeter will grow into midsize corporate apps. For now, we have two large offerings for the enterprise: one from IONTAS and the other from Fujitsu.

Many companies are conducting extensive business process interoperability (BPI) initiatives without exactly knowing how the process in question is actually being conducted. These APD software tools, with their process discovery focus, let organizations immediately discover human-generated processes as they are currently conducted, automatically, eliminating months of time and labor-intensive exploration. Companies can now see—in a noninvasive way—exactly how individuals and groups of users follow the process step by step. In addition, they can see how much time is spent on each step. Process maps clearly display the process path that users most commonly follow.

These flexible process maps reveal problems that, without this technology, are virtually unknown. The business process improvement team can now manipulate the visual display to show the desired amount of detail, from general trends down to individual users' actions and the timing of each step.

Process discovery automatically draws accurate maps of the actual process flows step by step, hour by hour, collectively and individually. The process involves installing a data collector, which runs transparently across the corporate network on users' machines. Companies can achieve multiple goals for process improvement at once. For example, they can:

- Identify process inefficiencies
- Detect unauthorized or noncompliant actions
- Determine best practices
- Jump-start initiatives with an accurate process discovery in a matter of days instead of weeks
- Establish accurate benchmarks
- Obtain visible insight into how employees use business resources to impact profits

This IONTAS Timeline Report (see Figure 5.1) categorizes efficient and inefficient activities and identifies longest duration by color (yellow, but shown here as different shades of gray). There also are drill down capabilities to analyze the process. Figure 5.2 shows an automatically drawn flowchart that highlights path frequency. These data visualizations not only provide important insight into existing processes and reveal hitherto unknown problems and exceptions, they also support the sustainability aspect of Lean. With these tools, we have made the invisible visible, enabling managers to prevent the old ways from creeping back into their environment.

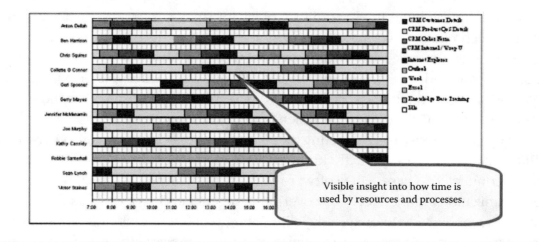

Figure 5.1   Timeline view of an automated process discovery (APD) tool.

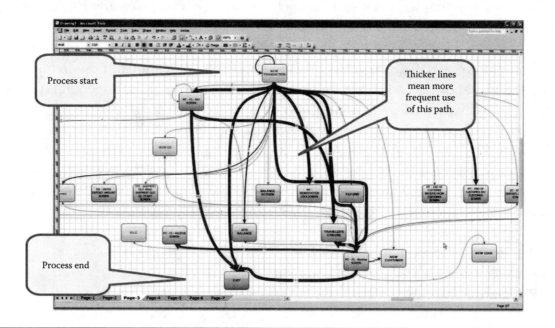

Figure 5.2   APD tools can automatically draw the process and quantify path usage.

Tool Tip: Fujitsu approaches APD as a service. Its customers provide them with existing database logs for the business processes they want to visualize. The Interstage software tool from Fujitsu runs through the data and helps customers visualize their business processes and also identifies potential areas for improvement.

The overall approach is broken into three phases (see Figure 5.3): (1) the data collection phase where thousands of instances of a process are collected from applications' data logs, (2) the analysis phase where the business flow model is created, and (3) the analysis phase where the implications of all the gathered data and the generated visual models are reviewed.

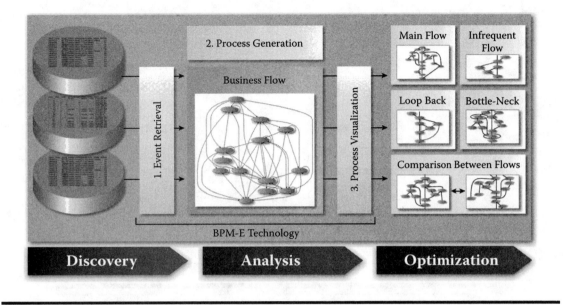

Figure 5.3   Overview of an automatic process discovery (APD) tool.

The advantages of having a large amount of accurate data come through in the final phase are (1) atypical flows are easy to identify, (2) variations between flows are easy to identify, (3) bottlenecks in the process are easy to see, and (4) statistics between activities are available for review. For example, if the standard deviation of duration time for a particular activity is small, it would indicate that this is a mature step, benefiting from standardization and predictable inputs. On the other hand, if the standard deviation is high, it would indicate a great amount of variability in processing time for that step, perhaps because of the quality of its feeding process, poor training of resources, or a poor process design that cannot cope with the range of inputs. This would appear to be a good candidate for improvement.

One of the interesting features of this tool is its ability to zoom in at different levels of detail. Figure 5.4 is a collage of screenshots of the process used in the Fujitsu demo. In each panel, you can see a slider bar in the lower left corner, which filters out levels of detail. In the first panel, the slider is set low and the process looks very simple and clean. In the second diagram, as the slider moves up, additional flows, not as frequent as the designed process but still common, become evident. Finally, with the slider all the way up, a vast hairball of a process is displayed. Although most of the instances may have flowed through the designed process, there are clearly many exceptions, probably expensive exceptions, hampering this process.

This approach has a great deal of promise, but it is obviously most valuable for large scale processes with many thousands of process instances from which to develop the process flow and quantify each path.

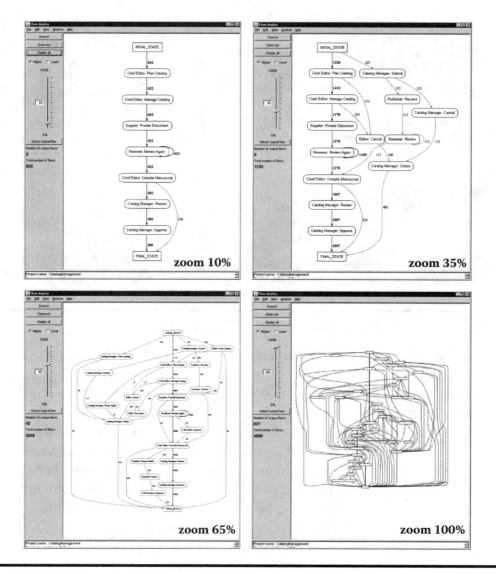

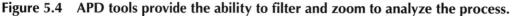

Figure 5.4   APD tools provide the ability to filter and zoom to analyze the process.

High-Level Design Principles for Information Lean

In a design and build environment of manufacturing, the factory receives a work piece where 100 percent of the requirements are known. The item to be manufactured is fully specified and it remains for the factory manager to perform the (still daunting) tasks of securing the supply chain, producing the items quickly, efficiently, and at high quality while satisfying schedule and shipping requirements.

On the other hand, the information process, relatively speaking, is built upon the shifting sands of incomplete requirements, in-process design changes, and unanticipated discoveries that can range anywhere from out-of-spec test results to updated business plans that seem to put the project in the red. The overall design for processes in this environment must be based on speed, flexibility, and the planned minimization of effects of these stochastic (random) events.

Case History: The Boss and the Rock

A junior associate received a simple assignment from his boss. "Go get me a rock," he said. The associate dutifully returned with a rock but his boss gave it hardly glance before saying, "No, a bigger rock." The associate returned with a substantially bigger rock and placed it on his boss's desk. "This rock has sharp edges. It's going to really scratch my desk. Bring me a big smooth rock." The boss's tone indicated that he felt this was obvious from the beginning. When the associate returned with a big smooth rock, he was told it was the wrong color. Obviously, everything in the office would be complemented by a white rock. "Get me a big, smooth, white rock," said the boss. The associate left, head hung low and muttering, in search of such a rock. Obviously, we can extend this example to several more cycles and it still wouldn't begin to describe some of the extreme cases we've seen or that perhaps you've experienced, but we think this is enough to set up the discussion.

Most people at this point in the story have one of two explanations. The first group sees this as a personality problem. The boss is a jerk or enjoys yanking the associate's chain. At best, the boss is so disorganized and selfish that he does not value the time wasted by his subordinate pursuing half-baked instructions that he plans to change anyway. The second group takes more of a systems view. They are convinced that the problem is in not having a clear definition upfront as to what is required. What in the system engineering world is called "requirements elicitation," the young associate in the story, notepad in hand, should have continued the initial interview as much as necessary to get a complete and full understanding of all the detailed requirements so that he could satisfy them on his first mission.

The problem with this answer is that it is wrong. It is not a question of completing all the design requirements upfront because that is neither possible nor feasible. In this illustration, two things are going on. First, the boss is busy with matters that he probably values more highly than rock hunting, and second, and this is the key, he doesn't actually know what the requirements are. He hasn't thought it through much further than "rock." Any attempt to drag these requirements out of him is going to be counterproductive—the most benign effect of an activity your boss finds extremely annoying. If the young assistant pleads his case well, he may get a meeting sometime on the busy calendar of his boss, which may give the boss some time to have his ideas percolate up.

The real point is that the boss in this story, by intent or accident, expects to evolve his requirements through the multiple iterations of rock reviews. Each review informs the next iteration of requirements refinement—a continuous improvement process analog (see Figure 5.5). He would not have been able to articulate all the requirements no matter how long or careful the elicitation session had been. The path to success here is to create several iterations as quickly as possible. Each rock fulfills established criteria, so real design work is accomplished, and each iteration helps the designers determine criteria for the next. It isn't rework; it's proper work.

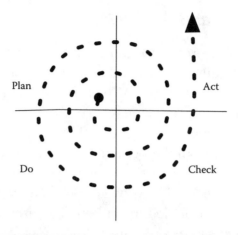

Plan

Act

Do

Check

Figure 5.5   The plan–do–check–act (PDCA) cycle and spiral design both rely on recursions.

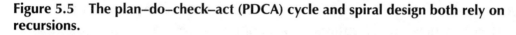

From a Lean waste perspective, the many rock-hunting trips look like waste at first glance. Poka yoke would suggest you find the right rock the first time! In fact, there was much less rework than there might have been if the associate had put a lot of time and effort into finding the perfect rock in an environment where rock perfection had yet to be defined. The point of each rock-hunting iteration was only to elaborate against known requirements, not unknown ones, and from that perspective there was no waste. We cannot hold the associate or the boss responsible for nth set of requirements because they were only made possible after reviewing the results of the nth − 1 rock collection.

The big requirements upfront approach, even if the meeting is delayed, may seem to have established all its requirements sooner than this iterative, or spiral, approach, but those are just paper requirements and risk project failure. It may be that the specified combinations of size and color are just not available in the garden, and the assistant will have to order a custom rock from the quarry at great expense. The spiral approach completes pieces of the design with each cycle, limiting and suggesting the next set of choices and minimizing the chance of major project failure.

CAUSES OF DEVELOPMENT WASTES

Missing or vaguely expressed requirements

Unknown desires or functional requirements not articulated or elicited up front*

Elaborating full functional or technical requirements for the sake of completeness

Orphaned requirements (dropped along the development path)

Base-lining requirements too early or too late

* There is a difference between unknown requirements and unexpressed requirements. We suggest that interested readers review kano analysis for some very important lessons in this area.

Late-arriving requirements changes
Forward-only design, failure to involve the early functional require-
　　ments team as design evolves

This formal approach has been around for about 20 years. The spiral model or spiral development model was proposed by Barry Boehm in 1988.* This interleaved combination of design and prototyping stages has been successful and variations were developed throughout the 1990s, among them chaos development, agile development, extreme programming, and SCRUM. All of these differ from the waterfall design† in that they rely to varying degrees on interim deliverables and prototypes, and tend to be far more flexible to changing or adaptive requirements.

The careful reader will note that this methodological boom came about during the fast-moving and highly competitive dot-com era when time to market was critical. Like all good ideas, one wonders why spiral/agile et al., design took so long. In fact, it really didn't take long. The process had been used extensively for ages in other areas.

Case Study: The Spiral Model

Think of a fashionable woman buying an expensive evening gown at an upscale couturier. The last thing the shopkeeper would do is to ask Madame to sit down while he completes a detailed requirements session. He asks a few general questions and immediately starts showing her gowns. Both parties learn something from each dress review and jointly begin narrowing in on a final selection. The process speed is governed by the cycle time: the number of models the couturier has and how quickly they can change.

The waterfall approach, on the other hand, would look something like this: The customer describes the gown in detail to the couturier, who elicits additional details. Madame is measured, and a boxed dress, unseen by Madame, arrives at her address just in time for the grand ball. Would you want to be the couturier and take the risk that the dress will be perfect on this basis? That no changes are desired or alterations required? That the color is just right in this new light?

This analogy may strike you as fanciful. Until you think of the Lean genesis. When Taiichi Ohno, the acknowledged father of the Toyota Production System (TPS), came to inspect Detroit's automobile industry in 1956, he left shaking

---

* Barry Boehm, *Software Risk Management* (Piscataway, NJ: IEEE Press, 1989).
† The waterfall model is a sequential software development process, in which progress is seen as flowing steadily downward (like a waterfall) through the phases of conception, initiation, analysis, design (validation), construction, testing, and maintenance. The waterfall development model has its origins in the manufacturing and construction industries. Often used interchangeably with the stage–gate process, which describes sequential flow from one stage through another with acceptance by each subsequent group in a gating process.

his head. There was no way the struggling Japanese industry could lavish the production line with the type of capital-intensive solutions the Americans were using. The Japanese could never get so much capital to lock in to the production processes, and therefore had to make do with less. However, during that trip, he noticed one particular American supermarket, Piggly Wiggly, and its system, which provided the basis of the pull concept in TPS. It is simple and highly responsive to customer demand since it replenishes the shelves as customers select, or pull, a product. This, coupled with Ford's assembly line production system, and with quality and statistical process control contributed by Deming and Shingo,* became the bedrock of TPS. So the fact that your corner grocery market held a process insight that would revolutionize all global manufacturing might help you put the dressmaker's requirements insight into context.

Now, let's take a simple example and put some meat on its bones. In a typical project, the project sponsor, more often than not a group of people rather than a single individual, will have a high-level understanding of what the functional requirements are. However, they tend to have only a vague notion of what the technical requirements might be. Usually, they have very little, if any, understanding of the different interactions among the design, schedule, and budget implications of these technical requirements.

Choosing a good requirements management approach, whether enabled by a software tool or not, will focus on completeness and the elimination of ambiguity. For example, marketing might have a requirement that "the screen must refresh quickly." This kind of vague unquantified requirement is guaranteed to drive the engineers who receive it batty. They might work for months without any assurance that the refresh rate they develop will be satisfactory. Sometimes they throw the requirements back to marketing and, with a stiff upper lip say, "please be specific," and the marketing department will eventually produce a quantitative number to underpin their arguments for what they perceive to be customer demand for really fast screen refresh rates.

The problem—and it is among the most pervasive problems in a waterfall or stage-gate development process—is the lack of feedback or context provided by marketing when they created their original specification. You can imagine what happens when, after six or seven months of design, after all that time and effort has been put into developing and designing the engineered item, and the software, the hardware vendors, and system integrators have been chosen, and all the potential suppliers have been interviewed and lined up, the engineers look at the requirements, shake their heads, and say, "If only this screen refresh rate were 6/10 of a second instead of half a second, we could do it with off-the-shelf components. Now we have to find a new screen vendor and start from scratch." The amount of time elaborating against requirements that were essentially

---

* Perry Gluckman, Diana Reynolds Roome, *Everyday Heroes: From Taylor to Deming: The Journey to Higher Productivity* (Knoxville, TN: SPC Press, 1990); Shigeo Shingo, *A Study of the Toyota Production System* (Cambridge, MA: Productivity Press, 1989).

placeholders to flesh out the original functional requirements tables can be immense in a waterfall design approach. If you are lucky, an engineer will push back and ask, "Why don't you just use a standard solution?" If you are not lucky, they'll build it the way you specified it because you're the boss.

In a large development organization, a waterfall requirements design starts with creating casualties among the requirements. Some are orphaned, some are canceled or descoped, and, before long, the downstream engineering groups will come to realize that not all requirements are hard and fast. The inevitable presence of early, uninformed requirements casts a pall over all the others.

Case Study: Waterfall Requirements

The world of mechanical engineering has a useful illustration for us here. In developing the thermodynamic cycle for a power plant, the water in the cycle goes through several broad steps: feed-water is heated (via diverted steam from the plant), the feed-water is then boiled and brought to high pressure steam, the steam spins the turbine and in doing so loses energy and reverts to hot water, that hot water is cooled in a cooling tower, and that cooler water is cycled back to again be heated, boiled, and so forth. Fairly simple; not too distant from the cartoons you've seen with a teakettle spinning a child's whirligig, but the reality is far more complex. There are multiple stages of feed-water heating each increasing the water temperature a fraction of its eventual temperature rise, there are multiple stages of turbines, each sized to match the energy of several different steam lines tapped at various parts of the cycle, and so on. This is done for efficiency, not elegance.

Lessons Learned

Sometimes business process management is overly influenced by a "clean" process that offers simplicity and standardization, but this should not drive your process design. The waterfall design is conceptually simple, and still quite common, but we don't think it should be the basis for Lean given its huge potential for rework, poor visibility and status, and tendency to promulgate many simultaneous projects staffed by overloaded, multitasking resources.

It is essential that the high-end design of the Lean information process be flexible and minimize rework waste by elaborating against only firm requirements. To do this, baseline early and often, leverage the high-speed communications at your disposal to create a Lean process that only looks redundant.

Knowledge Management

Knowledge management (KM) is typically an enterprisewide function and comes under the purview of corporate IT. They have the skills and the tools, even if much of the knowledge they manage comes from the rest of the organization. KM is critical, and the flexibility and customer centricity of the IT department is critical to its successful deployment.

During the 1980s and 1990s, many leading authors and pundits waxed lyrical regarding the power of KM. It was to be the savior of big business. There was good reason for this. Information was being generated and consumed at an unprecedented rate. Large corporations had scale problems; the knowledge was spread over too large a landscape to be useful. Organizations with turnover or with fast-changing industries had trouble keeping their material fresh. Companies with too much organization, widely distributed or autonomous groups, strong silo barriers, and so forth were creating and using material without collaboration or even awareness that several groups were developing the same material. In short, companies didn't know what they knew.

The ability to collate all this institutional knowledge and leverage it at the margin for the next piece of work, wherever in the organization it would take place, is a remarkably powerful waste eliminator. Too bad we mucked it up.

It has been said that generals are always preparing to fight the last war. Similarly, knowledge management solutions often tend to be based on the assumptions of the previous generation of information storage. Consequently, many corporate knowledge management sites suffer from excessive structure. The unspoken assumption is that searching begins by navigating to the right location. For example, if you are looking for information on the return on investment (ROI) around the benefits of automating design, you need to start by finding the part of the site "owned" by the West Coast CAE (Computer Aided Engineering) group, which has a subsection containing client case studies.

These KM systems naturally require resources to manage them, not just the maintenance from IT and storage space. Developing all the procedures and processes supporting the creation and submission of material takes time and effort, which usually comes at the expense of the resources' day job. *Waste: excessive care and feeding of KM systems.*

The submission and approval process with its emphasis on format and "strategic alignment" is less interesting to many information creators than the content itself. Once their new material is created, they are satisfied and neglect to place it on the KM site. *Waste: the knowledge that never makes it to the knowledge management system.*

Each group owning some of the KM real estate has its own messaging and organization, which are usually tied to its group mission or strategy. They also have their own guidelines about posting material to KM, the degree of review each piece receives, and the tagging or indexing (if any) applied. Naturally, the different groups place varying degrees of emphasis on keeping their KM up to date. *Waste: Researchers typically cannot find exactly what they need and so cast the net wider and gather far too much.* Now the "quick look" into the corporate KM system has turned into a major research time sink with 30 documents to review.

In addition, corporate KM sites become like the famous "roach motel": information checks in, but it doesn't check out. Few organizations go back and cull or update old material. Nor do they link it to updated references. *Waste: Outdated or superseded materials that have the look, feel, and provenance of the official company position. Work based on this material is at risk.*

Finally, managers of corporate KM systems are ignoring Chris Anderson's ideas in *The Long Tail: Why the Future of Business Is Selling Less of More.** Their Web sites have limited ability to showcase corporate documents, customer value propositions, and so forth. Increasing the natural language search will allow workers to more easily find the specialized material they may be looking for rather than the current Webmaster favorites.

All these knowledge workers are comparing their KM system against their other search experiences such as Amazon or Google. In other words, KM systems are often contrasted with the very best search engines in the world, and it's no surprise that they come off poorly in comparison. On Amazon, you could search for the phrase "they were the footprints of a gigantic hound!" and the return would be a rich, but targeted selection of various editions and commentary around *The Hound of the Baskervilles.* To find the same information on a typical KM site, you make various selections eventually leading you to Fiction/ Mystery/Victorian where you scan a list of titles and make the connection. In this example, you're lucky because the title provides a solid clue as to the content. Imagine you were instead looking for the great piece with the line, "Last night I dreamed of Mandalay." The content search will take you right there, but the structured files search won't help you match your search with Du Maurier's *Rebecca* because the title doesn't provide any clue to the content.

In many organizations, people still assign storage primacy to their own hard drives. For broad research, they go to the Internet and all its vast pools of content. For specific corporate materials, they use their internal KM system supplemented by broadcast e-mails asking for help in finding material. That's the problem. If the KM system doesn't measure up to the very tough standards of Amazon and Google, and if it isn't up to date, it falls into greater and greater disuse.

Tool Tip: A simple solution is to make it extremely easy to post material to the KM site and rely on the ever-growing capability of search engines and evolving user interfaces, such as Apple's coverflow, to allow users to find material by full text or even graphical content. The final element is a wiki feature where users can rate the document, apply additional tags, provide connections or links to related documents or later versions, mark material for deletion as inaccurate or superseded, and so forth.

---

* In his book *The Long Tail* (New York: Hyperion, 2006), Chris Anderson argues products that are in low demand or have low sales volume can collectively make up a market share that rivals or exceeds the relatively few current bestsellers and blockbusters, if the store or distribution channel is large enough.

Using Ross Mayfield's power law of participation,* we would have to categorize the vast majority of corporate KM users at the very lowest level: read only.

The next steps would be the ability to tag favorites, create rankings, subscribe to updates on the topic, and so forth, and the next levels of participation would include writing, collaborating, moderating discussions, and so forth. Unfortunately, most KM sites are like 19th century libraries: you go, you perform a categorized search, and you read (only). You don't add anything, and you had better not leave comments in the margin!

In our view, we should minimize or eliminate the corporate KM system and create a system managed by the users within the corporation. There should still be locations housing standard information or templates and forms, which are centrally managed, in an organization with thousands of users creating and devouring information at today's fantastic rates. The best solution is to get out of the way of the stampede and not try to force it into predetermined silos. The quantity and quality of information that emerges will be far greater. Your people will gain value from each other, not from a preapproved subset of aging information.

Lean Code Management: Lean *by* IT *for* IT

IT can influence Lean, especially information age Lean, throughout the organization. They are the key to enabling several important elements of improved flow and use of information. Wherever scale (big systems) is a factor, wherever security or external data transfer is a factor, IT will be there. Some things can be done on a small scale, but if the Lean charter is to propagate to the rest of the organization, then it is clear that we need IT. One or two brave little groups may develop their own Web 2.0 solutions, but it is unreasonable to expect that all future Lean groups will do this. The best approach may be to cast these initial Web 2.0 ventures as "skunkworks" to fully develop a working model and deeply understand all the user requirements; true companywide deployment of broad information tools must be an IT responsibility. Ideally, support in developing small tools can be assisted by IT.

IT also plays a crucial role in:

■ Supporting automatic process discovery
■ Supporting any tool that spans multiple organizations
■ Allowing Lean teams to test and adopt Web 2.0 and collaborative tools
■ Supporting visual management systems

---

* Ross Mayfield is chairman and president of Socialtext Incorporated, an enterprise social software company based in Palo Alto, California. Mayfield's power law of participation says that social software brings groups together to discover and create value. This is particularly interesting when you think about how a communications program might map to different levels of community engagement. According to this power law, content consumers thrive at the tail of the participation curve, so this is where companies have to be cognizant of user behaviors and practical about the engagement tactics they employ.

■ Developing and hosting corporate Lean tools such as ROI calculators, crowd-sourcing, open innovation, and communitywide sites

These considerations are for IT as a partner and enabler of information age Lean elsewhere in the organization. What about IT's internal core processes?

We group IT's sources of Lean waste into two broad categories: (1) those stemming from its business model and relationship with the rest of the organization and (2) those stemming from its development and production processes.

Business Model Wastes

These are the kinds of issues that arise in negotiating and delivering IT services to the rest of the company.

Examples of business model waste include:

■ A slow or cumbersome process to elicit and develop requirements
■ A standard development process, such as a waterfall, that does not support projects with fuzzy initial requirements or those that have short time horizons
■ Siloed focus on IT budgets and resources rather than a corporate view of the most economical solution for the company as a whole (the internal customer is weak)
■ An overreliance on large-scale external developers, systems integrators, or outsourced work that adds time or additional cost or scope negotiating cycles to the overall plan
■ The use of small-scale external or outsourced developers in the overall development process in a way that creates excessive handoffs or bottlenecks
■ Costs for services not valued by the internal customer
■ Insistence on organizations modifying their process to adopt a standard or off-the-shelf tool (buy vs. build waste)
■ The creation of tools or writing new code rather than adopting or modifying existing ones (buy vs. build waste)
■ Failure to invest in the ongoing training of programmers, and to review and adopt new tools

Most of these wastes are more or less self-explanatory. One of the common themes is the transactional, project nature of IT's collaboration with the rest of the organization. They review the internal customer's needs, using their own process and available resources, and usually respond with a development estimate and timeframe. Few internal organizations are specialists in all areas and may have a hard time competing with quotes for the same service received from external vendors. This is partly due to expertise and experience, and partly due to the perceived difference between an internal and external customer; most departments think they are getting better service and response from an external provider. The IT department's ace in the hole is that it is the ultimate gatekeeper for the solutions proposed by the external customer and can block or delay or tax any such implementation.

The total outsourcing waste can be quite significant. The business user needs an application or modification to an existing tool but has to enter into a blind negotiation cycle between the company's IT and the vendor. The lack of visibility into the process leads to suspicion and most estimates seem to reinforce the impression that every change costs too much and takes too long. The natural cycle of this process prohibits fast response or minor changes, and discourages users from seeking them. Consequently, they develop workarounds or learn to live with these problems until the next major release. In turn, IT learns to bundle all these minor requirements into a major upgrade project, guaranteeing a major project and reinforcing the "no small changes" culture.

The partial outsourcing waste can be equally significant based on the dependencies and tie-ins of the affected system. If the external vendor is working on a largely independent application, then there will be few ripple effects and the proposed cost will be close to the final evaluated cost. If, however, the vendor is altering a piece of code that is highly interdependent and has the potential to have far-ranging and late-arriving impacts, then this project has the potential to drive massive waste downstream. One of the uses of the DSM* technique described in the information element section (see Chapters 7 and 8) that has the potential of delivering huge returns for the company is the categorization of information activities into independent, dependent, and mutually dependent. This same approach can be used to categorize IT work and assure that only independent work is outsourced on a piecemeal basis. This is a key, often overlooked element of the buy versus build analysis.

Development Wastes

Development wastes are the kinds of inefficiencies and defects that come from IT's own core technical processes. Some examples of development waste are:

- Rewriting new code from scratch rather than reusing code
- Rogue or ad hoc changes to standard components, which cause problems downstream
- Poor documentation practices leading to multiple reviews of code and misuse of code components in later applications
- Modest customization of functionally similar code, which creates multiple separate maintenance streams
- Failure to capture, share, and leverage lessons learned from internal or external sources
- Defect fixes and security modifications performed on a project-by-project basis with little or no collaboration

---

* Design structure matrix. Sometimes also referred to as the dependency structure matrix.

- Optimization of individual projects rather than optimization of the portfolio of applications that share the same code and metadata
- Limitation of code discovery efforts to a particular silo in the organization
- Developers maintaining code with which they are unfamiliar
- Best developers assigned to creating new code while maintenance is assigned to new hires or less-skilled developers

Many of these wastes drive code divergence—different streams of functionally similar code with enough customization and variation to require different maintenance efforts and also prevent interoperability and reuse. Multiple and contrasting fix streams will enter into the code base and code searchers are likely to initially find similar yet incorrect artifacts for their applications. This leads to quality problems, rework, and a higher learning curve and knowledge transfer costs.

Three Lean IT principles can be applied to develop the specific practices of Lean code management to address these wastes:

1. Lean code creation (aka overproduction)
2. Lean code maintenance (aka poka yoke)
3. Lean code oversight (aka 5Si)

Lean code creation is heavily based on code reuse and leveraging existing ideas, components, and tools. Creating code that already exists is a violation of overproduction—the most fundamental of Lean wastes. Specifics will vary depending on the type of code you create and the nature of your business, but good guidelines to follow are:

- Maintaining an active library of reusable components
- Identifying, and encouraging, internal developers with API and framework expertise to support a culture of reuse
- Identifying key projects that have, or did have, potentially reusable code to populate this library

Of course, the type and number of software languages used is an issue. But this is specific to each IT shop and it would be impractical to say that all development must move to the latest object-oriented language. This is particularly impractical for maintenance when so much existing code already exists and there are so many interconnections. We merely suggest that IT departments apply these principles to all their families of code recognizing the need to focus development on new languages that new graduates are trained in, while carefully evaluating the ramifications of migrating code from past languages. Maintenance is not an issue for SAAS (software as a service) and Web 2.0 solutions, but this is just one aspect of any adoption decision.

Lean code maintenance is not so much about the fixes themselves as the need to understand holistically how these fixes can or should be applied against a portfolio of projects and applications. This is a key difference between IT and Factory Lean where improvements can be tactical and local (obvious considerations such as standard machinery and parts are exceptions). Realistically, physical changes to assembly line 3 cannot show up unplanned in assembly line 12. Code, like most information, is invisible and highly mobile and once these changes are written to patch, say, application 3, they might easily be later used in addressing a similar issue in application 12 with potentially negative results because of differences between the two applications.

Most developers are siloed and project oriented. A focus on "this fix" without an understanding of how the code change may affect other issues will lead to downstream IT waste. Therefore, Lean code maintenance is heavily influenced by poka yoke—the prevention or error proofing of software defects in the first place. The challenge is not to solve a defect but to reduce the defect injection rate into the maintained code stream. The undiscovered rework implicit in siloed code maintenance is one of the key drivers of downstream waste.

Lean code maintenance has to both fully understand the portfolio view and ramifications of the problem (impact analysis) and help ensure that sharing and knowledge transfer does indeed happen (fix sharing). Guidelines for Lean code maintenance are:

Dependency—Identify any other parts of the application that may be affected before coding.

Scalability—Assess the vulnerability and impact of a defect or fix across projects before making any decision on coding.

Research—Consider where else has a similar defect been addressed.

Notification—Once remedied, the developer needs to alert all the projects that may be affected or benefit currently.

Documentation—Clearly document the fix and also clearly identify where else it should be applied.

Root cause—Communicate the solution to those who may need to take remedial, preventive action to benefit projects in the future.

Lean code maintenance will reduce downstream support costs, reduce latent defects, and minimize code divergence. Lean code oversight (LCO) is the plan–do–check–act (PDCA) corrective cycle for maintenance. This is separate from the project view, or even the portfolio view, and concentrates on the process: Do we have diverging code maintenance streams? Are we managing our lifecycle maintenance costs? Are we efficiently refactoring our code to simplify maintenance, knowledge transfer, and reuse? Are we driving a culture that de-emphasizes rogue edits and modifications without burdening the day-to-day activity with bureaucracy? Are we ensuring that our developers receive training and there is sufficient cross-pollination to support a holistic view of the portfolio?

LCO serves the purpose of 5S for IT waste. Large IT departments will have a hard time red-tagging pieces of code and performing the sweep functions. This is not because it is inappropriate, just impractical. Unused code is much harder to identify than unused factory equipment. The IT department can begin with little-used applications and services—anything that can have a box drawn around its dependencies and evaluated as a stand-alone entity. However, the more important aspects of LCO are around the sustain aspects of 5S. Developers must be trained in code search tools to minimize the waste of overproduction. Developer forums must be created to facilitate sharing and provide situational visibility for impact analysis, and an effective, tagable wiki (to start with, more advanced applications to follow) can be used to maintain the library. The important thing is that the LCO be presented as a community of developers and not the Lean code police.

In summary IT is key to the success of Lean for the information age office for most medium and all large enterprises. IT cannot be the enemy of operations Lean, especially in the information area where they hold so much sway. First, if companies are to use "large" or "networked" tools such as APD, then they will need IT's expertise and scope. Second, if they are to leverage the innovation of the total global marketplace, then they need IT to guide the company's tool selection rather than act as "security myopic" gatekeepers. And third, they have to consider their resources. You cannot tell bright young engineers or marketers that they are limited to the "approved" toolset and to forget all the tools and Web sites they normally use, and expect them to be happy. It is a very real recruiting disadvantage. To paraphrase the famous post-WWI line, "How are you going to keep them on the IT farm once they've seen the Paris of Web 2.0?"

Small companies can easily leverage loose governance and small budgets into competitive Lean and Web 2.0 solutions that will dramatically increase their competitive position against their larger rivals. And that should be the biggest large-company motivator of all.

THE KNOWLEDGE WORKER'S LEAN FIELD BOOK

Chapter 6

How to Launch Your Lean Journey

Lean is often described as a "journey" because of its emphasis on continuous improvement, and culture or attitude change. Although this has a slightly mystical sound to it, in this chapter we will describe the Lean journey in a tangible, quantitative way and will demonstrate that the same elements that make Lean a journey make it an attractive choice for your improvement efforts.

It is common to speak of the Lean journey, which is the appropriate metaphor in many ways. In the context of continuous improvement, we can think of the effort to eliminate waste and improve efficiency as an ongoing process rather than as a project. Even though some projects are vast in scope, they nonetheless have end points. There is a little flag there in the lower right of the Gantt chart, but unless that flag is labeled "perfection," this isn't the right way to represent Lean activities.

Journey is a metaphor, but it is not a pleasure trip. The horizon may be always ahead of us, but we're not taking this journey out of a love of travel. We are on this journey to make money. We do that by some combination of reducing costs and increasing revenue. The direct levers are the elimination of waste and the increased attractiveness of your product or service in the marketplace, because of increased quality, improved design, time to market, among others, as well as the redeployment of critical resources to activities that more directly add value than where they had been deployed.

On the other hand, as the saying goes, if you don't know where you're going, any road will get you there. It doesn't have to be that way. There is an effective roadmap for the Lean journey, which also serves to highlight the advantages of the Lean approach, and in this section we will develop and use a representational technique to actually map the Lean journey.

Alternate Routes to the Lean Roadmap

Suppose you want to understand and quantitatively represent the as-is condition of any process on a coordinate system. Usually, the trade-off you are asked to make is performance versus cost, and in this example we'll use them as our axes, although we rename cost as efficiency (defined as 1/Cost). Looking at the first diagram, Figure 6.1, this makes the upper-right-hand quadrant the place to be; data points there are either more efficient or better performers, or both, than other data points.

Now assume you own a process with a measured cost and performance represented by point A on Figure 6.1 and further suppose that word comes down from above that all departmental budgets have to be cut 10 percent to deal with worsening market conditions. You have barely left the meeting room when you start developing some ideas. Since your group employs about 20 people, you are also thinking about which two people you are going to cut. You choose Jonathan and Maria, the two newest members of the group, although they provided expedited special handling and staffed the after-hours help desk. You decide you are going to have to live without those two services for now.

The group's performance has now shifted to point B on the grid. The cost has gone down and so the group *appears* more efficient. It is still providing the process but at a lower cost. However, the performance level, assuming you had a way to measure it other than customer complaints, has dropped because your department is no longer providing these two distinct services. If you were told that you had to cut some more next quarter, then the process cost and performance might move to position C on the grid. Once you connect those dots, you

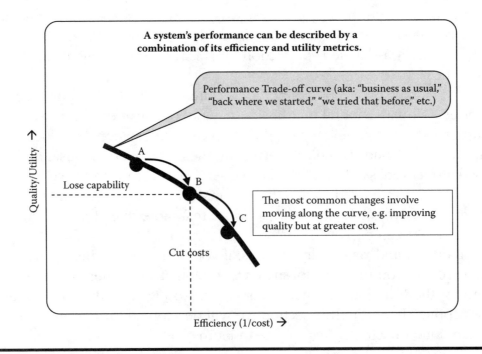

Figure 6.1 The performance trade-off curve.

have a trade-off curve that relates performance and efficiency for this particular process. If you gained budget relief next quarter you might rehire your employees or gain others, and your process would move back to A. Based on the systems and paradigms in place, you are naturally constrained to move up and down the trade-off curve.

This drives a key learning: any manager or organization can reduce cost, or add performance, to some degree by just moving up and down the trade-off curve. Such movement implies no process changes or improvements or changes to the system under which they are operating. In other words, once the budget heat is off, we can all go back to business as usual. Reason tells us that all companies with similar processes and departments must have a similar trade-off curve and they can each move up or down their trade-off curves relatively quickly by cutting back or adding resources to the services that would constitute performance. Yet experience tells us that if we very carefully benchmark several comparable companies with the same process we will find a wide variation in the graph plotted.

The logical conclusion is that the different systems, processes, and techniques at these different companies are what drive the location of their trade-off curve. Look at company B in Figure 6.2. Its trade-offs are similar to A's, but the curve is shifted to the right. This represents business processes that are inherently more productive and efficient than those of company A. They can produce more at the same cost and resource level or they can produce the same amount at lower cost. Since the vertical axis represents quality and utility as measured by value to the

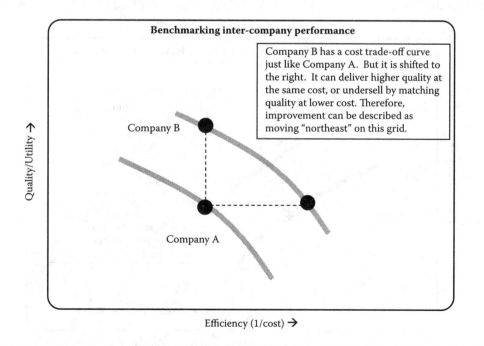

Figure 6.2 All companies have trade-off curves; curves shifted up and to the right are better.

customer and the horizontal axis represents cost and efficiency, this chart is a good working description of how Lean you are.

These are our Lean journey compass headings. To make our process Leaner, we need to move up and to the right on this grid, and there is more than one way to do this. Business improvement practices and techniques are constantly seeking this "northeast passage," and it is instructive to see how some of the recent improvement methodologies have gone about doing this.

The Benchmarking and Best Practice Adoption Hop

Adopting best practices is perhaps the most obvious way to move northeast on the grid. The idea is to identify a process improvement empirically by direct measurement or by reviewing data submitted by the other companies' process teams. Take care to filter out companies that have structural, commercial, regulatory, or cultural differences significant enough to make adoption of the best practice too challenging. Also, take care to ensure that you gather not just cost measurements or benchmarks but also relevant performance metrics. This is more difficult than it sounds because most subprocesses in most companies do not have explicit performance measures, and when they do, they are often subjective evaluations from an internal customer. Accurate and reliable comparative data of this nature is quite hard to get and often takes great effort. Figure 6.3 illustrates what happens when benchmarking and reengineering are applied.

Another challenge is competitiveness between the participating companies. It's easy to describe a benchmarking or shared best practices study as a win-win

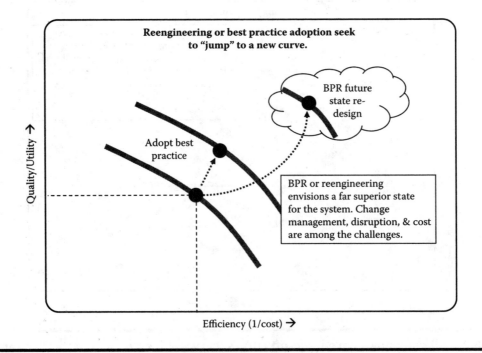

Figure 6.3 Reengineering and benchmarking are attempts to move to a better curve.

opportunity for the managers involved, but it often does not work that way. Managers do not like to quantitatively assess their department or process as inferior to another, especially that of a competitor in the same industry or region. Data from the "other guys" typically are met with skepticism and a great deal of time is spent describing the structural differences that might explain away any perceived performance or cost advantage. We will be very happy if we never hear the phrase "apples to apples" again. It's a pity so many managers seek to win the benchmarking comparison. The winner in this case is really the loser. The manager will have bragging rights, but will have gained no insights into how to improve. Conversely, those evaluated near the bottom have the opportunity to learn from the other members and dramatically improve both cost and performance. If only they saw it that way.

This competitiveness problem can partly be solved by benchmarking companies in very different industries; for example, evaluating learning user interface design from Apple, customer service from L.L. Bean, and efficient back-office operations from Vanguard. Managers are more likely to be praised for running in such fast company than chastised for falling short.

The challenge to best practice adoption is not uncovering what the best practices are but in actually making those ideas work and then making them stick. Best practices should not be confused with closely held corporate secrets. Most companies like to discuss, at a high-level, what their secrets to success are. This is good for recruiting, investor relations, and in attracting future business partners. Many experts have written books about best practices in their specialty, blogs, expert forums abound on the Web where state-of-the-art ideas are freely available, and consultants will be happy to share or develop best practice surveys as well as explicit investigations. Nevertheless, the fact remains that getting value out of best practices is a tricky business at best. Many business pundits now say that there really is no such thing as best practices; it's more like "the best for them" practices.

There are so many unseen and unquestioned cultural and structural differences, including the quality and training of personnel, that it historically proves hard to both adapt and maintain an externally derived best practice. The tendency is to design best practice projects for scale so that they are significant enough to warrant the effort and especially the attention that it will likely bring. Who wants to be the manager who comes back and reports that he or she studied some world-class companies' renowned process but learned nothing?

The change is usually rather broad in scope and not fully understood. For example, in accounting or back-office operations, managers might determine that the paperless office is a best practice they should adopt. There is certainly plenty of objective reporting and literature to support this, but they may have failed to take into account that their clerical staffs are not used to computers and see no real advantage to looking at images of documents as opposed to actual documents. The fact that many other parallel processes such as record-keeping, troubleshooting lost invoices, training and reporting, expediting, and so forth are dramatically improved does not sway the team that does the basic invoice checking.

Another example is outsourcing. No one could argue that this has strong best practice credentials, but still many outsourced operations fail to deliver because, among other things, the hidden costs of communication and rework that were not part of the original analysis. Although in Figure 6.3, the best practices approach incremental hop appears to the right, the hop comes with a high probability of regression back to the original curve (imagine someone moving from a slow moving escalator to a faster one and you will understand why).

The Business Process Reengineering Leap

Reengineering is a great idea, simple in concept and vast in scope. It is liberating for some and takes both courage and humility for others to admit that our processes are far from where they should be and that it would be easier to start with a clean sheet of paper. Turn the Etch A Sketch upside down and start over.

Most process consultants working today to some degree have made their living by reengineering. It seems wrong somehow to find fault with this approach, but the fault is there. Chief among the problems with the reengineering approach is the risk brought about by the scale of change. There usually is no clearly envisioned path from the current state to the end state until such a plan is developed, and there is many a slip between the cup and the lip.

Reengineering has the same adoption challenges as best practices except that the challenges are on steroids. It is not just the reengineering, that is to say identifying the as-is state and developing the business case or gap analysis, it is change management that's the problem.

These massive visionary changes, for which your people don't have the knowledge or skill, have to be delivered without shutting down your current operations. It's the old joke about changing the tires on a moving vehicle. In the years after Hammer and Champy wrote their industry-changing book,* reengineering seemed to become defined as large systems integration. That's very convenient if you are installing SAP systems for a living. What we don't like about this is that, except for a few project management and liaison personnel, the company's process workers have to take a backseat to the external experts—at least until the system turnover and training is accomplished.

You can guess that Lean practitioners, who believe in empowering workers and leveraging their ideas and institutional knowledge, might look askance at this approach. Of course, if you do need a large enterprise resource planning (ERP) system, it makes sense to launch a large ERP project, but this is really a different question from whether to use Lean approaches for continuous improvement. So, Business Process Reengineering (BPR) shows on our grid as high gain and high

---

* Michael Hammer and James Champy, *Reengineering the Corporation: A Manifesto for Business Revolution* (New York: Harper Business Press. 1993).

risk (see Figure 6.3)—a Hail Mary pass to the upper-right-hand corner, a pass that's usually incomplete. Today's literature cites a 70-percent failure rate for large BPR projects, which are also very expensive, very high profile, and tend to drive worker fatigue. Reengineering, as practiced, is definitely a project, not a process, and you need significant downtime between them for your resources to recover and stay enthusiastic. One or two failed mega-projects like this can be career limiting.

The Statistical Process Control and Six Sigma Turn

Statistical process control and Six Sigma improve performance by concentrating on the elimination of variation within the process, which ultimately leads to a drastic reduction in defects. These methodologies are characterized by rigorous systems and well-trained leaders, the famous Green Belts, Black Belts, and so forth, who support the broader base of workers and actually perform some of the more rigorous analytical and statistical activities. That Six Sigma processes usually move up in our graph is easy to grasp. They deliver a very high quality product. What's more interesting is that they also move to the right because they improve cost.

Many managers have a kneejerk expectation that delivering high quality is very expensive and is justified only in certain high-end product categories. Indeed if you look at the trade-off curves in Figures 6.1 to 6.3, that is the fundamental premise—the line slopes downward from left to right indicating that to move up and deliver better quality you are constrained to move left because to improve quality means higher cost.

Case Study: Higher Quality, Lower Cost

Six Sigma challenges this thinking. In many instances, it is actually more cost effective to deliver high quality than not. Suppose we make a consumer electronics product and have a certain defect rate at the time of shipping. Every defective product that reaches our customer triggers a whole series of costs: calls to customer care, cost of a replacement product, shipping, and some recovery or refurbishment costs for the original defective product. But the later in the process you discover a defect—component testing, system testing, or in this case a very expensive form of user acceptance testing—the more expensive defects will be. Much like the Lean principle of poka yoke, Six Sigma reduces errors, waste, and rework in the process in addition to minimizing all the post-shipping costs.

A Six Sigma program is a large and expensive proposition, ultimately worthwhile but not immediately so. In Figure 6.4, we represent three stages of a typical Six Sigma implementation process. In the first stage, our progress moves down and to the left indicating that initially there is both increased cost and a drop in performance as a result of all the training, investment, and methodological development required to kickoff Six Sigma. In the second phase, the performance

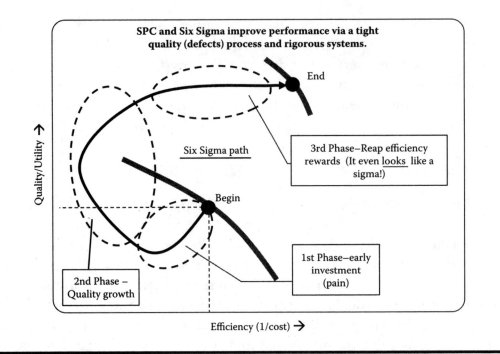

Figure 6.4 Six Sigma first invests heavily before working toward a better curve.

curve turns and product quality begins to increase even though our costs are still high because of continued support, training, and process refinement. Many of the cost advantages, such as fewer returns or payouts of warranty costs, are naturally on a longer cycle and have yet to be realized.

Last, our process turns again and finally starts delivering both continued incremental product quality and rapidly improving efficiencies and lower costs. This Six Sigma journey is a continuous journey, and its shape represents a classic invest and recoup business decision.

One of the greatest challenges to Six Sigma, however, is time. Without the proper metrics to evaluate the movement upward in product quality and utility, Six Sigma projects can look like costly exercises. Western management typically looks for quarterly returns, and the Six Sigma leader must be careful to demonstrate strong performance improvement in phases two and three and be able to predict when the line will cross the company's original trade-off curve at an orthogonal and truly begin to pay off. It is easy to remember the typical Six Sigma life cycle we graph here since it traces out a shape very similar to a lowercase sigma.

Creating the Lean Roadmap

The Lean journey, the one we are most interested in, includes elements of each of the alternate approaches but is really quite different from any of them. First, it is a journey but unlike the Six Sigma journey, it is an unguided journey. As Figure 6.5 illustrates, it is a series of short hops, each representing a tactical or

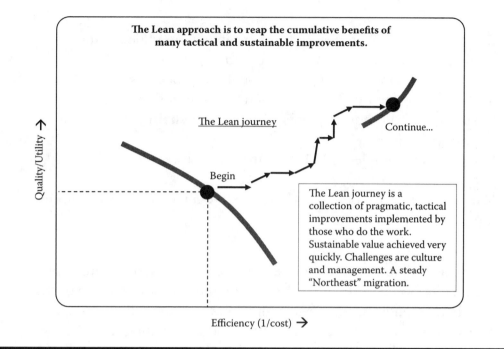

The Lean approach is to reap the cumulative benefits of many tactical and sustainable improvements.

The Lean journey

Continue...

Begin

The Lean journey is a collection of pragmatic, tactical improvements implemented by those who do the work. Sustainable value achieved very quickly. Challenges are culture and management. A steady "Northeast" migration.

Quality/Utility →

Efficiency (1/cost) →

Figure 6.5 Lean does not move via one big jump or one all-encompassing program.

pragmatic improvement, some of which may be primarily cost reducers and others may be primarily process or quality improvements. They may be dependent on each other or independent. They are likely to come from several different individuals or teams, and these individuals or teams are more likely to be process owners or at least company employees and consultants or software vendors. Unlike reengineering or Six Sigma, these improvements don't require the development of a formal business case. Although collectively their impact is very significant, individually they are simple, practical, and low cost. Often Lean ideas are represented in A3 format, what an American would call 11 × 17-inch or tabloid format because the whole problem statement and solution is expected to fit on that one sheet. It is important to note that these ideas are seen as being on trial. In an environment where you have a large number of small ideas, it's much easier to permit a couple of mulligans. This is a morale and confidence builder for your Lean team. In addition—and this is one of the most important points— since these ideas came from the process owner, they are individually small and practical and, therefore, can be put into place and deliver results quickly. *Lean changes tend to have a much higher adoption rate than other types of process changes and tend to be sticky.*

WHAT A LEAN PROCESS LOOKS LIKE

There are few performance trade-offs (flexibility as well as efficiency)
The value-adding processes flow and customer demand pulls the work through the process
There is very little waste or duplication in the value chain of activities

Customer focus, awareness, and involvement are critical issues
Workers and teams are empowered and largely self-directed
The Lean principles are applied throughout processes
Standard work and variability reduction programs are in place
Connections to other elements of the value chain are made using the Lean principles
Lean metrics (simple and visual) are understood, communicated, and acted upon
Management and supervisory practices are aligned to Lean thinking

All the methodologies (alternate routes) we have described are capable of yielding results. Some of them have come in and out of fashion over the years. Some of them, reengineering, for example, have gotten a bad rap because large software vendors, outsourcing consultants, and cost-cutting managers wrapped their very different initiatives in the reengineering banner. Your organization's needs may very well dictate the use of one over the others. Table 6.1 is a short comparison based on selected criteria. This table represents our high opinion of Lean techniques for performance improvements. Lean is the only fast, effective, and distributed approach; it also is one of the low-cost options.

■ Lean is the only method that empowers the workforce and delivers fast results at low risk to provide sticky results quickly; it also is sustainable. The challenge is in sustaining the cultural momentum of continuous improvement.

Table 6.1 Characteristics, Advantages, and Risks of Various Improvement Strategies

	Cost Cutting	Best Practices	BPR	Six Sigma	Lean
Action leader	Management	Management	Process owner	Management	Process owner
Thought leader	Management	External	Experts	Experts	Team
Time to results	Fast	Medium	Medium	Slow	Fast
Scale of results	Varies	Medium	High	High	High
Risk of failure	Low	High	High	High	Medium
Risk of counter productivity	High	Low	Low	Medium	Low
Risk of reversion	High	Medium	Medium	Low	Low
Knowledge transfer	Low	Medium	Medium	High	Medium
Sustainability	Low	Medium	Medium	High	Medium

- Cost cutting has speed, but it is an illusion. Most companies revert up their cost curve and risk cutting muscle, rather than fat, and injuring their operations in unforeseen ways.
- Six Sigma represents a great effort and is highly sustainable once achieved (similar to the way someone who has made it through boot camp is fit).

Preparing the Road for Knowledge Worker Lean

Before you start to involve the organization in the pursuit of practicing Lean, you and your fellow knowledge workers need to start by getting acquainted with the Lean philosophy. Have a curious and a bit skeptical mindset while doing this. Figure out what might work in your environment and what might not work. Remember that practicing Lean is nothing other than practicing common sense, but in a systematic way. There is no sense starting with the most advanced ways of applying it. First, learn the basic ideas and discuss them among yourselves; by doing that you will most likely see things differently than before.

A good idea is to formulate a framework for Knowledge Worker Lean by articulating the way you would like to apply Lean to your information intense processes. We use the model of the Toyota Temple of Lean in a pragmatic and bespoke way. The entity or temple (the framework) describes the system holistically. It is built upon the ground of standardization and stabilization. The two pillars of the temple are just-in-time and quality, and the roof is composed of customer focus and the atmosphere. The spirit of the temple is the mixture of teamwork and engagement.

By formulating how you would like your organization to relate to the dimensions of

- customer focus
- just-in-time
- quality
- standardization and stabilization
- teamwork and engagement

you are setting the framework for the deployment of Lean.

Selling Your Organization on Going Lean

> During times of transformational change, not only do new problems arise; old ways of understanding problems become problems themselves.
>
> **—Ray Jacques, *Manufacturing the Employee***

If you use Lean as a program, or some specific aspect of an improvement program, or if Lean is a new idea for your client or organization, you're going to have to sell it. Sorry. There's no way around that. Some executives or process leaders might be willing to take a half-informed gamble on Lean. Some may have decided to do so after reading the tea leaves, or because their boss expects it, or because their peers are doing it. Some will be following the improvement flavor of the month. You know the type: the bosses that alternate a major cost initiative with a reorganization every quarter or two to appear to have a capital strategy. Interestingly enough, this latter creates very fertile ground. Change and adaptability are muscles (OK, they're not really but you know what we mean) that need to be exercised to keep from atrophying. The kind of organization described facetiously here has a lot of experience in pursuing an operational change initiative and reporting back on it. The challenge to working with this group is that they don't really take it seriously. "This too shall pass" is a common defense mechanism. That's OK. It is far better than the many organizations that have become calcified in their thinking and process because they did not feel strong competitive pressures to change.

If you think that all organizations feel pressure in today's fast-moving and competitive environment, we disagree. Most customer-facing groups in a competitive environment certainly do. There's nothing to compare with loss of market share as a metric to drive behavior. Negative reviews of your consumer product vis-à-vis the competition cannot be easily explained away. However, many groups are insulated from such dramatic evaluations. There are regulated and natural monopolies such as utilities and city governments as well as all the support organizations, (accounting and legal, for example) that naturally tend toward risk aversion rather than process improvement. There also are the creative types in research and design, who are interested in the myth of the "fuzzy frontend" of development and naturally tend to design detail rather than cycle time reduction.

The next few paragraphs described one method for screening your Lean team members and evaluating process owners, in this case accounting, legal, and regulatory groups. Use this interesting test as you meet and get acquainted with them during the first few days of your Lean project. The simple question scenario helps you gain feedback on their creativity, pragmatism, and ability to handle change. Ask the group to evaluate the following scenario:

You are the owner of a small store and you suffer about $200 per week loss due to shoplifting. You notice that most of it happens in the afternoon in the two hours after school lets out. Should you hire a security guard at $40 per hour to stop this?

Most of these resources will focus on risk-intensive activities like fraud, regulatory penalties, lawsuits, and such. They play defense. Their background, education, and experience have trained them to look for the risk or the flaw. The costs of their approach, tools, and systems have typically been secondary; getting the job done is defined as avoiding these large-ticket issues. This, by the way, is reinforced by their metrics and performance reviews.

On the other hand, these people are smart. Smart enough to do the math implied in this scenario as fast as you say it: even if you hire the security guard for only two hours a day you're still paying $400 to avoid a $200 loss each week. They are also smart enough to know what answer you expect from them. The question is whether they give it to you. We have run this test several times and the most common answer is something like, "I see what you mean" or "That's an interesting question." Very few of them will give the harsh business answer that a $200 loss is better than a $400 expense as their initial response.

The issues are not about risk aversion but problem solving. The risk and cost elasticity for any process change or redesign will always be an issue to consider when evaluating solutions, which must be based on the cultural values and paradigms of the group owning the process for it to be accepted. The real question behind the question in this problem is whether the interviewee distinguishes between the requirement and the solution. Hiring a security guard is only one possible way to fulfill the requirement of not losing money. Many alternative answers break the limitations of the A or B scenario:

- I would hire the guard for the first week to send a message.
- I would install security cameras (or fake security cameras).
- I would put up signs warning of our prosecution policy.
- I would protect the most commonly shoplifted items.

The ability to develop the alternate solution is the key thing. It's not about risk aversion; it's about change aversion. *Star Trek* fans will recognize this as the "Kobayashi Maru" scenario. Neither of the two predefined outcomes, lose $200 or pay $400, is acceptable. You must create an entirely new option. The ability to generate a game-changing design solution is not a luxury; it is an integral part of Lean thinking.

The good thing about selling Lean to your organization or customer is that there are so many ways to approach the task. We have always felt that there are four basic ways to convince someone that an idea is a good one. There are variations and subcategories but they fall within four fundamental types of arguments.

Argument 1: The Good Idea

We always think we have a good idea; the self-evident, "Why didn't anyone ever think of this idea before?" When you put this in front of your customer or a company executive, you expect them to slap their foreheads as they grasp the brilliance of the thing in a flash. "Oh, that is so simple, yet so clever." This does happen, and it's quite wonderful, but it is rare.

What often happens is that the person doesn't get it quite as fast or to quite the degree that you do. This can be because the person presenting the idea has been living more closely with the problem and the elaborated solution and can't quite put himself or herself in the shoes of someone seeing it for the first time.

Sometimes the new set of eyes, or different evaluative criteria, of the person being sold detects more flaws or implementation challenges than the seller does. At any rate, if the idea is this good and obvious, you should be successful most of the time, but not all.

Argument 2: The Consensus Approach

The consensus approach is the "4 out of 5 doctors recommend Brand X" sales pitch. It has benchmarking and best practices implications and can be very powerful. This is bread and butter for Lean selling. After all, it worked wonders for Toyota, is being said even when it isn't being said. *The Economist* magazine wrote that Lean was one of the fundamental drivers for productivity gains throughout the Western world over the last decade. Strong stuff! It gives the person you are convincing comfort that it has worked elsewhere and reduces his or her personal risk of adoption. That falls under the "nobody ever got fired for buying IBM" sales mantra from the big iron computer hardware selling days. The real problem for Lean here is that it is so ubiquitous the brand will be diluted. Many initiatives will be sold as Lean even when they are really not, just as reengineering was partially hijacked and morphed into large ERP projects throughout the 1990s.

Argument 3: The Expert Opinion

What does Warren Buffet say about the stock market? What does Henry Kissinger say about the Middle East? What does Steve Jobs say about the next wave of personal computing? Whether you accept the position stated or not, you're likely to give it some weight. Lean is also very strong in this area, although it's less personal and more corporate. You might think of Jack Welch and Six Sigma as sufficiently paired to be mutually supportive, but Lean heroes such as Shingo are less than household names in America and Europe.

Argument 4: The Analysis

The analysis is the evaluated data-based expression of the benefits of the choice. The chief problem is that you can't use the analysis before you do the analysis, so most methodologies rely on analysis from previous similar opportunities or employ this technique at the end of a diagnostic phase to support implementation and expansion.

One of the beauties of Lean is the eye-opening realization of the magnitude of waste that exists in an organization once you've learned to look in the right way. This makes the preliminary sample analyses very strong. Even better, a quick-and-dirty value stream calculation can be used in practically all scenarios to quantify the opportunity. For example, look at a sequential paperwork process such as reviewing an application or matching invoices to receipts and paying a bill. In one short interview, you can outline the number of steps and the estimated minutes required for each one and contrast that to the (likely) many days required to complete the process. Once you have articulated that it is taking 15 days to do 15 minutes of value-added work, it's hard to argue that something can't be done to recoup some of that wasted time. Some of the problem statement facts will help you structure the Lean argument. We had a very large consumer electronics client whose new product development effort was chronically late. Senior executives complained that it was choking the company and posing a threat to its continued existence. Yet when you picked any particular product under development, you'd most likely find that it was idle and not being worked on at all. Toward the end of the development cycle, of course, all hell was breaking loose and tiger teams were formed to concentrate on the products and complete them.

This scenario has all the classic symptoms: a push-based system, congestion brought about by dependency and variability, huge work in progress, incorrect metrics, and heartfelt congratulations for the heroic last-ditch effort that finally saw the product completed at the end. A tremendous amount of the work was completed in the last phase when a dedicated team worked on it in sharp focus. What is so strange about developing a production system that relies on that strength as its normal mode of operation rather than as the emergency exception?

Up to now we have discussed the whys of Lean for the information age including the high-level rationale for selecting and justifying Lean using the bidimensional Lean journey. Now it's time to dig deeper into information flow and develop some tools and representations that highlight the differences between it and factory-style process flow.

Chapter 7

Model Information Flow: The Information Element and the Information Matrix

Before you can continue our Knowledge Worker Lean journey, you need to be grounded in some new representational and analytical techniques. We describe the concepts of the information element and the information matrix.

The development and exchange of information is the single critical factor affecting many design and development activities. This applies to such diverse realms as new drug development, consumer electronics product development, new financial derivatives, software design, and so on. However, the groups may be organized physically, a rich and complex Web of information flow invariably characterizes the groups responsible for these concept-to-commercial activities. Despite this unofficial information network, most companies have official processes that describe a linear, idealized version of their work processes; this is illustrated in Figure 7.1.

The Difference between Information Flow and Process Flow

The business of white-collar design groups is to solve problems. Information is their currency and the main component of their work. Processes, projects, and organizations are all abstractions meant to coordinate and measure their use of information to solve problems. The implication is that most company procedures and process diagrams are of linear processes or a combination of linear development steps. There are places where the process may branch (decision diamonds in normal flowcharting technique) and alternate paths, of course, but these

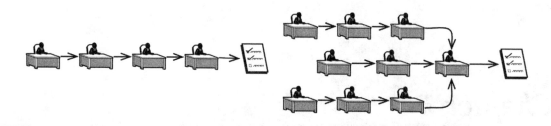

Figure 7.1 Most processes envision an idealized linear flow of one path or converging paths.

represent parallel paths and most work is assumed to "advance" along one of them.

When a company's engineers and designers understand what the factory or field forces require, they are able to create designs that can be manufactured with minimal retooling or can be easily integrated into the existing physical plant. Similarly, the manufacturing or product testing groups can readily shorten product development cycles by applying concurrent engineering principles and participating during the concept phase. In this way, operational requirements are given their due early in design and a great many rework cycles are eliminated.

In reality, however, such a simplistic example only scratches the surface of design iterations in a modern new product development cycle. There are scores, if not hundreds, of opportunities for iterations. Some of them are planned, as during the proof of concept phase, where the phrase "back to the drawing board" is both literally true and wholly appropriate. These planned "assume/test" iterations are a key factor in good design.

However, many design iterations are unplanned and are the result of new information, design errors, changed assumptions, inappropriate task sequencing, or poor communication. When these iterations are based on proximate tasks in the development cycle, the damage is relatively contained. Often they occur far apart in the cycle, perhaps in totally separate organizations within the company, and the personnel responsible may not be in good communication with each other. In some cases, they may not even be aware of the details of each other's work and their close interconnection with the evolving design. When this happens, not only does it generate rework between the two activities, but also there almost certainly is a significant, and as yet hidden rework penalty embedded in the work of all the intervening tasks. It is easy to imagine a new product going through this cycle many times as the original defect and all its ripple effects are slowly discovered and worked out.

The Impact of Modern Communications on Product Development

The advent of e-mail, cell phones, corporate intranets, and so forth have all quickened the transfer of information. In some ways, this speed increase can mitigate the iteration problem noted earlier. If you are cycling much faster, you can afford more cycles. On the other hand, there are other negative effects to enhanced communications. We find that these new tools have irrevocably changed the product development process and created communications links that can enhance, or subvert, the normal process flow.

Most process designs are still based on paper flow and face-to-face review meetings, but e-mail, for example, allows organizations that are relatively far downstream to get the proof of concept results at the same time as the proper "in sequence" organization in the developmental chain. This creates parallel paths, in some cases many parallel paths, and unofficial loops of information that can lead to wasted or redundant effort as well new sources of error and rework (see Figure 7.2).

Modern communications act as an accelerant, a force multiplier for the challenges of new product development. The information dimension is a fundamentally different, derivative one from the process diagram or project activity metaphor we are used to. We need to harness this new dimension of information flow rather than be victimized by it.

High-Level Process Design and Its Implications for Information Flow

Most processes are designed with a left-to-right bias. If you look at most IDEF* process diagrams, or Gantt charts, or milestone schedules, you will naturally look to the upper left corner for the starting event and the lower right for the finish. The unspoken assembly line metaphor is there, a legacy of our experience with

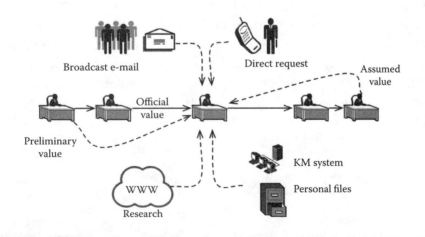

Figure 7.2   The modern knowledge worker has many more unofficial information sources (dashed lines) in addition to the official process.

* IDEF stands for Integration DEFinition, a diagramming method used to model decisions, actions, activities, and organization in a system. There are several detailed variants but, in casual usage, they are essentially the same as flow diagrams.

the physical assembly processes: start here, add something here, add another thing here, and so on.

The orthodox approach to new product development is the stage–gate approach, which is also referred to as waterfall development because of its sequential left to right, top to bottom diagram. In the last two decades, several new process paradigms have been introduced, largely from the core knowledge worker group, the software developers. The most common techniques—spiral development, rapid prototyping, agile development, SCRUM, and extreme programming—all veer drastically from the waterfall paradigm. They emphasize shorter, iterative cycles with interim deliverables, or as we would express it, they all tried to address the information flow wastes of the waterfall approach.

In the waterfall or stage–gate approach, the project requires a broad scope definition up front ("make sure you get *all* the requirements") on the belief that late-arriving requirements are the problem. We believe that working with poorly elaborated requirements from the beginning is far worse. The early requirements in a waterfall approach are laced with assumptions, guesses, and placeholder values. Many of these are carried along with the design for long periods, many hard choices are made based on soft requirements, and much rework is occasioned.

The other modern approaches are more inherently Lean in their approach to information in that they only use good information. If only some of the requirements are known, then work is done against them. That process informs the team and helps to develop additional requirements for the next iteration, and so forth. Bad data or unmanageable requirements are quickly sorted out. In a waterfall, the effects of an early bad value can ripple throughout the entire chain and, since there is much less visibility in a waterfall than a spiral, subsequent downstream groups may never even learn that a certain value was only a placeholder. They move heaven and earth to fulfill an actually quite elastic requirement.

The stage–gate approach brings disciplined reviews at certain selected points as a new product design matures. There are many variants, but a typical set of stages would be concept, requirements, design, test, integration, and sometimes deployment (see the left side of Figure 7.3). Between each of these phases, there

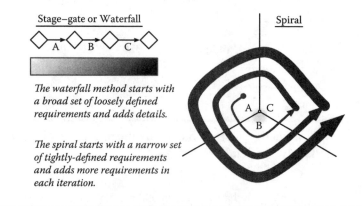

Figure 7.3 Approaches to development: stage–gate and spiral.

is a pass/fail review gate. The gate serves two purposes. The first purpose is to ensure that the original business cases and rationale for the product are still valid in light of the increased understanding that each stage of development brings. The second is to gauge whether the design is complete enough to support the activities of the next phase. The stage–gate approach presupposes that the problems inherent in each stage are self-contained. Once resolved, design can progress.

The problem with these review gates is that passing, in itself, becomes the focus of development efforts for each stage. This often leads to dressing up the pig or throwing it over the fence. The natural tendency for a design group, especially one in a competitive, high-pressure business, is to do its job as quickly and effectively as possible and get its project to the gate review. Three results, two of them good from the perspective of the design group, are possible: (1) the project passes the gate review and becomes the property of the next group; (2) the project is killed as being infeasible or uneconomic and thus is also taken off their hands; or (3) the project is rejected for lack of completion or insufficient documentation (the only bad result). In the third case, the gaps must be filled by the submitting organization. However, this is the rarest of the three possible outcomes for several reasons: (1) the submitting organization presumably would have postponed the gate review if it was not ready; (2) the more important documents are likely done and if earlier predecessor work is missing, it can be explained away as moot or implicit in the final results; and, most important, (3) the downstream organization is likely to feel the pressure of its own targeted delivery gate or the rapidly approaching in-service date, and takes on the incomplete project and fill the gaps itself. At least its destiny will be in its own hands.

All of these behaviors reflect an essentially internal focus for each organization in the process. Except for complaining about those so-and-so's upstream, most modern development groups have so many projects and so much pressure that they remain focused on their own activities. They lack situational visibility. We have repeatedly found that most engineers in our clients' organizations are somewhat surprised to see who eventually uses the information they generate or that different groups use the same source information they do for their own purposes.

The traditional project management tools do little to improve this situation. PERT (program evaluation and review technique) charts, Gantt charts, and other common scheduling tools were created to help managers plan, schedule, and resource large construction projects such as building factories or ships. However many thousands of tasks a complex project may entail, the principles are still simple and the sequence of events highly predictable. These tools depict tasks or activities, often grouped into phases of work, and they illustrate higher-level dependencies. Process flow charts may convey more detailed information, but their boxes and arrows format is relatively inefficient. If you were to capture every detailed task in a major new product development in this format, the ensuing plan would run on to hundreds of pages and it would be very difficult to trace an interaction between two boxes separated by 20 pages.

Product development is very different. It is about innovation and complex learning, which requires complex information flow, often in feedback loops, and the ability to easily represent coupled tasks or pieces of information.

Conventional planning and project management tools use the dimensions of tasks and time, such as the critical path method (CPM).* The expectation is a clean "left to right" flow because time cannot flow backwards, but information flows loop back forming closed circuits; these can be concurrency, rework, requirements planning, clarification, and so forth. This information flow will clash with the organizational hierarchy or the presumed work breakdown structure (WBS)[†] of the project. The neat project plan may not reflect it, but there is no escaping it: designers are problem solvers, who will find the subject matter expert, data repository, or external source that has the information they need to solve their problem. They will circumvent process gates or procedures to do that.

Much of this problem goes away in a spiral-type development approach, which is inherently Lean because the initial development work is performed against well-established, if fewer, requirements. In stage–gate (or "big up-front development" as it has been called), the early requirements documents are populated with assumptions. They have to be unless this project is a near duplicate of a previous one. As Figure 7.3 implies, stage–gate design is a broad line getting darker while spiral design is a dark line getting broader.

Both stage–gate and spiral development styles can be represented by conventional tools such as milestone charts, Gantt charts, and PERT diagrams. Conventional tools answer the question, "What is my critical path and the shortest possible schedule?" However, we can do better. We can ask ourselves, "How can I use the information needs and flows to redesign my process and reduce cost and rework?"

We can apply the Lean mantra to project management: Your job is no longer to just do the work. Your job is to do the work and improve the way you do the work.

How to Represent Information Flow: The Matrix

There are many potential ways to represent information flow. Adding commentary or document symbols to a standard flowchart is perhaps the most common. Adding the information component as another dimension to the flowcharts (line

---

* CPM is a common and powerful technique in project management whereby algorithms determine the longest path, and therefore shortest possible project time. This is typically based on fixed or probabilistic durations of tasks. Any extension of these "critical" tasks translates into an extension of the overall project.

[†] WBS is a technique for specifying the organization and classification of subtasks as the overall project is parsed into smaller elements. WBS is often indexed along resource, skill set, or location lines, and can miss information flow dependencies.

width or color) is another. Software can be used to display tagged information components as alternate views of a process representation. All these approaches start with the process view.

We are interested in the creation, use, and consumption of pieces of information. Their physical flow is not important in the modern office, where we only need to show their inputs and outputs (their dependencies). Such a technique already exists; it is the design structure matrix. Developed by Donald Steward of NASA, it is a two-dimensional grid mapping relationships that has been used to understand the connections between systems, project management, and now information flow. Software has been developed to automatically rearrange the matrix and, in our case, streamline flow. First, let's examine the basics of the technique.

Sequential Flow

We will start with the simplest process, a linear flow from A to B to C. The left side of Figure 7.4 shows a flowchart representation of this process. The matrix shows the predecessor and successor relationships in two dimensions. For larger processes the matrix approach is much faster at identifying relationships than tracing flow lines.

If you look down the columns instead of across the rows, you will see that the Xs represent the destination of the information generated in that column. For example, if the knowledge worker in B ever wondered what happened to her analysis, she could look down the column and see that it is used by C. This is a simple example to illustrate the point; it's just as easy to trace destination in a 100 × 100 matrix. You can do it at a glance. To retrieve the same information with process diagrams you would be tracing many lines with your finger across many pages.

In general, rows indicate sources, and columns indicate destinations.

Parallel Flow

Figure 7.5 is an example of parallel flow. A and B are developed independently and they both feed C. If you look at C, you see an X in each column; however, no relationship or dependency between A and B is indicated in the figure.

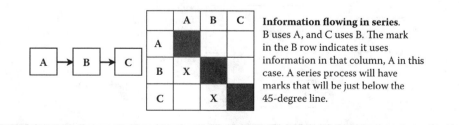

Information flowing in series. B uses A, and C uses B. The mark in the B row indicates it uses information in that column, A in this case. A series process will have marks that will be just below the 45-degree line.

Figure 7.4 Serial information flow analyzed in a design structure matrix.

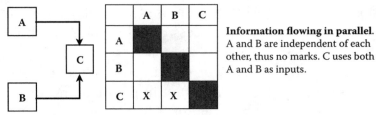

Information flowing in parallel. A and B are independent of each other, thus no marks. C uses both A and B as inputs.

Figure 7.5   Parallel information flow analyzed in a design structure matrix.

Note that A and B are "combined" and not "integrated" at C. If C integrated A and B, for example if A was software and B hardware, we could not show them as independent in this way because somewhere upstream both A and B would have had specifications and requirements as inputs that would allow them to be integrated into a larger unit at C. In the case of integration, the values and attributes of A would affect B and vice versa. What this diagram represents is enveloping two independent values into a third information element (Infel; see later for additional information). For example, A could be a required delivery date from an engineer and B could be a price quote from a buyer combined in a purchase order in the accounting department.

Circuit Flow

We call mutual dependency circuit flow (a term borrowed from Donald F. Steward, but circular, recursive, or chicken-and-egg will also serve). As you can see in Figure 7.6, C is dependent on A, but A is also dependent on C. This kind of iteration is very common. Often, it is easier to assume a value and determine its implications than it is to come up with a procedure to obtain the optimum value. We've all taken this trial and error approach many times. When an individual uses trial and error, it's an unremarkable technique. When two nearby coworkers who collaborate frequently use it, the results are usually fine except for the occasional miscommunication. On the other hand, if you and your collaborator are in different locations or organizations, in addition to delays in completing the iteration, errors frequently occur and the placeholder value can become the official one.

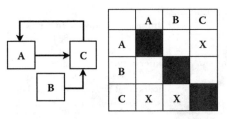

Information flowing in a circuit. C uses A and B as inputs. But A also is dependent on C in a circular fashion. Mutual dependency is not a logic error, it is common. A usually begins work with an assumed value of C's output.

Figure 7.6   Circuit information flow analyzed in a design structure matrix.

THE TROUBLE WITH DOCUMENTS

Take a minute to examine an important point. Most documents contain more than one piece of information. Some, such as a functional design requirements document, might contain dozens. Figure 7.7 illustrates two different matrix representations: one indexed at the document level and the other at the information element level.

The situation illustrated in Figure 7.7 is sometimes referred to as a transitive dependency. Is the information in A a pass-through to C or is it "consumed" in the creation of B? In Unified Modeling Language, for example, transitive dependencies are not acknowledged, but this presupposes that programming best practices are adhered to. What actually happens on a larger scale when information is passed among knowledge workers in an organization is a hybrid of the two. Constructing the information matrix superficially and relying on the official process and procedures will result in something like the left matrix. The left matrix is the official representation of the process; however, the knowledge worker responsible for C has learned to get the information directly from A. (This can happen in a number of ways: e-mail request, asking to be cc'd when A transmits to B "for information only," using the value from A's last output, some form of the electronic water cooler, etc.) That is why we always recommend interviewing knowledge workers to elicit these alternate paths. Questions like, "Suppose Bill were on vacation, how would you get the A information?" This will yield an answer like, "Well, I get cc'd on A anyway when it's originally created. That way I can get an early start and not have to wait for the B document." Now you have two paths for the information to reach C, and two versions of the information.

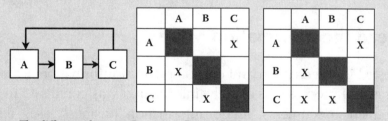

The difference between Document flow and Information Flow.
Documents are typically comprised of multiple information elements that tend to mask true information usage. At the document level (middle graphic), C appears to only use B. In reality, information created in A is repackaged in B and passed thru. The final graphic shows C using A information once the information has been freed from the document envelopes.

Figure 7.7   Information flow must be analyzed at a detailed level.

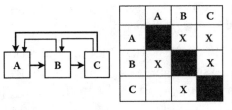

Multiple Circuits. In this example there are either 2 or 3 complete circuits (depending on whether the A:C dependency is real or transitive). Scattered across a large process flow these circuits would be hard to trace, and the DSM matrix and software really shine in situations like this.

Figure 7.8 Multiple circuit information flow analyzed in a design structure matrix.

Multicircuit Flow

Figure 7.8 illustrates multicircuit flow. This situation is actually quite common although it is often invisible to the process workers because the A–B–C Infels may be quite distant from one another, perhaps even in different organizational entities. We've compressed them here to illustrate the idea, but bear in mind that dependency (sometimes design) structure matrices (DSM) software clusters this information very effectively.

Note: Nothing is wrong with the logic of these relationships, there are many such mutually dependent steps or analyses or objects of code. The challenge is to sequence and structure, that is, cluster, them tightly together to minimize the waste of rework. Initially, with a raw matrix, these circuits will be large and scattered; the redesigned matrix will cluster them.

We have illustrated these simple matrices starting from process diagrams, but you can translate them from other representations such as a project schedule template or list of deliverables, or a stage–gate description or a spiral description. Each of these will only generate a high-level matrix. Developing the detailed Infel-level matrix requires more work including eliciting true information use from the knowledge workers involved in the process and parsing the process documents into information elements.

How to Read the Information Matrix

We are interested in the creation and consumption of information across a complex, cross-organizational process. Historically, information was contained in design documents, requirements documents, vendor information, business cases, test results, and many others, which were comprised of many smaller bits of information. (We termed these document fractions or lowest common information denominator the Information Element, or Infel, and it is similar in concept and pronunciation to pixel, short for picture element.) The larger design documents were reviewed (at gate meetings or other acceptance meetings) and moved from one group to the other.

As said before, we have found that e-mail and the other communications accelerants have changed that paradigm. Today, designers seek out very specific pieces of information and bypass or ignore the rest. For example, a systems integrator will receive the test scripts from the concept stage months before the

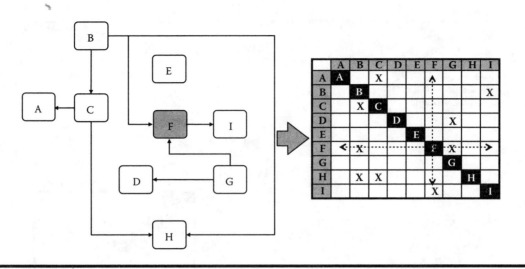

Figure 7.9   A process or flow diagram and its corresponding dependency matrix.

---

project has progressed through the intervening engineering groups. Once a component vendor is selected (or even before), many developers will go to the vendor's Web site and download detailed specs without waiting for their upstream colleague to do so and pass on the information with whatever value-added analysis that colleague performs.

To illustrate this, Figure 7.9 combines these building blocks into a slightly larger diagram that illustrates them all. By now, you should be able to easily read Figure 7.9. Concentrate on element F. It is dependent on B and G as the incoming arrows in the process sketch show. We can see Xs in the F row under columns B and G. Element F feeds I. If you scan down the F column, you will see an X in the I row.

Discerning the dependencies in the information matrix is far from all you can do. The matrix itself provides several important clues, and, with a little experience, they will jump out at you.

Figure 7.10 is an annotated Infel matrix outlining the classes of information flow that can easily be spotted in this representation.

Four basic clues are immediately available:

1. Assumptions—Any marks above the line represent an input from a "latter" element, one that is expected to happen later in the process yet is somehow providing an input. This is possible if you use an assumed value. The farther removed from the 45-degree line, the greater the risk of rework to bring that assumption, and all the subsequent work dependent on it, into line.
2. Circuits—These are assumption–development pairs. A small circuit can represent a simple iteration of two collaborators and can be quite effective. A large circuit almost never is. This is a key clue.
3. Out of sequence—Any mark significantly below the 45-degree line represents an out-of-process early pass-through of information. Many knowledge workers believe this is a good practice and that it enables "preparation," but,

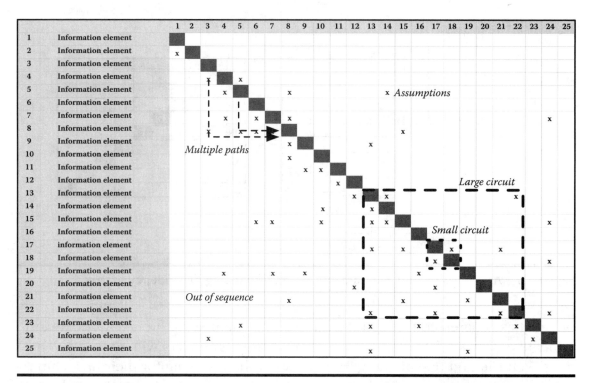

Figure 7.10 **An information flow matrix is packed with hints and symptoms useful to the Lean team and can be a more effective workspace than a traditional flow diagram.**

more often, it creates confusion and rework because the early value is subject to change as it goes through the official process. Most of the prep work is wasted.

4. Multiple paths—It is common to find more than one way to get an Infel. The question then becomes which one to use. This and clue 3 are more representative of "just in case" thinking than JIT or continuous flow.

These clues are almost immediately revealed in the matrix representation. Your kaizen discussion is working on something tangible in the first five minutes.

If we take these ideas and what we have learned about the implications of dependency placement on the matrix and extrapolate them to the general case, we get Figure 7.11. (With a nod to Sergio Leone whose terminology we've appropriated).

Just below the 45-degree line is "good" in that it represents an orderly sequence of steps adding value. Slightly above the 45-degree line or significantly below it suggests trouble—too much recursion or out of sequence work. Any dependencies in the upper-right-hand corner are truly an ugly problem and should move to the top of your improvement ideas list. After reviewing all the symptoms and clues of an "opportunity rich" information matrix, it is a good idea to examine a well-designed one. Figure 7.12 is illustrative and highlights the major points we want to make.

First, note that Figure 7.12 contains only 22 items (rows) instead of 25. A review of the columns in Figure 7.11 revealed three empty ones, information that

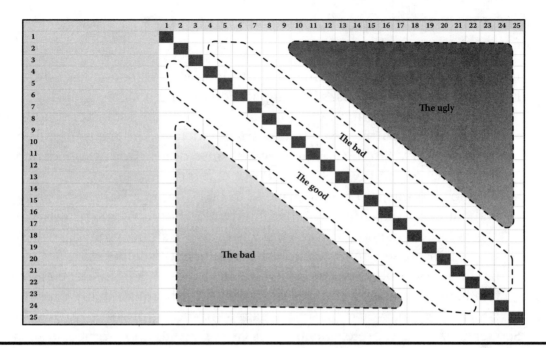

Figure 7.11   Marks in any of three distinct zones provide a quick assessment of the degree of out-of-sequence or recursive information flows in any process.

was not needed and never used. This allowed us to immediately capture cost savings or waste reductions.

Next note that there are fewer dependencies. This largely happens "off the page," but we eliminate multiple paths and out-of-sequence information flows. They are a safety crutch that adds no safety yet introduces waste. Finally, we see a characteristic shape represented by three zones: independent, dependent (or

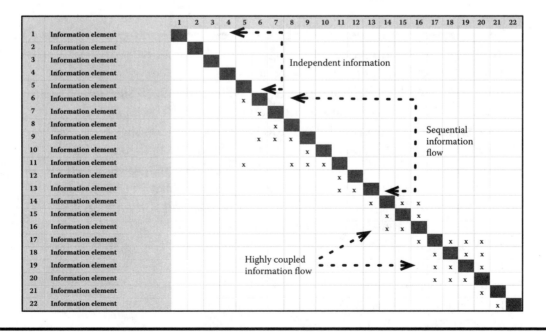

Figure 7.12   A redesigned matrix will group information into three distinct areas.

sequential), and highly coupled (or clustered). These three zones provide another set of suggestions to feed your improvement efforts:

1. Independent zone—These elements are truly independent and are only used later in the process. The uses and implications of these elements include:
   - Outsourcing/partnering—One of the main problems with exporting work to a vendor or partner is that the wastes of defects and miscommunications can outweigh the apparent cost savings driver. However, independent activities can be safely moved out of the organization.
   - Workload leveling—These activities can be done on a start/stop basis without negatively affecting other information flow needs. Therefore, they can be used as temporary assignments or as a training ground.
   - Inspection phase—In any hand-off environment, whether from an internal group or vendor, these penalty-free activities should be done early to familiarize the team with the specifics and to determine if any gaps or issues exist that would cause the team to reject the project.
2. Sequential zone—These elements are a great place to apply concepts such as line balancing, continuous flow, or Kanban. This should be the largest part of the process.
3. Highly coupled zone—These elements are highly iterative, and project duration and cost are highly sensitive to performance in this area.
   - Consider assigning your best or most experienced resources here.
   - Likely the source of your process constraint, therefore, focus management attention, monitoring, and reporting here.
   - The iterative and team nature of these information activities can lend themselves to a cell structure. Consider an information age cell staffed with colocated, cross-functional experts.

Tool Tip: The information matrix approach to Knowledge Worker Lean is based on dependency (sometimes design) structure matrices (DSM). An excellent central resource for DSM is the Web site www. dsmweb.org, which contains a knowledge base, links to a DSM community, and discussions of several tools. Noteworthy among these are PSM32 by Donald Steward (the originator of the DSM), Lattix, Adept, and DeMAID as well as several Excel and MATLAB macros that can be used. There are many other custom tools built for software dependency analysis or similar specialties in part because talented software engineers are good at developing bespoke tools.

A poor man's DSM tool is an Excel table, without any analytical partitioning or clustering macros, that would serve to represent the matrix. Some of Excel's traceability tools and circular reference warnings might provide minimal insight into the matrix, but if you intend serious use, you should graduate to one of these other tools.

The Uses and Benefits of Infel Design

The Infel methodology can be used in several ways to add value. For one thing, the matrix view is a far more dense representation of the interconnections than a typical node diagram. When the number of nodes grows too large in these diagrams they look like a confusing hairball of lines and arrows. The matrix view is far more efficient, and it brings the simplification of Infels with its focus on information dependencies. This means that we can typically replace several "action" steps in a flow diagram with a simple Infel. For example, in a process diagram, you may have a sequence like write test scripts, secure lab time, run tests, evaluate tests, and write test results, whereas with an Infel this is all replaced with "test results." We can focus on the nouns and ignore the verbs. The following observations highlight some of the insights that you can gain from a kaizen review of the completed information matrix.

Situational Visibility

The Infel dependency matrix is an excellent tool for providing detailed information at a glance. Information flows are easy to follow across multiple groups. Smoothly sequenced tasks are clustered just below the 45-degree line; any Infel above the 45-degree line represents coupled tasks or an information circuit. Infels significantly above the 45-degree line represent a dangerously large circuit with significant rework potential. Infels significantly below the 45-degree line represent parallel or duplicate paths of information. In some cases, these merely represent additional, nice-to-have supporting evidence. In other cases, they might represent the bypassing of an interim group or the duplication of effort since the information has multiple possible paths with different developers' input and they might converge with different results downstream, which would imply significant rework and conflict resolution.

Task Resequencing

Software tools can analyze the Infel dependency matrix using Boolean algorithms to resequence the Infels (and the tasks that produce them). This is one of the key benefits of the Infel approach. Infels with no dependencies are given priority and displayed at the top of the matrix, and Infel circuits are cut and reformed based on precedent values assigned by the analyst. For example, if there are two coupled Infels, you can assign a higher priority to one of them (it makes the first assumption) based on the greater experience level of the associated resources or any other relevant parameter such as data quality. The resulting matrix either falls completely below the 45-degree line or else is tightly clustered with the coupled Infels, that is, adjacent to each other forming the smallest information circuits possible.

Legacy workflow represented in an Infel matrix often shows several circular or "circuit" information flows (any entry above the 45-degree line indicates that a subsequent process is really an input). Each of these will require a knowledge worker to make an assumption regarding the downstream task, which can be a source of internal rework if that assumption is incorrect. Often, several other tasks will build upon that first, not-yet-corrected, assumption. These Infel circuits are inherently expensive and managing them requires extra communication across sub-teams. The larger the circuit (height above the 45-degree line), the more costly in terms of rework it is likely to be. Note that a resequenced matrix has all dependencies below the line except for some unavoidable tight clusters.

Cost Reduction through Task Elimination or Exporting

The Infels represent deliverables and the Infel dependency matrix clearly identifies the input sources and downstream customers for each Infel. This translates into a practical value scale for each component produced for the group. The cost of each Infel can be estimated using interviews or observation. It is straightforward to determine the value of each Infel by noting its downstream use, or lack thereof, and interviewing the customer organizations to determine the value they place on the information. Infels that are received from an upstream group and passed on with little value added can be allowed to bypass one or more steps. They can be released so upstream providers and downstream consumers can connect directly, and whatever effort was previously expended to gather and modify these Infels can be spared.

Identification of Independent Tasks

An optimized Infel matrix will elevate the independent tasks (those with no subsequent internal dependencies) to the top of the matrix. These tasks are extremely useful to the project manager for resource leveling since they cannot have ripple effects resulting from the creation of undiscovered rework. They can also serve an inspection function, since they can be done immediately upon receipt of the project, and whatever is learned about the project's completeness or viability can be used in planning or halting subsequent tasks.

Reduction of Rework

Task resequencing is key to the implicit reduction of rework. Coupled tasks are adjacent to one another; the coupled tasks that remain can be sequenced so that those in which you have the greatest confidence can be done first. If you are going to have assumptions and iterations, it helps to start with your best guess. Independent tasks also allow for risk-free inspection of the upstream work. If something is missing or deficient in the new product after it is handed over is discovering this during the performance of independent steps incurs no undiscovered rework penalty.

Simulation Friendly

Out-of-sequence activities and suspect information have long been key components in developing dynamic simulations of rework cycles. The Infel methodology provides a solid rationale in support of scenarios and parameter sets fed into a design–build simulation model. The two products work extremely well together, and allow you to quickly develop alternate task/Infel sequences and simulate their hourly resource costs very quickly.

Earned Value Analysis

One of the first applications of Infel was for the benefit of a conceptual design group. Since Infels represent work product, it was possible to assign earned value credits for each Infel in the process and determine a pragmatic percent complete score for projects. For anyone who has ever worked on the fuzzy end of new product development, this is an invaluable tool. Early concept work is so apt to change that most designers are loath to distribute their work for peer review or even commit it to formal writing. The small scale and discrete nature of Infels, however, were less inhibiting, as they rarely call for major conclusions. We were able to encourage designers to publish their early Infels and even developed an automated peer review process. The benefits of teaming and increased visibility during the early design stages were very significant.

Organizational Design

We have also produced dramatic results by applying the Infel methodology to organizational design. Process views are too macro to provide much insight into organizational issues, but a detailed tracing of information flow across an existing hierarchical organization can yield surprising results (see Figure 7.13). In the case illustrated, we readily determined that a typical project was subject to 14 information and process handoffs within just one group in the product-development chain. Further, many of these information flows were in parallel but subject to the varying priorities and availabilities of the different individuals and teams handling them. A separate time and motion study indicated that as much as 80 percent of the project cycle time was wasted in transit or in waiting for information from others.

The Infel resequencing strongly suggested that several coupled Infels (test requirements, test scripts, test results, etc.) be clustered within one group. Previously an engineering group was doing requirements in the company headquarters and the testing group was translating them into test scripts at its own laboratory facility. (This is only one example of Infel-based reengineering.)

Several Infels were eliminated or exported, and the overall process was dramatically simplified as illustrated in Figure 7.13. A process with 14 handoffs, many of them across organizational boundaries, which afforded practically no

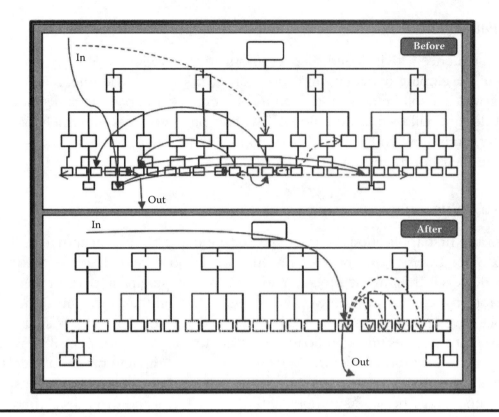

Figure 7.13 Before and after information flows.

situational visibility, was dramatically streamlined. The reduction in handoffs eliminated much of the justification for and reliance on multitasking since waiting times for external input vastly decreased. Rearranging the existing pieces like this can create significant reductions in time spent by eliminating the rework and inefficiencies inherent in the "before" process.

KEY BENEFITS AND PROCESS INSIGHTS OF THE INFORMATION MATRIX

Simplifies the analysis by reducing many process actions to a smaller number of information elements (verbs to nouns).

Provides the direct Lean benefits of waste identification and task resequencing.

Enables situational visibility, a large canvas view of what goes where.

Enables identification of the three tiers of activities—independent, sequential, and coupled—which provides a starting point in kaizen brainstorming for improvement ideas.

Infels are less formal than documents, are less likely to be governed by procedure, and can be easier to change.

Using the Information Flow Matrix to Identify Lean Wastes

The information matrix can provide hints for Lean teams seeking to improve information flow in modern organizations. It can also serve as a vehicle to map traditional Lean concepts of waste to the modern office process.

Overproduction

Two major categories of information overproduction are identifiable using the information matrix. The first is orphaned information. Some information is created or modified in a step, but is never actually used. Such information can be spotted by locating any empty columns on the matrix and can be eliminated, and the time spent creating them put to valuable use. Large documents such as reports are relatively easy to find; this is low-hanging fruit that can be captured via interviews. Going to the Infel level of detail will uncover many more pieces of documents and reports that are not of downstream interest. In fact, if the analysis is done at the report level, you may find that most reports survive this orphan check because there is usually something of value in them for which they are rated as valuable in a survey-type process. Often, only a small part of the overall report is used, and much of it should be seen as waste.

When we spoke of the paper-based Administration Lean, we suggested stopping the production of reports to see who noticed. This is far less effective for computer-using knowledge workers who can find a proxy value for the information they need through unofficial channels. It also creates false negatives. Sometimes people will notice a missing report or document and request it even though they really only need one of its 10 Infels.

The second example of overproduction is not necessarily creating more information than we need but supplying it or packaging it twice or more times. This is identified as parallel flow in our DSM map. The recipient gets similar information from more than one path; the information probably arrives at different times and is slightly different. Which information should the recipient use? If work begins based on the first Infel to arrive, do you revise it based on the perceived reliability of the source or begin a multiparty review to determine which is best?

Waiting

It is safe to say that waiting occurs where multiple pathways converge since, by definition, the Infel being created is using all of them as inputs. The more converging paths there are in the Infel flow, the greater the chance that most of them must wait for the arrival of the last key Infel. Some convergence, such as the assembly of several information streams into a final document, is desirable, but midstream processing steps that receive multiple Infels will fall victim to the multitasking scapegoat. Many balls are up in the air while we wait for the last one. As we have discussed, multitasking tends to breed more multitasking and the late arrival of one Infel on a specific project can delay many unrelated projects because they congregate at the same desk. These complex nodes in your information flow network should be carefully examined by your kaizen team.

In addition, many pass-through Infels create both waiting and a form of excess transportation waste. We will describe them later in the transportation section.

Defects

Defects can occur naturally in the creation of any one Infel; they can also leak into the product due to the process structure and information flow, and it is this that we are most focused on. Reusing information is very attractive and easy to do, but it leads to errors. Cut-and-paste errors are extremely common as is incorrectly, or incompletely, modifying a similar document selected as a template. Many tools allow you to create a template version that has all the structure and formatting but not the information content, which makes it less likely to introduce this type of error if you use the formal template rather than previous files of the same type. The templates can be centrally managed and updated with desktop links so that users can get to them as easily as opening up the last version from their "recent documents" menu in their operating system.

Another critical source of defect waste is making the wrong assumption. As we've described, there often are mutually dependent Infels. If they are separated by several process steps, or organizational barriers, they can be powerful defect and rework generators. Identifying these information circuits, eliminating the unnecessary ones, and placing the remaining ones closer together is an excellent way to address information-defect waste.

The best solution is to make these mutually dependent steps contiguous, in an ideal world a sort of partner desk or set of adjacent cubicles, where the iterative loop is so tight as to be unnoticed elsewhere. If the circuit cannot be eliminated, extra management and process attention should be arranged to control it. The more experienced "assumer" of information should go first to minimize the iterations by initially generating a better seed value. If the circuit is still large or spans organizational or corporate barriers, then it should be treated as beta; create a tiny spiral within the process where the interim steps go only as deep in their Infel development effort as warranted by the first values/iteration of the process. Minimize the minispiral as much as possible and don't let it reenter the main process until the circuit dependencies have been resolved.

Transportation

Many Infels are simply repackaged in larger collections (called documents or files). A knowledge worker generates an analysis with three pieces of information: A, B, and C. The next person uses the B and C Infels to develop a new Infel D. The next person in the process doesn't care a hoot about B, C, or D, but has to wait until the new document is created and the A Infel is transported to him or her. Essentially this A Infel should have gone directly to its user or consumer instead of meandering via cut-and-paste through the steps using B and C to develop D.

Suppose that A is the design of the supporting columns and beams in a building. B and C might be their type and quantity, and that information is used to place the order with the steel supplier and generate the cost, D. The next designer is waiting for the procurement negotiations to finish so he or she can get the layout drawings in order to add the machine locations, E. That person doesn't care about the price, and the layout drawings should have come to him straightaway.

Motion

Motion is a tricky dimension for the knowledge worker. One of these wastes is the additional keystrokes and mouse clicks required to do a task or find information; for example, hard to find information that requires navigating through cumbersome knowledge management systems, asking for information via e-mail, using inconvenient or poorly organized reference libraries.

One of the keyboard/mouse click tools is dictation software. Modern versions of this software are very good, though still far from perfect. They are great for spraying large amounts of text, and particularly valuable for workers who are faster talkers than typists. Dictation creates an insidious type of error, the incorrect word that spell checkers cannot find. Therefore, the significant rework and editing must be balanced against the much faster initial dump. More accurate future versions and context word-use checkers rather than mere spell checkers will soon bring about an era where speaking will be a very important, probably parallel, way to interact with your computer. Whether all this talking will create offices as noisy as the mechanical typewriter-filled newsrooms of the 1940s, usher in a new era of private offices, or create wealth for white noise generator companies is too soon to tell.

The other kind of motion waste involves moving the whole body and not just the data appendages. You won't have a hard time convincing most businesspeople that meetings can be a waste of time. Usually one person speaks while others listen, which makes meetings good for broadcast but not necessarily so good for elaborating the information. Twitter and e-mail can do a great job of broadcast. Collaboration methods based on Web 2.0 software tools can do a great job of actually getting the work done. Now virtual meetings with participation and polling, visual chats with two or more participants, and desktop sharing, can capture all the tone and body language of face-to-face meetings without travel or interruptions. And they are even better at providing supporting documentation because the participants are at their workstations and no one has to promise to forward missing or requested documents once they get back to the office.

Despite these tools, meetings are very important and we have a strong tradition of meeting people face to face, especially when the chips are down and things have to get done. We could take a page from SCRUM software design and keep the meetings frequent but ultra short, employing standing-room-only rules to reinforce this.

Processing

Examples of excess processing include creating long reports, repeated handling of the same information (all that cut and paste pass-through and redundant approvals), inappropriate software, and the use of outdated forms and reference materials.

Inventory

There are two kinds of inventory waste: excess support information and work-in-process. The excess support information is all the little known databases; underutilized knowledge management systems; unread e-mails; and unnecessary meeting minutes, procedures, or instruction manuals. These are the day-to-day rat race of information. Other examples include the many back-and-forth e-mails shepherding PowerPoint presentations in development, and systems and databases that were built and exist to support the knowledge workers, many of whom don't know of them or use alternate means to gather necessary information.

Work-in-process represents the large amount of information that comes from multitasking and an accept-all approach to work management. This is in direct contrast to continuous flow and other Lean principles, and is a key waste contributing to poor throughput.

Infels and Therbligs

Earlier we mentioned Frank Gilbreth as one of the pioneers of time and motion study. Gilbreth invented the term *therblig* (his name backward except for the *th*) as the smallest component of motion. Complex motions could be described as a combination of therbligs: lift hand, rotate hand, and so forth. Gilbreth developed this idea years before Logo or any concept of the computer languages used to describe robotic motions. Among his applications was to streamline the number of motions used by soldiers in field stripping and cleaning their rifles, an activity that is repeated many thousands of times and could mean life or death.

We have created the term *Infel*, from Information Element, to represent the smallest component of an information deliverable. An Infel can be a diagram, text, a price quote, a calculation, an approval, and so forth. Documents usually comprise several Infels and work can be described as the motion of information as it collects and assembles its necessary Infels. The notion of Infels is key. Documents are just too big and their movement is the "official" process movement that masks the true information flow. You can cut and paste an Infel from an older similar document. You can copy an Infel from a Web site. You might get an Infel by being cc'd in an e-mail on an FYI basis or the number you're looking for via short message service (SMS) or IM chat. None of these is part of your official process flow.

Like Gilbreth, we realized that any attempt at optimization needed to be indexed on the least common denominator. Infel analysis allows us to break information flow into its constituent parts in an attempt to find the one best way to perform the process. We realize that therbligs are not part of the daily workplace vocabulary, but creating new frames of reference and terminology is a daunting task. We have great sympathy for all who attempt it.

In Factory Lean and Paper Office Lean, we were mostly concerned with process flow. Now we know that it is not enough to describe the operations in a modern computer-filled office. It is as if we had limited our study of the body to the circulatory system and only recently realized that there is a nervous system as well that we have to consider. The information matrix is a powerful visualization. It is both a heuristic guide and freestanding analysis engine. Properly employed it can be of great value in redesigning information flow. Now that we are armed with the key visualization and analytical method to make the previously invisible, visible, we are ready to put it to work in Knowledge Worker Lean.

Chapter 8

How to Implement Knowledge Worker Lean

Here we put it all together and explain how to deliver Knowledge Worker Lean in a practical way. We include not only the tools and theory, but also the "soft stuff" because it is so critical to success.

Overview

We begin with the premise that your organization is new to Knowledge Worker Lean (KWL). Because it is a first-time KWL lean effort, it is going to have many "project" characteristics. Our goal, once Lean is implemented, is to make projects obsolete, since they are to continuous improvement what fad diets are to a healthy lifestyle. But we have to start somewhere.

Lean Methodology: A Snapshot

We can illustrate the overall KWL process on the back of a napkin—and we have (see Figure 8.1). Our work concentrates on the "nouns" not the "verbs"; we focus on the actual pieces of information and where they are created, used, or consumed. Rather than focus on vague phrases like "perform test," we use the information inputs and outputs such as "test plan" and "test results." As we've stated, knowledge workers won't wait for the official process or the project to catch up to them; they will work out of sequence by downloading information from a vendor Web site, by e-mailing a colleague and asking for information early, or by using information stored on their computer from a previous piece of similar work.

Much of Lean is predicated on learning to see and understanding muda (waste). This is hard enough on a factory floor where you have to teach yourself that things like excess inventory are bad. In an office environment, where

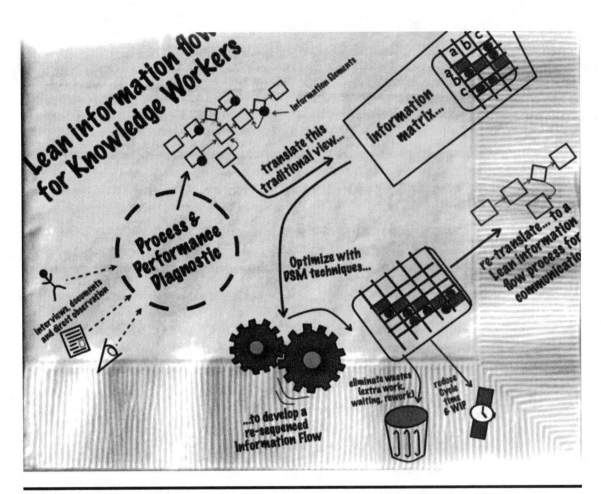

Figure 8.1 The Knowledge Worker Lean approach explained on the back of a napkin.

information flow is invisible, this is a difficult concept. You can observe two very neat and efficient workstations next to each other and not see the painful waste—one of them has information critical to the other on his or her hard drive, but neither knows it.

Information Matrix

To improve information flow, we have to make the invisible visible by:

1. Starting with a diagnostic to understand the nominal process and basic performance parameters. A special subset of Lean diagnostic tools is used for KWL.
2. Carefully noting where documents, or parts of documents, are used. These information elements are the common denominator of information flow we will track.
3. Starting and maintaining a risk and change management strategy from the very beginning of the journey.
4. Translating the process diagnostic into an information matrix. (As we outlined in Chapter 7, this very dense representation of the overall process will provide situational visibility.)

5. Basing your kaizen efforts on this dense representation of information flow. (We suggest using DSM [design structure matrix] to highlight wastes and resequence the information flow.)
6. Highlighting and eliminating wastes such as orphaned information or rework.
7. Discussing and setting priorities with the team for more complex improvements to be implemented.
8. Reexporting the matrix view to flow diagrams or before and after Gantt views as needed.

We will examine each of these steps in more detail in the subsequent sections.

Process Improvement Maturity Model

Applying Lean in an information age environment poses a problem—actually, it magnifies an existing problem. Most process improvement methods present themselves as an advance over existing management practices, or at the very least a more recent development; but modern technology and innovation advances so quickly that we find ourselves interpreting these tools in the context of existing Lean methods.

Figure 8.2 illustrates that the gulf we must span is not merely from management science (M) to process improvement (P), but rather from M to P to technology (T). The greater the mismatch between levels of maturity, the greater the adoption challenge. (Just try to get most accounts payable groups to accept a delivery ticket via Twitter as opposed to a signed original or fax, and you'll see what we mean.) To implement KWL successfully, you have to be careful to select new tools that reinforce and enable it without triggering a "change management rejection reflex."

States of Maturity: Where We Are Now

Technology is continually emerging and rapidly changing. Entire new technologies can be widely adopted in two years or less. The maturity level for the technology that knowledge workers are exposed to is state of the art.

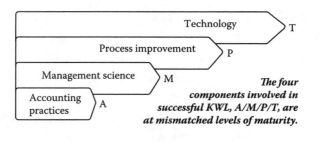

Figure 8.2   The Knowledge Worker Lean maturity model.

Process improvement techniques tend to advance in a more measured way. The book introducing Lean to the West, *The Machine That Changed the World,* was published in 1992 and The Agile Manifesto was written in 2001.* Both are ancient in Web time. The maturity level of process improvement technologies is from circa the Vietnam War era through the recent past.

Management techniques, so critical for Lean adoption, and change management move even more slowly. Whereas psychology has moved on to cognitive science and neuropsychology, management techniques remain based on carrot-and-stick behaviorism that would have been familiar to Pavlov or Skinner in the mid-20th century. The maturity level of most management techniques is circa WWII.

Cost accounting is still based on the GAAP (generally accepted accounting principles) established early in the 20th century. Although there have been notable attempts to bring accounting in line with process improvement—activity based, lean accounting, and throughput accounting—they are still quite rare. Typically, the maturity level for cost accounting in most companies is circa WWI.

Practical Applications of the Lean Toolset

Lean is a big, practical tent that incorporates a broad range of tools and analytical techniques. The principles of Lean are consistent, but we have found that some tools and methodologies lend themselves more to one setting than another. As Table 8.1 demonstrates, not all Lean tools and techniques are equally relevant or effective across all three potential workplaces: factory, paper office, and information age office.

In Table 8.1, the applicability of these tools and the feasibility that your Lean team can successfully apply them in each of these environments are represented relative to each other. That is not to say that a "low score" for any one tool might not yield significant results for a particular process. They are guidelines and a useful notational technique to explain our rationale for the methodologies we choose for implementing KWL.

Workplace communications. Posters and newsletters (including hand-drawn messages and charts) work fine in physical workplaces where everyone can see them. They are easy to create, and they reinforce the right messages. The information age workplace is more virtual, is spread across multiple locations, and has teleworkers. Furthermore, the knowledge worker class simply feels more comfortable working in the Web; it is natural for them and they have the skills. Wikis and blogs to start, custom sites and apps as Lean progresses.

Kaizen meetings, brainstorming, and problem solving. These are traditional face-to-face meetings in Factory and Paper Lean. Some of this dialogue and problem solving can move to online collaboration tools for knowledge workers.

---

* The Agile Manifesto is a statement of the principles that underpin agile software development drafted by a group of developers.

Table 8.1   Practical Applicability of Lean Tools

Tool or Technique	Factory Lean	Paper Office	Info Age Office
Posters	●	◕	◔
Newsletters	◕	◑	◔
Wikis and blogs	○	◔	●
F2F kaizen meetings	●	◕	◑
Online kaizen	○	◔	●
VSM	●	◕	◔
Takt time	●	◔	◔
Pull/Kanban	●	◑	◔
APD	○	◔	●
Cumulative flow	●	●	●
Poka yoke	●	●	●
5S	●	◑	◔
SMED	●	○	○
DSM	◔	◔	●
Heijunka	●	◔	◕
Muda	●	◕	●
Mura	●	◑	●
Muri	●	◔	◕
OEE	●	○	○
Gemba	●	◑	◑
5 Whys	●	◑	◕
Jidoka	●	◔	◑
Andon	●	◔	●

There is little need to spend group time annotating the whiteboard at the start of the kaizen session when this can be done in real time during the week, which would allow others to build on it prior to the kaizen session.

Value stream mapping (VSM) and takt time. These are great tools, especially for linear, sequential process flows, but can be difficult to use in recursive flows and feedback loops. In addition, it can be especially difficult to gather accurate task metrics due to the tremendous amount of multitasking in white-collar work. They can (and should) be used at a high level to roughly outline the diagnostic phase in Information Lean.

Kanban and pull-based systems. These are superior to push-based systems for knowledge worker project work, but it is often difficult to get the pull signals at task granularity rather than at the groups-of-tasks level (the equivalent to a pull-based stage–gate approach). Still, this is a big improvement for an environment with uneven flow.

Automatic process discovery (APD). It is impractical to capture knowledge worker task and performance times with a stopwatch and counter. We need an IT-enabled data logger that can monitor applications, documents, and activities on knowledge workers' computers from which we can extract useful data.

Cumulative flow diagrams. These are useful visualizations that are applicable across all types of Lean—anywhere process flows. Perhaps not as useful as VSM for physical flows, they provide useful high-level insight for Paper and Information Office Lean where detailed information may be hard to get.

Poka yoke. The principles of mistake proofing can be applied universally. In a paper-based environment, such as processing payments, you can ensure that vendors apply the appropriate tax treatments to reduce corrections. In an automated system, you can require duplicate entry of e-mail addresses to minimize your customers' error rate. Mistake proof whenever you can.

5S. Traditional 5S is a pure factory component and efforts to translate it to the office world can fail or even be counterproductive, and may drive home the message that Lean is superficial and nitpicky. Most offices do not have shift workers and few people need to instinctively know where you keep your stapler. What we call 5Si (information added to 5S), however, is valuable and includes such things such as file naming and storing conventions, shared electronic assets that are easy to find, visual management and progress systems, and so on. These tools translated to the virtual space are the key.

Single minute exchange of die (SMED). There are some applications for this in the office; for example, in terms of resource scheduling and the ability to apply human resources quickly across projects and clients, but largely this is a physical process tool. You will encounter resistance using this approach as anything other than a metaphor for a change in work process. White-collar workers and knowledge workers are not used to detailed time and motion suggestions.

Dependency (or design) structure matrices (DSM). Understanding complex dependencies and flows is vital in scenarios where you have them. Sequential processes such as physical and document assembly have enough to worry about with line balancing, continuous flow, and constraints without DSM. On the other hand, DSM is a key component in our approach to unraveling, simplifying, smoothing, and finally redesigning processes that have complex information flow.

Heijunka. This is a Japanese technique for achieving even output flow. This simple visual progress-monitoring system is very effective in the physical process world. Our ideas about collaborative project management tools, 5Si, and virtual visual management all derive from it. Progress and status should be very easy to determine at a glance at any time during a project's lifetime.

Muda. The unnecessary or nonvalue activity waste is a very powerful argument in Factory Lean and KWL. It is less so in Paper Lean because many such processes use definitions of value such as "paper complete" and "per procedure" rather than speed or throughput.

Mura. Japanese word meaning "unevenness or inconsistency." Unevenness in work and just-in-time considerations are somewhat less critical in Paper Lean because there is less consequence of inventory—unlikely to need additional space, travel time, or inventory carrying costs. Information Lean, however, can experience severe consequences from mismatch in information arrival time as knowledge workers find or develop proxies for the information they need. Work based on these proxies is often reworked.

Muri. Japanese word for "overburden." Standardized work and workflow can be a key element in "fuzzy" knowledge worker areas such as design and development, as well as wherever the subsequent tasks are dependent on the results of the current task.

Overall equipment effectiveness (OEE). This is a very popular Factory Lean metric that can be stated as OEE = Availability × Performance × Quality, and is meant to be expressed and calculated algebraically. We doubt that Paper Lean workers focusing on getting their documentation correct or knowledge workers being creative would react well to this type of measure.

Gemba. Japanese for "the actual place." Going to see for yourself is key to Lean. Most reports and metrics are an abstraction derived from what actually happens and there is no substitute for direct observation—even immersion. However, in Office Lean, it is simply much harder to see the wastes and opportunities. Often the best way is to detect them by inference: Why is such-and-such document delayed? Is it usually delayed? How many do you have waiting to be processed? Going to Gemba in the physical world provides direct information via observation; in the information world you must supplement it with questions, hypotheses, and fact finding

5 Whys. This root-cause investigation technique is very useful in interviewing, fact finding, and problem solving though it is as much art as science and very difficult to do consistently. Moreover, it is least effective in paper-based Lean where many of the activities are done for legacy reasons, so by the time you get to the third or fourth why everyone is embarrassed to admit that no one knows why they are doing certain things. External consultants can be tripped up here too, as they are assumed to be experts and so many questions can make people doubt their industry experience. Always tell interviewees that asking why is part of a specific exercise.

Jidoka. Japanese term referring to the ability to stop production lines in the event of problems. Although a cornerstone of physical production systems, the ability for workers to halt an assembly line to reduce errors is not easily translatable to paper work or even information work. The suspect work in these two situations is simply stopped and set aside with little direct impact on other work. In the case of a technical project, however, the series of tasks can have effects up and down the line. The improved analytics and risk management capabilities of online collaborative tools will probably lead to increased KWL jidoka and will enable knowledge workers to identify and address problems and defects earlier. This should reduce the "Green ... Green ... Red" project status surprise so common today.

Andon. Japanese for "lamp" or "signal." A physical visual notification system is very common in factories but, outside of call centers, is practically unheard of in the office environment. As with Jidoka, new tools will be able to automatically update risk, predict project completion or software release dates, and so forth, and serve a strategic andon function.

Starting Off on Your Lean Journey: Your Charter, Your Customer, and Your Plan

Lean improvements are bottom-up driven from the direct contributors; but Lean, as a program and before it becomes part of the culture, must have active and visible executive sponsorship. We won't belabor a point that is covered by every other book on Lean, but we're careful to include it in the "must have" column. Executive support and visible sponsorship (such as participation on the blog on your Lean Web page) is crucial in supporting culture change as well as paving the way for your Lean team to ask tough questions or gather data and so forth— air cover for all the mechanics of the project.

In addition, the sponsor must also have enough grounding on what Lean is to effectively support efforts rather than undermine them. For example, your success in eliminating waste and increasing process speed and quality will be dashed if the sponsor looks up from your presentation and asks how many jobs can now be eliminated. The sponsor needs to clearly understand the difference between Lean performance metrics and traditional cost metrics and believe that the connection exists, even if we have never asked the question in quite this way before.

The successful KWL implementation is equal parts team, process, and tools (see Figure 8.3). We will describe each of these in the next sections. You can

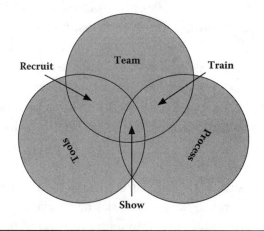

Figure 8.3   The three dimensions of implementing Knowledge Worker Lean.

train the team in your Lean process, but you must recruit existing tools skills into the team; there just isn't time in this critical early stage of Lean. Finally, you must "show" the value of the overall effort.

Lean Team Formation

You need a strong team to make these early KWL efforts successful. There can be no explicit rules, but we find teams of five to seven to be just about the right combination of resources and span of control and communication.

> **TEAM FORMATION GUIDELINES**
>
> *The right mix of skills*: Lean awareness, analytical problem solving, open-mindedness and creative skills, process content knowledge, and up-to-date computer and Web skills (this is KWL after all). It's fine if the team members have skill gaps so long as someone on the team has the skill. Focus on team members' strengths, not their weaknesses.
>
> *The right attitude and perspective*: Open-mindedness and ability to handle change and convince others, creativity, and persistence. Members should be the kind of resources that naturally consider "systems-based" explanations rather than personality-based explanations. The use of "they" and "them" can be poison to an effective root-cause analysis.
>
> *Awareness*: You can't have the team run off and start bumping into all the furniture. A seasoned sergeant can help guide the team through the organizational and cultural obstacles.

Take a clue from The Agile Manifesto, which recommends team members who are lazy, bored, and curious. Lazy because they are always looking to maximize the amount of work not done, which is an excellent definition of waste. Bored because that's the type of resource who welcomes and is stimulated by change rather than overwhelmed by it. Curious because that's what keeps the team members asking why and seeking to increase the breadth and depth of solutions.

What this boils down to is one team leader, one tool guy/gal, at least one process expert, at least one people person (the resource you will send for the tough interviews and to smooth any feathers that may have gotten ruffled), and at least one sergeant (the person who understands the organization well and how it really works; just like their counterparts in the military, they are the crucial connection between the theory and the troops. The sergeant has the respect of the process workers). Of course, some individuals may wear more than one of these hats.

Team Process

In the beginning, the overall process has a simple goal: to gain a detailed understanding of the process in question—its structure, performance, metrics, delivered quality, and so forth. This is done via direct observation and interview, and heavy use of the 5 Whys-type root-cause questions. Data gathering (more on this later) is important, both reviewing existing performance data and generating more. You must also request and review all the relevant descriptive documents: flowcharts, procedures, and training guides, as well as a list of sample in-process documents (secure one or two examples of each).

We define *process understanding* along six separate dimensions (see Figure 8.4):

1. How—This is the fundamental level of understanding. Typically, it is represented by a flowchart or a list of steps or procedures. If this does not exist, the team must create one; even a simple one will be valuable to all aspects of the project.
2. How much—A quantifiable sense of performance. What metrics are used? What is the value and trend of these metrics? This is useful for building a case for action as well as to understand the (perhaps unarticulated) sense of what the organization values.
3. Where—Where in the organization and the physical plant does the process take place? In particular, how many organizational lines are crossed?
4. Who—The resources responsible for the process. Their background and skill level is important because they are key components in developing solutions that will be accepted.
5. When—Process durations, cycle times, and variance. How is planning done? How are schedule changes managed?
6. Why—What causes delays? Defects? Initially these are hypotheses garnered during interviews. Later they are tested and new ones are developed.

Note that we cannot predict which tools or analytical techniques from Table 8.1 will be most relevant or applicable to any specific process analysis. The data and the process discovery steps will suggest them. You have to emphasize to your team that there is no detailed plan from start to finish. What you discover during the understanding process dictates the analysis, ideas, and experiments that follow.

A lot is contained within the little "understanding" icon in Figure 8.5, of course. Much of the rest of this chapter is dedicated to expanding it. Figure 8.5 provides a high-level view of this early diagnostic stage.

The roles and responsibilities of the team are also part of the process. A responsibility–accountability–consulted–informed (RACI) matrix provides a good shorthand description of the team's roles (see Table 8.2). The dark horizontal line separates the Lean team from the other interested parties: management,

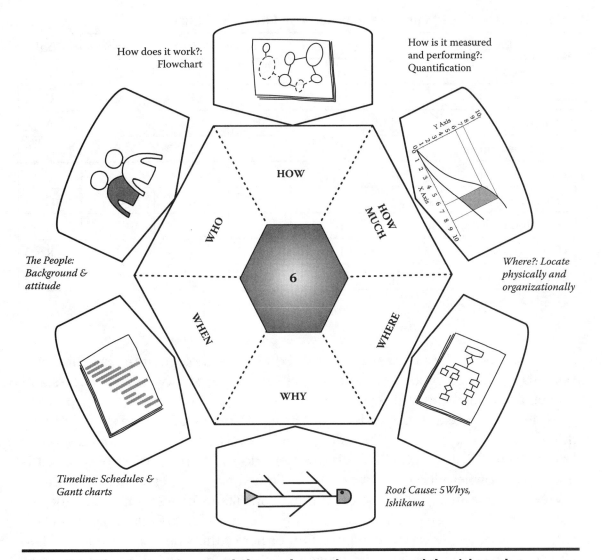

How does it work?: Flowchart

How is it measured and performing?: Quantification

The People: Background & attitude

Where?: Locate physically and organizationally

Timeline: Schedules & Gantt charts

Root Cause: 5 Whys, Ishikawa

Figure 8.4 The six questions needed to understand a process and the right tools to answer them.

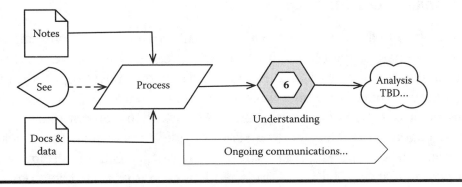

Figure 8.5 The process to understand the process.

Table 8.2 The RACI Matrix Clarifies Roles and Responsibilities

RACI Role	Management	Risk	Process	People	Tool
Team leader	A	A	R	A	R
Process expert	I	I	R	C	C
Tool guy	I	I	C	I	A
People person	I	C	C	R	I
Process owner	C	C	A	C	C
Process worker	I	I	C	I	C
Extended process owners	I	I	C	I	C
IT	I	I	I	I	R
Lean sponsor	R	R	C	C	I

Note: A, accountable; C, consulted; I, informed; R, responsible.

those involved in the process, and extended key stakeholders in intersecting or potentially affected processes. Note the process owner still owns the process and acceptance of the team's ideas is not automatic.

Note that the Lean team leader is ultimately accountable to management for the success of this effort as well as for people issues, such as disgruntled stakeholders, which will also be laid at the leader's door. We emphasize, however, it is the process owner who owns the process. Sometimes this person and the Lean leader are the same. In the case of external consultants or internal Lean experts, they are not. It is therefore incumbent on the Lean leader to collaborate closely with the process owner and convince him or her of the value of these ideas. Two effective ways to achieve that are active participation and phasing; most process owners can accept two or three improvement ideas, but not twenty. You must develop the roadmap for these ideas collaboratively and allow the success of the early ones to accelerate (or attenuate) the adoption rate for the rest. Note also that the Lean leader is accountable for risk management, which is our next topic.

Risk Management Techniques

Risks are often treated as project risks (after all, what could go wrong?) and typically become part of the planning phase as represented in Figure 8.6. Risks are identified, conditions that trigger them are listed, and mitigating action plans are developed. There is nothing wrong with this as far as it goes. However, if improvement is to be continuous, then surely risk management must be as well. If risk management is relegated to a series of questions or tests to be ticked off prior to launch, you are ignoring both the dynamic aspects of certain risks and presupposing that those risks are independent of any project developments, discoveries, or mistakes.

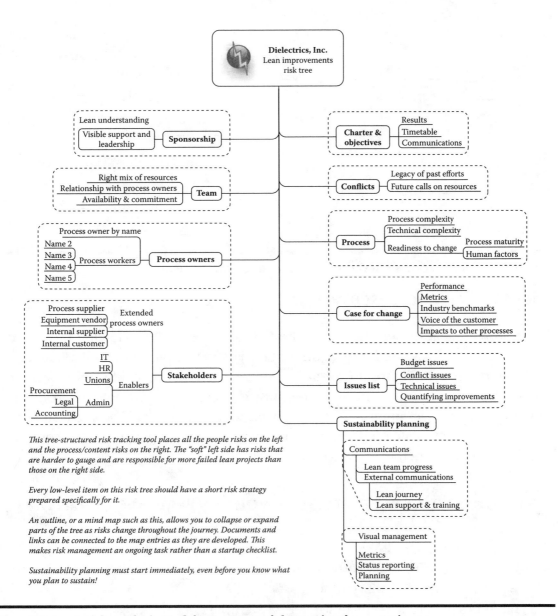

Figure 8.6   A risk analysis tool for a successful Lean implementation.

Figure 8.6 is an example or template that the Lean team leader may use from launch until whenever, since we incorporate sustainability into the risk tree and begin to think about it from the very start. The tree suggests growth and continued branching, and gives us the ability to hang things such as documents or links or comments on the branches. You can certainly use a word processor or an Excel spreadsheet to outline a similar structure if you are more comfortable with one of them because you should refer to this document a lot.

Lean fails because it is abandoned, not because there are no such things as waste or its analytical tools are invalid. Therefore, sustaining Lean within the organization and spreading Lean to other organizations is the path to success. The next step is the most important step on the journey. Your job as Lean leader is not just to eliminate waste and improve performance, but also to demonstrate and quantify these improvements, to convince others, and to enable the spread of Lean.

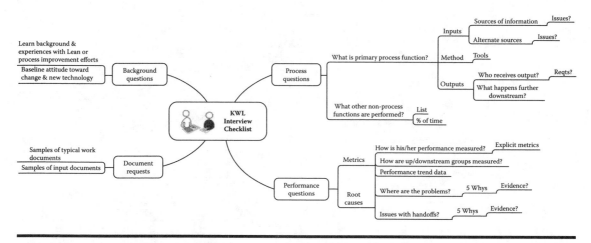

Figure 8.7   The interview checklist for Knowledge Worker Lean.

Fact Finding and Discovery

Fact-finding and discovery begins in the logical place by interviewing the process workers and the extended (upstream and downstream) process workers. Refer to the mind map in Figure 8.7 for an organized interview checklist. You want to learn about the process, especially the information inputs and outputs. You want to gather relevant documents. You also need to gauge the interviewees' attitudes about the risk and stakeholder maps. Finally, you want to gauge the process performance and the metrics used to establish that performance.

> **KEY QUESTIONS TO INCLUDE IN YOUR INTERVIEW REPERTOIRE**
> Can you tell me how long things take at a task level (or has multitasking obscured this)?
> What are your primary (official) inputs?
> What are your secondary (unofficial) inputs?
> What do you do if you cannot get these inputs?
> Describe the quality and timeliness of the people who feed your process.
> What tools or methods might help?
> What are some of the things you would change? Why? Why? Why? …

While you are conducting interviews, take the time to directly observe the process and process environment. Do people appear to be overly busy? Is there a lot of individual work or group work? How is status reporting done? Is there a lot of finger pointing and exaggeration? Can people tell you the status of projects within a few minutes, without guessing? Do people take pride in "the extraordinary" rather than the "ordinary"? In other words, do you hear stories about the crunch last month to make a scheduled date or are things calmer? Is this an organization of firefighters (sirens, smoke, excitement) or plumbers (no excitement and no water on the floor either)? The interviews and answers to these questions will give you a good start. Some other key elements in your discovery phase should include:

- Hypothesis list—Start your list of potential problems and their root causes early and include all the ideas that your interviewees provide. Treat their war stories as symptoms, not causes, at least until some analysis is complete.
- Document list—Create a document list or document hierarchy and be sure to get one or two examples of each item on the list. You'll need this to understand the deliverables, to gauge times needed to complete the documents, and to be able to parse them into Infels.
- Performance data—If previous reports or performance data exists, great. Otherwise, you may need to create it. You can sample documents to gain in-and-out timestamp data. You may not be able to understand all the task times but you will know when projects came in to the group and when they exited. Sample data; don't try to be exhaustive. You are looking for hints to discuss with a knowledgeable team, not ironclad proof.
- Voice of the customer interviews—What is the process's perception of its internal customers? Take the opportunity to range further downstream in the process, not just the immediate handoff point, to understand the internal customers' perception of quality and timeliness.

Figure 8.8 is an Ishikawa diagram of an interview with an engineer who was trying to explain why his group was habitually late in their phase of the development process. Table 8.3 is a sample transcript of the same interview showing how the 5 Whys technique can elicit information to go from a symptom to the root cause. Notice how the discussion begins with personal blame and works its way to a systems-level explanation. This is the real benefit to 5 Whys and other root-cause techniques because we can fix systems far easier than we can fix personalities.

A problem with applying VSM to Knowledge Worker Lean is that an information age project can exist in more than one place at a time. As you conduct

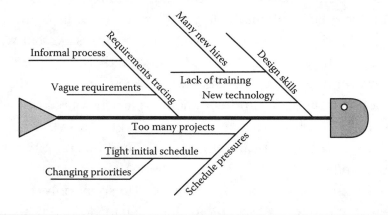

Figure 8.8 The Ishikawa diagram is a tool for root-cause analysis.

Table 8.3 The 5 Whys Method of Causal Investigation

5 Whys	Symptom/Driver: "We Take Longer Than Planned."
1	Because many of the designs we receive from "them" are incomplete, we have to fill their gaps and fix their work.
2	They just don't have the skills or discipline to get the job done in sufficient detail in the time allotted.
3	There is a lack of training in both our procedures and typical design specs. They reinvent the wheel a lot.
4	Mostly it's all the new hires. They just don't know what we're looking for.
5	We've been growing too fast and hiring like crazy, and the best designers are working on critical projects rather than training the new hires.

interviews and ask knowledge workers what they are working on, several will mention the same project. This would be fine if they were collaborating, but what if they have different functions that are supposed to happen at different times in the development of the work. In the same way that multitasking can mask how much time and progress an individual spends on an activity, this multilocational phenomenon makes VSM difficult. Rather than the linear sequential progression of the assembly line, you have a grid of interconnected activities where the nodes blink on and off as the multitasking workers shift attention to and from the project in question.

How to Retrieve Low-Level Process Performance Data

After your first round of interviews, you will have only a vague idea as to quantification. You will have received a lot of valuable subjective information but probably not enough numerical information to understand something like percent value time for a project in a certain phase.

One of the standard techniques to gather previously uncollected data in any detail is to ask your interviewees to help create a sample. The "day in the life" log, such of the one illustrated in Table 8.4 is an example. It has the very real advantages of simplicity and helping drive home the message that waste exists, and can help you gather missing data and understand where time and effort may be wasted; however, their accuracy and completeness are often suspect. Getting the team to jot down problems and comments is a rich source of ideas for round-table discussion. Its disadvantages are accuracy and the Hawthorne effect. In the sample log (Table 8.4), the software engineer claimed he spent two hours coding, yet he was frequently interrupted and, in addition, had a parenthetical support task to produce some delivery date information. He spent only 40 minutes (back from lunch early!) creating his PowerPoint status chart despite time spent looking for the template and recreating it from scratch.

Table 8.4 "Day in the Life" Data Collection Template

Task	Start	Stop	Value	Deliverable	Problem/Flow Issues	Comments
Check e-mail	0830	0920	No	None	None	Typically this takes longer
Review project notes	920	1000	Yes	None	Missing data, had to stop to make calls to backfill	This always happens
Code	1000	1200	Yes	New object	Phone kept ringing	Had to stop to send new delivery dates to Phil
Lunch	1200	1250	No	None		
Update status	1250	1330	Yes	PPT chart	Last version was PDF'd, had to recreate template	We should have the templates available online
And so on ...						

One of the hidden advantages of KWL data gathering is that most of the work is done on computers, which are very good at status monitoring and data gathering. Using automatic process discovery (APD) software (such as Slife, Fruitful Time, or Rescue Time), we can quickly gather accurate task duration data. These tools can query the user's keyboard, mouse, and screen activity every few seconds and collate this data against specified categories and activities. The accuracy and completeness of the data (speaking as consultants who have spent most of their careers trying to gather this kind of data using interviews) is astounding.

We created an APD graph based on a software developer's work in a product development organization (see Figure 8.9). This is an environment where young engineers work notoriously long hours fueled by pizza delivery and Red Bull. If you were to survey these software engineers, you would be told they work 10- to 12-hour days and are highly productive. However, if you look at the activity breakdown data, you see that the single biggest discrete task was status reporting (shown as the black section of each column on the histogram), which was defined as time spent working in PowerPoint and MS Project. Despite several work marathons that resulted in 12- and 14-hour days, many days show only 4 to 6 hours actually at the computer. The rest of the time was spent in meetings. Despite the massive (unpaid) overtime and hard work, the percent value time measured against a normal workweek was only about 35 percent as opposed to the implicit 150 percent from the timecard. A 4:1 nonproductive ratio goes a long way toward explaining process shortfalls.

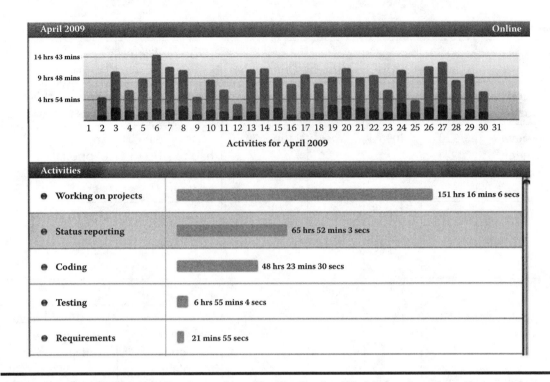

Figure 8.9   Automated tools can replace the day-in-the-life logbook and easily provide summary views.

To generate specific task durations, you can collect this time-spent data at the explicit document level. Despite all the pernicious effects and confusion of multitasking, you can still analyze data on total time spent on a specific task accurately, for example, the sum of times spent working on Project No9.xls + Project No9.doc + Project No9.vsd + …. You can also prorate some of the generic time spent on e-mail, and perhaps meetings, against the active projects. You will get far more accurate and useful data from this than from any estimate or manual time log.

In addition to individual and task data gathering, there is another aspect that is of particular interest: the nodes or points of handoff between one group and another. In some cases, these are no different from process flow between two individuals in the same group, but often they are much more formal and the process can be a great source of hidden waste.

There is an additional (and often overlooked) key discovery technique besides interviewing and gathering documents and performance metrics. We term this *handoff discovery* (see the checklist in Figure 8.10), and it should be done wherever the process flow and certain other critical information flows cross an organizational boundary. In development work such as waterfall design process, this includes all the gate review meetings where the downstream group formally takes possession of the project.

In nondevelopment work, these handoffs are still easy to spot, although it is not accompanied by as much fanfare as at other times, and it is less likely that

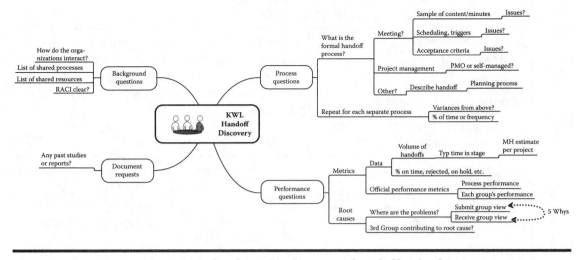

Figure 8.10   Discovery analysis for the critical process handoff point between groups.

useful data or meeting notes will be available for a historical review of performance. Splitting the process work has the advantage of leveraging expertise in a functional area, and this is the most common rationale for doing so. However, performance is also affected by things that have nothing to do with the process itself: a budget or workforce constraint in a small specialty organization, for example, can have a ripple effect throughout the entire organization that needs its particular input far beyond what might be expected. This type of KWL bottleneck is common when you have a small specialty group with nontransferrable skills; the legal department, the regulatory compliance review group, and the business case specialists are good examples.

Figure 8.10 outlines our suggested approach to discovering what happens at the nodes in the process. If this is a pure one-way handoff, a "border crossing," the most likely sources of waste come from a mismatch: different expectations of requirements, different expectations of scheduled delivery date, and different understandings of priority. Probe to learn how the downstream group monitors and expects delivery. Analyze how they balance workload to ensure that the upstream group doesn't rush to finish a project that has very low priority for the downstream group or let expected critical work sit idle.

Sometimes the process is a peninsula rather than a border crossing; it moves to a specialty group for value-added work and then comes back to the processing group. This double-crossing can be extraordinarily difficult to line balance. Investigate the levels of visibility the process group has into the peninsula. Are they negotiated? Are they flexible? If this is an outsourced task, it can be affected by perceived contractual risk, and comes with play-it-safe time estimates that add further waste.

The most common design solution is to minimize handoffs by consolidating tasks (insourcing) or rearranging them. In the early process discovery and analysis phase, many basic clues may be uncovered that can suggest investigative

Table 8.5   Pre-Kaizen Clues: Ideas to Investigate

1	Large number of resources touched by process.	These are symptoms of too much complexity in the process. Priorities can be mismatched. A long pipeline also enables high WIP by having many projects in development across all stages.
2	Handoffs and crossing barriers generate wait time and delays.	
3	Large number of handoffs in the main flow of the process.	
4	Long process duration.	Several boundaries crossed (organizational, physical, etc.). Symptomatic of poor performance and noncontinuous flow. Often associated with too much dependency and the waste of delay.
5	High variability in process time.	
6	Low value–time ratio.	
7	Hidden defect rate.	Hidden defects refer to midprocess rework that is manifested as delays or repeated steps. Processes done across siloed organizations lack visibility and tend to explain problems as failings in the upstream group's skill or schedule.
8	Nonsystems view of defects or root cause.	
9	Low situational visibility.	
10	Complex work breakdown structure; multistreams.	Processes combining multiple development streams can benefit from line balancing and information systems to aid coordination; apply Theory of Constraints (TOC). Multiple ownership problems can benefit from a responsibility matrix; apply RACI.
11	Complex WBS; multiowners.	
12	Low or casual opinion of official tool sets.	Lack of coordination and collaboration. Simple communications done via tangled e-mail strings. Waste of information inventory. Knowledge workers find their own solutions to information flow.
13	Point-to-point communications.	
14	Parallel project management.	Can lead to lack of scheduling credibility, adversarial estimating, and many starts and stops due to reprioritization, which extends times and increases WIP.
15	Manual status reporting.	Waste of nonvalue time to compensate for poor systems. Lead to surprises and redirection that decrease continuous flow.

areas during kaizen. The purpose of this discovery and fact-finding phase is not to prove anything but rather to inform the kaizen sessions that will generate and promote Lean improvement ideas. Many of the findings during this phase are just symptoms and further discussion, discovery, or analysis is needed. As an aid, see Table 8.5, which maps common information flow symptoms to suggested root causes and areas for further investigation.

Early Change Management

To say that the people side of Lean is critical is like saying that the blades are an important part of the lawnmower: without them there is a lot of noise and activity but no results. Since the soft side is the greatest source of risk, it should also be your partner in the strategic design of your Lean efforts.

- If the organization is on the fence, then design your program to demonstrate quick early wins.
- If the extended process groups are skeptical or opposed, then prioritize your ideas and implementation plans based on visibility and direct benefit to those groups.
- If the organization tends to use a limited IT toolset, then emphasize more face-to-face discussions and fewer "black boxes" and new gizmos.

The important thing is to make an actual map of stakeholders' attitudes and their ability to influence Lean and build a simple communications plan for each one (see Figure 8.11). Revisit each stakeholder several times. Understand what types of arguments and results each personally finds compelling. Understand the level and method of communication they are comfortable with (don't tell a group of people that they will get blog or podcast updates if they don't know what they are and don't ask people to participate on wiki sites if they are not comfortable with that). *Ignore this step at your peril!*

Role

Initial response to Lean	**Part of the Target Process**	**Part of an Extended Process**	**Enabler Group**
Theoretically supportive	**Mgr - Process owner** Design engineer Design engineer **VP - Lean Sponsor**	Design engineer Test engineer Test engineer	Test engineer **VP - marketing** Product manager Product manager
Undecided	**Product Manager** Design engineer Design engineer Design engineer Test engineer	Design Engineer **Mgr - Process owner** **VP - Engineering**	**HR - manager** **IT - CIO** IT - Manager
Theoretically opposed	Design engineer	Design engineer Design engineer Design engineer Mgr - Process owner	**IT - Tools group**

Figure 8.11 A stakeholder map for the Lean team's risk and change management efforts should highlight key challenges.

Figure 8.11 is a simple stakeholder map for the Lean team's risk and change management efforts. The most influential individuals are shown in bold. This map illustrates a typical "new to Lean" organizational attitude with many undecideds. The key points of attention are outlined: the influential undecideds. The Lean sponsor is also dangerously close to undecided and needs either immediate reassurance or quick results.

For a new-to-Lean organization such as this, nothing succeeds like success. Therefore, one approach might be to start with some demonstrated success in the first column: the target process. At the same time, you must demonstrate that you captured important inputs and contributions from the undecided members of the extended processes that interact with your target process.

The relatively high percentage of content workers in other processes who are opposed is also typical and is, in part, a reaction to "those guys" getting attention. The combination of early wins in the target process plus demonstrating that these workers contributed valuable input as internal customers usually makes this an easy group to win over.

The IT group on this chart looks like a challenge, but if you can demonstrate success and enlist their aid in delivering what promises to be tangible improvements to the corporation, they should come along.

Doing the Analysis: Developing an Understanding of the Process

We need two types of process representations to support the analysis phase: the what diagram and the so-what diagram. The what diagram is a process depiction or description. The so-what diagram is quantification. It should describe the degree to which this process is broken, the reason why you are all standing around looking at it.

The most common place to start describing a process is either with a process diagram (a flowchart or workflow diagram) or a procedural step-by-step description. Many companies already have these, they understand this type of view, and it's a great place to start.

One of the problems with flowcharts is that they are often more detailed than we need them to be and can be quite unwieldy. They graphically represent a list of steps or tasks that we can usually combine or contract into a smaller number of documents or deliverables, what we've elsewhere called converting the "verbs" of process into the "nouns" of information.

In Figure 8.12, we use a product development process from an electronics firm as an example and will build on this in several other illustrations. In the diagram, we have condensed several pages of process diagram into a single page of document flows or dependency.

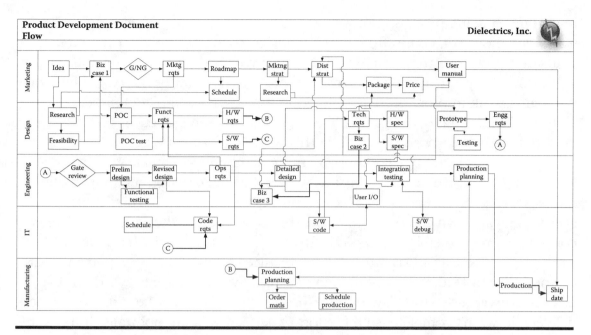

Figure 8.12 A condensed process map based on document flow, "nouns," not process details, "verbs."

The next step is to create the so-what diagram. A value stream map is a wonderful example of a so-what diagram, but it can be hard to generate for knowledge worker processes because of the multitasking, multilocation, and out-of-sequence flows, not to mention the difficulty of gathering detailed time data. A less satisfactory alternative is a simple black box value time calculation based on either time or effort.

- Time-based black box value calculation—The sum of the implicit time to create all of the process's documents divided by the total time in the process as measured by arrival and completion dates.
- Effort-based black box value calculation—The sum of the group's entire number of resource hours burned during a period divided by the number of projects completed during the period.

Either of these approaches delivers valuable symptomatic information, although they are a little simplistic. The following technique requires very little information but provides powerful visual feedback and reinforces the throughput; that is, the uppermost thinking we like to see in Lean.

Measuring Performance via Cumulative Flow

Let's drop a black box around our group or department of white-collar knowledge workers and think of them as if they were a single machine. In process design, we can look at this element using the supplier–input–process–output–customer (SIPOC) methodology. Understanding all five of these elements is important to doing process improvement since each is critically important. The true value, however, comes from maximizing the output. No matter how much you load up our design machine with input (projects, designs, whatever the work to be done is), you can't convert any of it into actual value for the company while it remains work in progress. The only good project is a completed project.

In the United States, the generally accepted accounting practices (GAAP) does not allow a corporation to credit this work-in-process (WIP) and carry it on the books as value. Therefore, by definition, adding too much WIP in an information-intensive process is just as wasteful as having too much raw material or spare parts inventory in a factory process. Money has been spent to accrue things for which your company cannot get credit. When we were young consultants, we remember telling our first project manager how hard we had worked over the Labor Day weekend to advance our project. We expected a pat on the back. Instead, we got something far more valuable; a little wisdom that has stayed with us to this day. He just shrugged and said that he didn't care; the deliverable wasn't complete, so the effort expended was unimportant. "I measure output, not input." At the time, it was disappointing, but we have come to see the wisdom of it. Keeping this mantra before us, what kind of performance metric should be used for our design machine?

Industrial engineering employs a very useful diagram to represent cumulative flow (see Figure 8.13). By tracking and graphing the arrival time of each project, or piece of work, as it arrives at your design machine, you get a simple curve where the vertical axis represents the accumulating number of projects and the horizontal axis represents time. Similarly, if you time-stamped each project as your design machine completed and delivered it, you would have your second curve. The dark area in the diagram between the two curves represents your WIP. In Figure 8.13, that dark area resembles a funnel, narrower at the base than at the top. At a glance, you can see that your design machine is slowing down, the processing time for individual projects is increasing, and the backlog or WIP

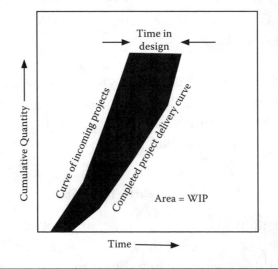

Figure 8.13 The cumulative flow view of project portfolio performance.

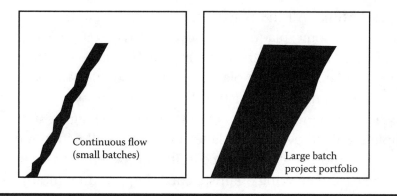

Figure 8.14 Cumulative flow diagrams highlight the far greater WIP of large batch processing.

is also increasing. This one simple chart, used as a performance metric, will highlight the current output rate, the WIP, and your performance variance over time. All this is done in a simple, at-a-glance way that is easy to communicate to the team of knowledge workers.

Figure 8.14 uses this cumulative flow diagram again to illustrate an experiment that contrasts two different ways to use your design machine. In the first approach, you run your design machine in a continuous flow mode accepting one or two projects, and working them exclusively and intensively until they are completed (the diagram on the left). As each project is delivered, a new one is accepted. Alternatively, you can run your design machine in batch mode, accepting a large number of projects all at once. If you examine the cumulative flow diagram for our design machine in batch mode (the diagram on the right), you can see that you really don't start generating any outputs until all the inputs have come in. There is far more dark area in the project portfolio diagram than in the narrow continuous flow diagram. The amount of WIP, which is waste, has gone up by an order of magnitude.

In the continuous flow diagram, the arrival rate of projects is the same, but because you only have started work on a couple of them (a much smaller batch size), you have slashed waste with no change in capacity or resources. This is the same principle as just-in-time in a factory. The width of these dark areas at any point represents the project duration in whatever time units are used. Projects on the right are in development far longer than those on the left, and you can cut cycle time dramatically by rearranging your process this way.

One of the things that has always intrigued us about organizations that use large batches in organizing and resourcing their projects is their seeming denial of the benefits of another approach they also use, the SWAT team. Invariably, whenever trouble strikes in the form of a deadline that's about to be missed or if there is a sudden surge in senior management attention to a particular project, they form a special, handpicked team. The call goes out to stop everything else and focus on this urgent project. They do this because it works. This tiger team focuses on the project, interteam communication and collaboration far exceeds normal levels, resources are cleared for use, and the deadline is met in the nick of time. All the players then congratulate themselves, human resources distributes some plaques, and everybody goes back to their normal routine of multitasking multiple projects in a large batch—the approach that got them into this trouble in the first place. A continuous flow approach is merely standardizing, streamlining, and institutionalizing their own successful plan B. Nevertheless, most organizations seem determined to juggle 30 projects poorly than to complete 3 well, even if the latter approach will actually complete more projects over time and do so for less cost. It's a puzzlement.

As WIP increases, delivering against schedule pressures mount, and customer calls become more insistent. The most common solution is called *expediting*. Special attention is given to one of the projects in this large batch. Naturally, this happens at the expense of all the others. It is a shell game that provides only temporary relief and is guaranteed to generate additional escalations as projects that were put on hold begin to clamor for their fair share of design attention.

The most compelling symptom of a poorly designed information process is frequent project escalations or arguments around project priority. In those organizations that use a formal project pipeline or database, project priority soon becomes meaningless. Everyone knows that only priority 1 projects get attention, so the game becomes designating all your projects as priority 1. It's not surprising to find pipelines where 80 percent of the projects are "top priority."

The next most common techniques to combat WIP are to slip schedule or reduce scope. In a design project, reducing the scope is typically done by either relaxing requirements (slower, smaller, etc.) or eliminating features altogether. This is becoming even more common than slipping schedule because the official schedule is so much more visible and missing dates is more directly associated with poor project management. Dropping features or scope from the work product can be more easily explained as the natural development of things learned during the design stage, including the viability or practicality of some of the original requirements. As an old thesis advisor once explained, "It can be late and great or on time and sloppy. But it can't be late and sloppy." Unfortunately from the Lean information perspective, many projects today are exactly that, late and sloppy, based on developmental and managerial practices that are replete with waste.

Our design machine is far from running at its optimum level. It is juggling far too many simultaneous projects; it is overloaded and working inefficiently; it actually values its large WIP rather than recognizing it as waste; its focus and mind share are scattered across a wide portfolio of projects; the dependencies and interactions among these projects are poorly understood; it has created a scenario of nearly constant escalations and priority shuffling, which lead to a lot of starting, stopping, and wasted effort; its use of multitasking makes process measurement impossible and hides areas for improvement; and, when the chips are down, they toss their process and assemble a SWAT team to finish a

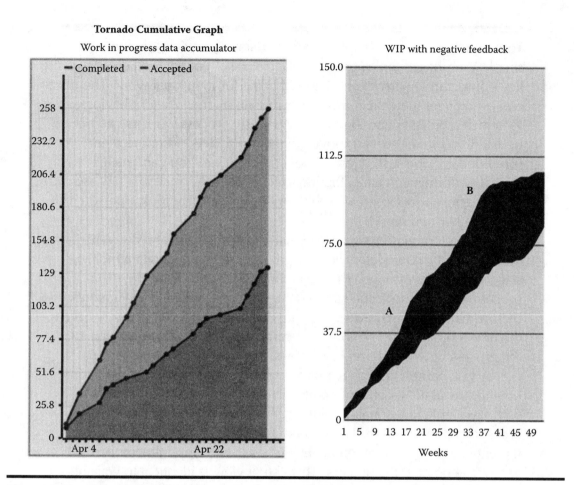

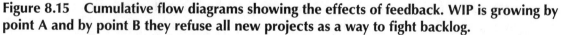

Figure 8.15 Cumulative flow diagrams showing the effects of feedback. WIP is growing by point A and by point B they refuse all new projects as a way to fight backlog.

project with eleventh hour heroics. (We will talk in more detail about some of these wastes.)

As a data-gathering exercise during the Lean discovery or early kaizen phases, it doesn't much matter which technique you use to capture cumulative flow data. If a historical record exists, which allows you to time-stamp historical data and create an accurate picture of last years' data, it would be a good choice since it can be done by the Lean team without intruding on the workflow.

Figure 8.15 contains two examples of cumulative flow charts: In the example on the left, the data is gathered at two separate points: when the project is introduced or accepted (the first step in the process), and when the project is completed and handed off. These two data streams are combined in a Web tool accessible by the two individuals working at distant parts of the process. The example on the right is a typical spreadsheet. In this case, it is a review of historical time-stamped data from project meetings and records. On the right, we can clearly see a behavior change at point B; the project lifecycle had grown so much that the group throttled back heavily on accepting new projects (the slope of the top line drops significantly) until it could reduce the backlog. Unfortunately, this example is all too common.

Tool Tip: If you need to capture sample data, one quick solution is a simple Web-based tool such as Zealog. In this scenario, workers at two key points can log arrival and handoff times for individual work. They can even tweet the data in from their mobile phones without having to launch a browser and log onto a Web site. Process workers can be updated by Twitter (for fast moving data) or RSS feed for more measured updates. It is fast, unobtrusive, and effective. You can change critical performance data gathering to real-time relevance in a few seconds of effort as opposed to week-old PowerPoint that took a person a day to gather and report.

For more comprehensive reporting than the basic in and out WIP measurement of cumulative flow diagrams, you can generate a multi-stage view of flow through the development process. If, during the process, there is good time-stamp data, such as e-mail announcements or transmittals, project review meeting dates, and so forth, and you have the time to collect and scrub it, you can create a more detailed view of the process flow with Excel PivotTables. You can use parameters—project ID, task names, task class/group, review meetings, physical location, organizational identifier, and potentially others—to construct a table with PivotTable functionality, which can be filtered and rotated by properties, class, and so forth. This can be used to create multiple views of the pig-in-a-python graph on a weekly basis or to graph the implied WIP at any one point in the process. This virtual view is identical to walking around the factory (Gemba) and observing multiple small inventories of WIP scattered around the shop as feedstock to various functions.

In the absence of reliable historical data, you can generate some samples to inform the discussion even though you may not have enough to be statistically conclusive. In a paper environment, workers can time stamp a routing slip attached to a document. In an information office, you can use e-mail forwarding or delivery receipts or microblogging to track progress through a process and feed your pivot analysis. It's one way to make the invisible visible.

Discovering Root Cause through Aggregate Data

In Chapter 4, when examining parallel project management, we discussed the effects of juggling multiple projects and of having an organizational boundary or disconnect between process workers and project managers. One of the manifestations of such an arrangement, especially in a high workload environment, is the institutionalization of constant firefighting.

Fortunately, there is a handy diagnostic trick, which may help you uncover this possible root cause to poor process performance. It is related to the shape of the person-hours curve through the duration of the project phase by phase.

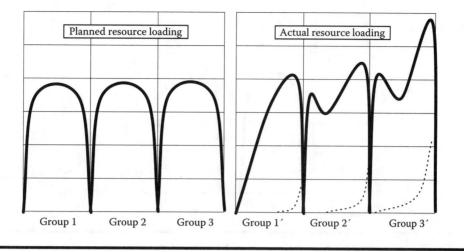

Figure 8.16   The actual dynamics of resource loading usually differ from the planned.

Implicit in most projects is some form of normal person-hour distribution, a bell curve, which begins with some kind of tail, proceeds through a period peak resource loading, and then tails off again (see Figure 8.16, left). In a multiproject multitasking environment what actually happens is a saddle- or mitten-shaped curve (Figure 8.16, right), with an initial peak followed by a valley followed by a larger final peak because no project is "critical" in its initial phase—at least not as critical as other projects the organization is trying to get out the door. Therefore, the organization tends to borrow or reassign resources from noncritical projects to critical projects (this is captured in that central dip of the curve).

During your data-gathering efforts, you may have access to timecard data that, if you're lucky, will provide time spent on a project-by-project basis allowing you to recreate a curve from historical records. We emphasize that, in our experience, the historical data is not as accurate as it might seem because multitasking is confusing and the workers completing the timecards are not going to do a great job reconstructing their hour-by-hour activities for the week. Automatic process discovery, if you can convince a few of the workers to do a test install and provide data, will provide better results.

The good news is that the saddle shape is usually so pronounced, and comprised of the contributions of a large number of resources, that it's fairly simple to recreate from interviews by overlaying the timelines of a few projects and asking your interviewees which project they were working on. Even though some of them will provide faulty data from memory, the average will still be useful.

These mitten graphs are not only symptomatic of some of the Knowledge Worker Lean wastes; there is also direct quantifiable evidence of poor process performance, which will be very useful in building your lean case. As you can see from the graph in Figure 8.17, the mitten shape does not represent a trade-off since the area represented by B is usually significantly greater than the reduced area represented by A. This is the direct effect; shifting resources to that rush-to-finish stage is not cost effective. There is also an indirect effect, since the second peak will come close or even exceed the overall resource capacity of the group.

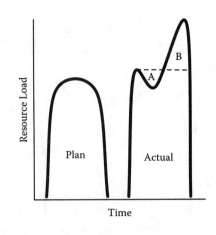

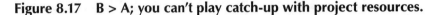

Figure 8.17 B > A; you can't play catch-up with project resources.

This will create other wastes such as overtime and fatigue, which will reduce productivity, increase errors, and lead to low morale.

There are other direct types of performance data you can capture during this phase that can be useful in building a case; however, you will frequently be faced with data quality problems. If your organization has not been gathering data in a certain way, it's unlikely that you will be able to get it. The safest data is time-stamp data from which you can infer flow through the process. Before you give up on the idea of creating cumulative flow diagrams because of poor data, consider capturing milestone slippages such as frequently delayed or rescheduled project review meetings or missed shipment dates. For diagnostic purposes, simple cumulative flow diagrams are often enough and difficult to refute.

Creating and Working with the Information Matrix View

At this point in the process, you have gathered a large amount of subjective and objective data, created a flowchart or document dependency chart, and are ready to create an information matrix.

There are two ways to get started: (1) create a simple information matrix at the document level (a document dependency matrix); or (2) break down the documents into their constituent Infels, create an Infel map, and use that as the index for the information matrix. Staying at the document level may be a first-pass compromise as you spiral toward a more detailed view. Figure 8.18 illustrates the process of parsing documents into information elements. There is some art and judgment to this. In general, if several pieces of information flow together from a single source, they should be grouped as a single Infel. If one or more of those information elements come to the worker from multiple sources, they need to be tracked independently.

This is a dynamic process. Even though you split information flows to capture parallel information element pathways, you are likely to eliminate all but the

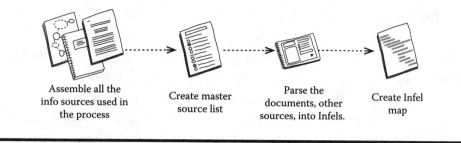

Figure 8.18 Creating the map of information elements.

best path as waste. With only a single information flow path, you may be able to group several information elements (that previously took different paths, but are now consolidated) into a single macro Infel. As a rule of thumb, information matrices start out complicated and daunting as you map known information connections in the process and discover many unofficial ones, but they become much simpler and cleaner as you eliminate duplicates, parallel flows, and assumptions. Figure 8.18 illustrates the overall transition from raw documents and process knowledge to the detailed Infel map.

You are now ready to create the Infel matrix (see Figure 8.19) from the document-level flow. At first glance, this is a tidy process with most of the entries under and close to the diagonal.

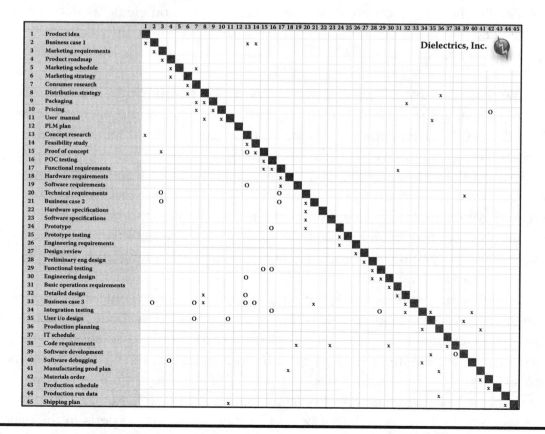

Figure 8.19 An example of an information matrix based on document-level dependency.

Even at first pass, we can make several observations:

- Xs represent dependencies implicit from the documented process flows; Os represent information use uncovered during our interviews.
- There is quite a bit of "early warning" as downstream processes receive unofficial results from upstream processes, which creates more problems than it solves, since these parallel paths often deliver different values and because the unofficial upstream results that come much sooner are likely to be less firm. There is a significant potential for rework if the knowledge worker begins processing based on the early unofficial data.
- There are a few entries significantly above the diagonal. These should be investigated. They are likely to be assumed values taken out of sequence and are another potential source of rework. For example, in this matrix, product pricing is based on an assumed value for material costs long before there is anything approaching a final design and firm data on which to base pricing. This may be a simple matter of updating the pricing once the vendor and material costs are known; on the other hand, distribution strategies and sales commissions may have been calculated based on incorrect data and those negotiations also will have to be reopened.
- There are a few circuits, or circular references, in this matrix, which you should try to cluster more closely together as you work to improve this process.
- Finally, there are a couple of orphans, i.e., information elements that are created and never again used. Business Case 3 with an empty column 33 is such an example.

Now that you have the process flow, information matrix, and the results of discovery, you are ready for your first brainstorming kaizen improvement session. Keep this KWL kaizen approach simple and stay connected to the knowledge workers aiding you in process improvement.

Some of the techniques may not be easy for your brainstorming colleagues to accept. They may have trouble using the results of automatic process discovery software, for example, especially when the results are likely to be shocking and indicate that workers spent far less time being productive than they have always assumed. However, an even bigger challenge is the partitioning and clustering algorithms of DSM software.

It is almost an oxymoron to go into a kaizen session with some kind of a computer-optimized solution. You will be viewed as geeks without common sense, who ignored consensus, and relied on a predetermined solution. If you go into a kaizen session and say, "I plugged in an information matrix and here's the answer," you will lose the audience and you will have a hard time recovering. We do not advocate the expert or deus ex machina approach. Remember, process workers are experts at their jobs and, certainly, they are experts in the exact process manifestation of their jobs.

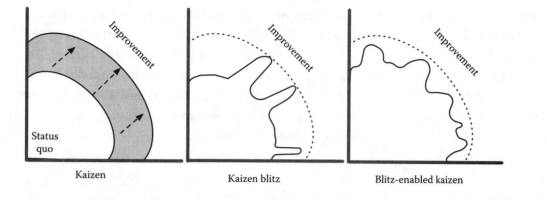

Figure 8.20   Kaizen blitzing on a few pilot projects can lead to uneven, unsustainable development. We advocate more communication and implementing Lean on a broader front.

If you want KWL to succeed, you need to treat the information matrix as brainstorming input, not output. The DSM tools should be used heuristically to inform and guide the kaizen sessions.

In the best of all possible worlds, in an organization that has deeply embraced lean principles, kaizen looks like the left side of the diagram in Figure 8.20. Improvement (represented here by movement up and to the right) is happening everywhere, continuously, across a broad front of organizations and processes.

In organizations that are new to Lean, particularly in the West where fast results are paramount, the approach looks more like the kaizen blitz (Figure 8.20, center) with its concentration on just a few targets. In this instance, two or three pilot projects are receiving a lot of attention and probably delivering very significant improvement results. However, there is a risk that these projects, simply serving as examples, will not be enough to make Lean spread and take root throughout the organization. The pilot projects are so keen to move forward, the participants forget to look around to see if anyone is moving with them. If the rest of the culture has not embraced Lean, these improvement peninsulas will probably not be sustainable. They will not get the support they need from other groups, appropriate Lean metrics will not be adopted by management to reinforce Lean, and worker mobility in and out of the groups will dilute whatever they have learned and any progress they have made.

Note: There is probably an IT component to these peninsular successes. However, if these are isolated experiments, it is also likely that IT has put a chain link fence around them and relaxed some of their concerns about these processes, although they have not done so for the rest of the organization. This will certainly hamper tool adoption, among other things, which may be necessary for other Lean projects.

We believe the rightmost graphic of this triptych (Figure 8.20, right), which we call blitz-enabled kaizen, is the right method, because it is more focused on communicating and promoting Lean through the organization than in having a few successful pilots. This focus on "adoption elsewhere" creates many parallel reinforcements in terms of resources, metrics, expectations, and so forth, and tends to make results more sustainable. This attitude reinforces the heuristic approach to the use of software tools. You need to be as inclusive, transparent, and simple as possible. You are striving for gradual yet steady improvement even if you have to sacrifice a few initial successes. A couple of isolated showcases are not as valuable as careful change management and communication, and may even be counterproductive and generate resentment.

Kaizen Phase 1

Figure 8.21 provides a high-level roadmap for the initial kaizen process. Begin with the Infel Map and the six dimensions of deep process understanding (Figure 8.4) to populate our information matrix and then annotate that matrix and the process flowchart (the "what" diagrams) with all the results, symptoms, suggestions, observations, and ideas to generate input for brainstorming, which characterizes and quantifies improvement potential (the "so what" diagram).

Remember your parents' answer when you asked for a bigger allowance, "If you don't earn it, you won't appreciate it." Even if the Lean leader or team members have some ideas about solutions, this is not the time to bring them forth. They can be added to the brainstorming session as possibilities; you can oh so subtly steer the team in that direction. It has to be a group decision. There is an old adage: If you can't properly explain something that's probably because you don't understand it. If you can't convince your kaizen colleagues of the merit of an idea, it's likely because the idea is not as good as you think it is. You likely have failed to resolve objections or quantify it properly.

Try to restrain yourself from leaping to the latest generation of tools, software, or perceived best-practice solution. We need our solutions to be accepted broadly by the average process worker and not just the early adopting techies. It takes a year or two for new technologies to cycle through from "strange new thing" to

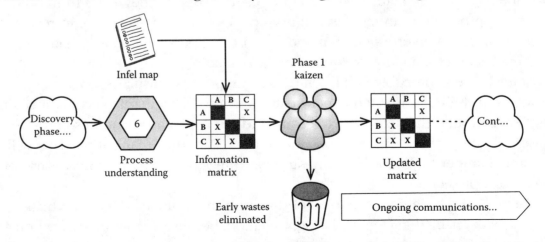

Figure 8.21   High-level roadmap for the initial Lean kaizen process.

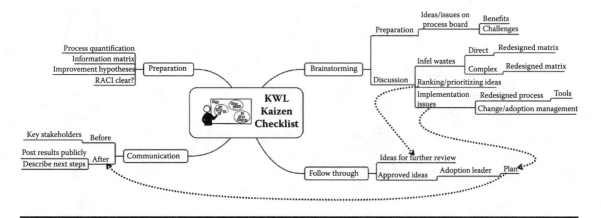

Figure 8.22   For a KWL kaizen to be effective, you must thoroughly address four broad areas.

relevance. New tools and techniques only become socially interesting once they have become technically boring.

The details of what happens in the brainstorming session, (Figure 8.21, center) represented by the people icons and nestled between the two information matrices, is governed largely by the skills, creativity, process knowledge, and interpersonal dynamics of the team members. Figure 8.22 summarizes the brainstorming component and puts it in context of the overall kaizen mission. The brainstorming itself is only one part. You must not forget the elements of preparation, communication, and follow through. Great ideas kept in a locked room, which may or may not eventually produce some process improvement, are not going to spread Lean.

Figure 8.23 is an annotated process flow with simulated results of a first kaizen session. Around the perimeter of the diagram are three graphed sets of data representing some discovery-type analysis. The cumulative flow diagram in the lower left suggests growing work in progress. The resource curves in the upper right corner imply that there is a lot of multitasking and firefighting and the graph in the lower-right-hand corner indicates that a large percentage of ship dates are missed.

Some of the discoveries made possible by the information matrix have been mapped back to the process flow. For example, you can clearly see (Figure 8.23, middle) that Business Case 3 seems to gather a great deal of data input from multiple sources to generate new information that is not used by anyone. The assumption can only be that by the time a project reaches the stage, in this company, it is rarely killed and the business cases are simply window dressing. A couple of simple solutions that the team might discuss are (1) it can simply cancel Business Case 3 and spend that effort elsewhere, or (2) it can put more effort into making a stronger Business Case 2 that might actually be used to cancel certain projects that are not warranted by their financial projections.

Some assumptions are also identified: Marketing is developing a price based on vendor and material costs that won't be known for some time. The consequences may not have been evaluated, but, if they were, standard pricing terms

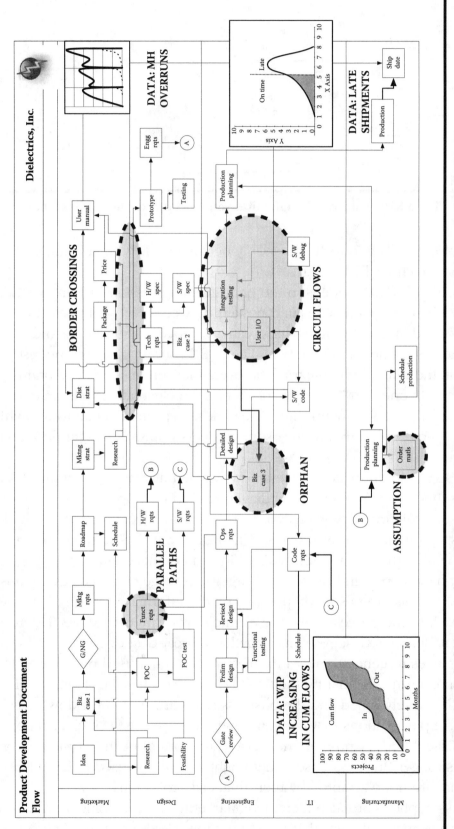

Figure 8.23 Problems identified via the information matrix and kaizen can be mapped back to the typical flow diagram.

could be established with known vendors to minimize risk or automatic change clauses could be built into any distribution or commission processes that might be dependent on price.

A large number of parallel paths are identified. The functional requirements document, in particular, seems to have a life of its own. Parallel paths are trickier than orphans, assumptions, or information circuits, which are readily understood. Most workers still have a why-not attitude toward parallel information flow. They feel that they are in the loop and that this is early warning or just-in-case type information. When parallel paths are so prevalent, they can be the significant driver in information flow even if they seem relatively innocuous compared to some of these other wastes (we will discuss this further later in the chapter). What we call Phase 1 kaizen, whether it is literally one brainstorming session or a month of them, really refers to that part of process improvement where we are capturing the early wastes—the low hanging fruit, to use the consultant's cliché (see Figure 8.24).

In addition to orphans and duplicate pathways, you can also see low-value and high-effort activities. A hint of their existence is the identification of any element that was receiving multiple inputs, which were used only once or twice and even then parallel to or duplicative of other Infels. It is quite possible that the organization could get along fine without this expensive element.

It is important to remember that we cannot only be interested in how efficiently information flows around the organization; we should also be interested in how efficiently that information is generated to start with (see Chapter 3 for a refresher).

This is another reinforcement of the principle of using team brainstorming for kaizen rather than best practices, expert opinions, or the output of optimized software tools. The combination of human creativity layered on top of the information matrix and process diagram is where the true value comes in; for example, when one of the team members circles five or six disparate parts of the

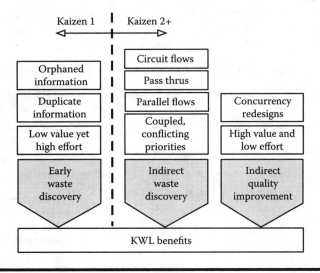

Figure 8.24 The initial wastes are quickly highlighted and resolved while continued kaizen sessions address the more complicated ones.

process diagram and says something like, "Instead of ferrying this document all along this tortuous path, why don't we just use an evolving document collaboratively on a Web site that we can all see?"

Kaizen Phase 2

Kaizen phase 2 represents a shift in the level of difficulty of the KWL ideas we are discussing. During kaizen phase 1, we are essentially collecting the evidence wastes on the surface and quickly achieving significant results.

The ideas of kaizen phase 2 are usually marked by the insidious phrase "on the other hand." Some kind of a penalty usually is involved in accepting and implementing the idea. That company might be gaining approval for a nonstandard tool, significantly altering the procedure, or the change management challenge may come from touching upon a sacred cow.

One of the most difficult implementation challenges to resequencing or clustering activities is the attendant movement of personnel across organizational boundaries. In theory, it's pretty straightforward to say something like, "writing test procedures and executing the tests are very tightly coupled since the test results often suggest changes to the procedures, so these two activities should be done by the same resource or by a two-person team working closely together." It happens that the engineer who normally writes the test scripts and the lab technician who executes them are in two separate organizations and neither of their superiors is interested in giving up the head count (especially when "cost cutting" seems to be going on).

Figure 8.25 illustrates the core of the information age kaizen process. You begin with the information flow description (in this case, we suggest the Infel matrix). You brainstorm and generate alternatives based on the information in

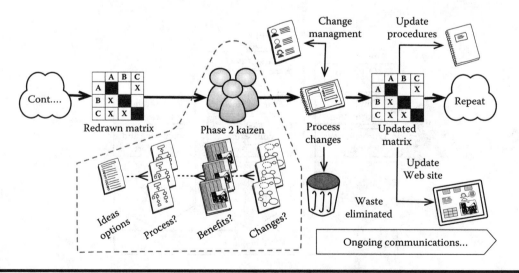

Figure 8.25   The second wave of kaizen involves more collaboration and discussion of alternatives and their benefits than the first wave.

front of you. You evaluate the best ideas based on their implied process changes, potential benefits, and any other infrastructure or organizational changes that may trigger issues. This cycle will generate an improvement plan of one or several changes or new ideas. Capture, describe, and, if possible, quantify the eliminated wastes. Charge your people person with handling the change management with any affected stakeholders. Update your matrix to the new state. Rewrite any procedure or documentation. And don't forget to claim success by updating your Web site and Lean communications vehicles.

This process will be repeated over and over again, so often, it should become a fundamental part of the job, so often that it's not even identified as a separate task. It is the same as thinking of your strategy as a chess game. There should be no distinction between planning your moves, anticipating your opponent's moves, and actually moving the pieces; it's all part of the game.

Selecting Kaizen Phase 2 Ideas

Due to the ramifications associated with kaizen phase 2 ideas, we have divided the discussion of the process into two parts: (1) idea selection and (2) the lean process implementation steps.

To determine what Lean ideas should be considered, the team should:

1. *Keep a list of potential ideas and options, and add to and trim it with each new discussion.* This list was initially populated with the process "mythology" (our term for those issues or causes that were widely held to be true even though there was no real evidence for them). As brainstorming sessions and data gathering proceed, these ideas become much more focused and quantified, and their potential benefits and rationale should be clear. We recommend the A3 tool, where all the elements of the process redesign have to fit on a double size sheet of paper.
   - Be certain you understand how this suggested change will affect the rest of the process. Fortunately, this is exactly what DSM was invented to do and is actually quite simple.
2. *Articulate the benefits of the change.* Presumably, the team understands the benefits of the suggested change pretty well or else it would not have bubbled to the top of the ideas list. But a common mistake is to suppose that because the kaizen team or process workers recognize the benefits of the idea that others will, too. This Infel is going to drive some important information flows: you will tout this benefit on your Lean Web page as a victory, make sure your Lean sponsor hears of it, and be ready to pull it out in future discussions with stakeholders whenever the value of Lean is brought into question. Do a good clear job on this.
3. *Manage change.* This is critical to success. You have already analyzed the process and information flow impacts of this change; now you have to consider the soft part of those changes. Typically, this is the people side, but

it can also be the policy side. You will quickly learn which of these types of obstacles is hardest to overcome in your organization. Perhaps it is legal or regulatory; perhaps it's anything that people think is a pet of the CEO; or perhaps it's just tradition. Whatever it is, think it through and be ready to scuttle or postpone any idea that poses too great a change challenge. Remember, there will be many ideas; there is no need to crash your Lean boat on the first set of rocks. As success mounts, your team will be able to tackle greater adoption challenges and you can revisit some of the ideas you postponed.

Implementing Kaizen Phase 2 Ideas

By now, your Lean team is functioning like a well-oiled machine.

- Your tool guy is taking the new material and immediately uploading it to your Web site (which is starting to look like a rich source of improvement and Lean education; soon others will be copying it).
- Your people person is delicately approaching whoever may be affected by the latest suggested change. Depending on the nature of the ideas, this is either sharing good news or the beginning of a delicate campaign that will demand that person's contribution and stewardship of change.
- Your process expert updates the new flow and information matrix, and any new company procedures that may be affected.
- The entire team takes time to talk to anyone who will listen about the latest great new change.

Then, you get to do it all again. We envy you.

We have used modestly sized information matrices to illustrate the technique. As with any such method, its value increases with the complexity of the problem. You certainly don't need DSM to analyze a 2 × 2 grid, but you would be leaving many great ideas on the table if you try to analyze a 200 × 200 cell matrix with paper and pencil. Figure 8.26 is a representative example of an engineering design process information matrix. It can be tackled piecemeal on paper by brainstorming teams or it can be analyzed using DSM software—the choice is more a cultural one than a technical one. Bear this in mind when selecting your kaizen phase 2 methodology.

The best use of DSM software in the kind of blitz-enabled kaizen process we are discussing is in the background. Rather than trying to explain the software tool and algorithms, or getting multiple team members involved in completing or validating the dependency entries in the matrix, we think the Lean leader or certain designated team members can use DSM in the background, essentially unknown to the rest of the team.

Look at Figure 8.27. There are probably 20 separate sequencing changes from the raw matrix to the processed one on the right. It is impractical to suppose

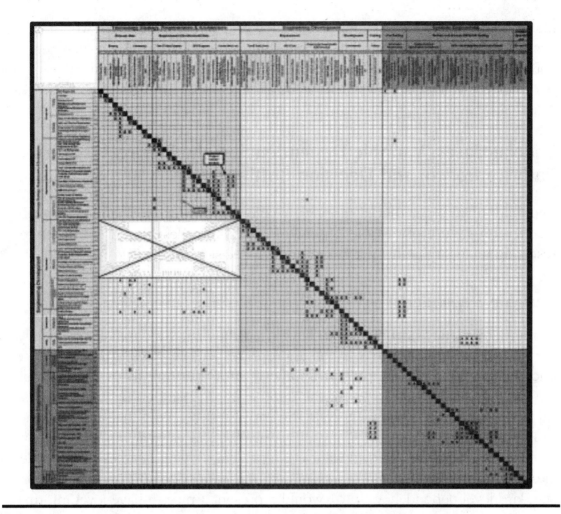

Figure 8.26 **An example of an actual information matrix describing a design process between three separate groups. This type of diagram would form the basis of a second wave kaizen session.**

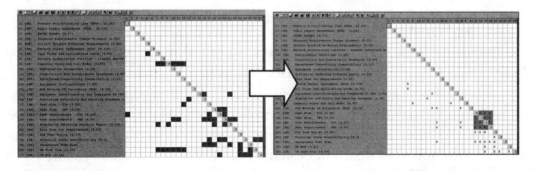

Figure 8.27 **An example of information flow redesign using DSM software tools.**

that a half dozen process workers can digest anything like this number of changes within a reasonable timeframe, not to mention the synergies of all of them simultaneously.

Instead, a couple of the team members should immerse themselves in DSM and use the tools as a way to suggest ideas, which they would bring to the kaizen team and which they would put on the table just as if they were inspirations that came to them while singing in the shower. The team members would discuss these ideas in the typical magic marker and yellow Post-It note manner without using software—at least not until a large number of team members became very comfortable with this technique.

Special Cases: Variable Dependencies, the Desire Path Approach, and Decision Bottlenecks

There are three other special cases we would like to touch on before closing this chapter: (1) the use of variable dependencies, (2) the "desire path" approach to resolving multiple parallel pathways, and (3) decision bottlenecks.

Variable Dependency

In the dependency documents we have used thus far, we have represented dependency with a simple X in the appropriate cell, and to illustrate the difference between the official and the unofficial information flows in one example we substituted an O to represent the unofficial information flow. This is a useful convention and it helps illustrate the early start problem that is so common in KWL.

You can also use numerical values to represent varying degrees of dependencies. You can easily use 3 to represent a critical dependency, 2 could stand for a standard level dependency, and 1 would represent a nice-to-have level information. This can be a little confusing when done in the team brainstorming session and there will be discussions about the interpretations of these variable tendencies, but once it is done, it helps with any tie breaking and eliminates duplication. However, we have found that when working with information matrices in a group setting, variable dependencies are less useful. Any tie breaking is done in an ad hoc manner for each case, and the level of effort needed to establish multiple dependencies can be more of a distraction penalty than it's worth.

Variable dependency delivers benefits when a small group of analysts is using DSM software to analyze a large and complex matrix. Depending on the design of the DSM tool, the analysts can examine individual clustering choices, and this is a very useful guide in matrix redesign. Some DSM tools include multiple levels of dependency, and if sufficient care is taken to accurately categorize these levels, the resulting partition and clustered matrices can be most impressive.

The Desire Path

Architects and planners sometimes delay landscaping and visit a new building site shortly after it opens to observe the natural pedestrian paths that emerge because pedestrians are highly mobile and naturally seek the most efficient path.

Only then do they create walkways along these desire paths—the natural, discovered pathways—rather than those the architects initially envisioned.

In the same way, we can examine the information flow matrix to determine what is the desire path for information. This may deviate from the official process flow diagram and often does. Another way to discover the desire path, such as in the example of paper-based Administrative Lean, is to stop delivering the information along the official information pathway and observe which alternates, if any, spring up. Often there are enough parallel pathways to shunt the information path. This is because electronically assisted information flow in a high-tech environment is very different from the paper-based information flow of the past. In the latter case, if one department ceased to officially issue a report, monthly sales projections for example, the dependent reports such as actual versus projected sales would not be issued because the group that issues the reports could not do its job. Nowadays the downstream group is likely to visit the intranet page where the information is kept and generate its own table of projected values, or get it through back-channel e-mails to members of the projections team, or ask the regional groups that feed the projections team for the information directly. With the speed of the e-mail and computer tools available, the missing report is at most an inconvenience. Soon the downstream group will have smoothed the path to the regional groups and will begin asking for the information on a routine basis (in case the projections team is ever late again, they will be ready). Why not? The e-mail servers won't get tired. Soon, this becomes the desire path—after all, those guys in sales projections are just cutting and pasting data from the regional groups, so why shouldn't we get it directly?

Decision Bottlenecks

One of the sources of waste in any networked process is decision delay. There is a famous story of a Microsoft program leader who had a sign on his desk, "Decisions in ten minutes or your money back." We need more of that.

The reason decision bottlenecks are important is that they are a legitimate and meaningful source of delay but are wholly contained within one of the boxes of the process flowchart or one of the cells of the information matrix. The presence of decision delay cannot be inferred from the topology or structure of either of these documents, but is implicit in the nature of the decision maker.

Big decisions have big ramifications, and so they are pushed back until all the facts are in, consensus is reached, so-and-so is back from vacation, and so forth. However, because tasks hinge on these decisions and other tasks hinge on the outcome of those tasks, the downstream result can be a very large number of potential courses of action, all dependent on the decision.

There are three ways to attack this waste of decision delay:

1. *Clearly identify who owns this decision and who is expected to have key (decision altering) input.* An excellent format for this is the RACI matrix also referred to as the responsibility matrix. This is a table identifying who is responsible (R) to provide significant input, accountable (A) for the decision (the final authority; there can only be one), who should be consulted (C) prior to the decision, and who should be informed (I) once the decision is made. As simple as this sounds, you can learn a lot about the organization by trying to develop a RACI, especially one-on-one with the decision makers. You will usually find a great deal of authority conflicts, disagreements as to who should be consulted, and occasionally a few orphaned decisions that no one seems to think they own.

2. *Detailed, up-to-date project information.* As long as information is distributed in meeting notes and e-mail attachments, then every project suffers to some extent from partial status latency. Multitaskers or people returning to the project have to get up to speed to support a decision. This often involves status meetings and briefings, which is time wasted for the percentage of people in the room already up to speed. A graph of status congruency, the degree of up-to-dateness for all the project participants, looks like a sine wave or a saw tooth diagram. At these status meetings most of the team (including the decision makers) catches up quickly, but the group's collective understanding begins to fade almost immediately. Most of the peripheral team members don't bother to keep up with the project for most of the calendar time. They're busy and, after all, that's what the briefing meetings are for. We believe that collaborative project management and visual management systems address this problem.

3. *Lack of situational visibility at the portfolio and enterprise levels delay decisions.* The ramifications and ripple effects of the decision are unknown. There are many kinds of dependencies—both external and internal—and they usually come in varying strengths and degrees of direct impact. A delay in the design of a printer cartridge project will delay the printer project; that's an easy connection to make. What is less clear is that the resources working on the printer cartridge project are also key to the stepper motor shared by three developing designs. The wrong decision could delay them all. A good portfolio management system helps, a DSM-style representation of dependency helps, but the most important mitigating factor is reducing the number of in-play projects in the first place and moving to a continuous flow design.

Chapter 9

How to Sustain Knowledge Worker Lean

To sustain Lean you have to develop mutually supportive feedback between demonstrated success stories, the propagation of Lean to other parts of the organization, and the continued support and sponsorship of senior management. IT is critical to reinforce the cultural and attitude parts of Lean with evidence of success. Visual management tools provide the tactical support to do things in a Lean way as well as the strategic feedback to sustain Lean.

Not too long ago, when we were trolling the Web looking for the latest and greatest ideas about Lean (continuous improvement is a demanding mistress), we came across one of many free, downloadable white papers on a Lean topic. The topic was 5S, one the fundamental pillars of the Lean approach. While scanning it, we could not help but notice that this white paper was being offered by a label manufacturer. Somewhat cynically, we wondered just what take a label manufacturer would have on 5S. No doubt there would be an emphasis on organization and tidiness and it would probably require a great deal of, shall we guess … labeling.

We downloaded and read the piece and, frankly, it was pretty good. A strong and useful summary of traditional Lean 5S with some useful, and we think correct, insights on implementation. We couldn't help but notice the emphasis on the visual (factory) workplace and we noted some distinctions that we thought were useful in understanding the 5S challenge as applied to the high-tech information intensive office workspace—what we call 5Si.

Overview of 5S

English-language Lean practitioners have looked for the equivalent words to the Japanese that began with S. Different books use a slightly different list, and some add a sixth S for safety. The list we suggest is standard: sort, sweep, straighten, standardize, and sustain. One of the dangers of the 5S program is that these words and their superficial meanings look like a housekeeping task, the same steps used to clear out a closet or straighten the garage. That conceptualization diminishes an elegant methodology. We think *elegant* is the right word to describe the combination of simplicity and depth of 5S. From the following descriptions, some are likely to say that this is absurdly simple. You would be wrong. These 5S programs are simple in the same way that playing the piano is simple; after all, you just have to hit the right key at the right time.

1. *Sort—The identification and elimination of the unnecessary.* For practical purposes, unnecessary is defined as "unused" or "redundant." In a factory setting, you would use a red-tag program where workers literally put red tags on all the equipment and material that seems to have been pushed to the side and is gathering dust. If these items are actually in use, it is incumbent on the user to spot the red tag and salvage it. Otherwise, it is discarded after some period of time. Red tag programs are ruthless and always reveal surprising results. There is a vast amount of unused material taking up space and getting in the way. On the information side, the equivalent step is to identify not only legacy equipment (typewriters? fax machines? drafting tables?), but also documents, procedures, and systems that are legacies or were carried over out of habit, not design.

2. *Sweep—Literally, a cleaning and tidying step.* The idea is not cleanliness for its own sake; rather it is to clear the field of vision so that abnormalities, defects, missing items, things out of place, and so forth are easier to spot. We can't help but think that there is a none-too-subtle message that has to do with discipline and pride involved here. It is the difference between the deck of a shipshape naval vessel versus the average merchant ship.

3. *Straighten—The step that creates order, especially visual order, in the workplace.* A place for everything and everything in its right place. Instead of a pile of tools on a workbench or a toolbox on a shelf, each tool would be hung on a pegboard with a marked outline so that not only can you access each one directly, but you can immediately see if any tools are missing. This might sound a little obsessive compulsive but realize that a worker on a different shift will have no idea where the previous shift's machine operator, in particular, keeps the needle nose pliers.

   Visually ordered systems, as a requirement, need to be so simple that a new, inexperienced person can understand them at a glance. To put it in a high-tech perspective, think of an iPod interface compared to your typical 40-button VCR remote control. Now extend that concept to the company's intranet site where process information, documents, knowledge management, and all the supporting information for day-to-day operations are maintained and you will have an idea of what we are talking about.

5Si straightening activities might include consistent file naming, tagging, adding Google search to your intranet knowledge management system, being able to place a bookmark on your frequently used intranet subsite, or building some of the procedural checks and balances directly into the workflow.

4. *Standardize—This is the harvesting step.* In the first three Ss we have been making improvements; now we stop to write and codify them. In a physical work environment, it has become quite common to communicate using posters with a high emphasis on simple diagrams, cartoons, or illustrations depicting the process and the results.

Office workers who are used to long, wordy documents describing their procedures might find this a little too cute, but these simple diagrams have the advantage of conveying a lot of information very quickly, and, of course, they are contextual. For example, the diagram about how to load the truck is located right next to the loading dock. You can't do that with a long list of office procedures, unfortunately. The office worker first needs to know that there is a procedure covering this issue, then where to look for it, and then must find it and actually read it. Each of the steps takes time and effort and has a failure rate, so it is not surprising that most procedures are not read. Until they have been violated, of course, and are then assigned as remedial reading. Imagine intelligent machine-generated voice messaging automatically broadcast on your computer before a specific milestone and repeating the procedures for entering the next stage in the project.

5. *Sustain—This step is the foundational mechanism of Lean and the most difficult.* Now that you have completed discovery, identified and tilted at legacy equipment and processes, reorganized everything with visual and elegant solutions, rewritten all your procedures, and documented your enhancements, you get to do it all over again and try to ensure that things don't revert to where they were.

This step showcases the change in philosophy and attitude that perpetuates Lean and continuous improvement. It is the difference between getting your teenage son to clean up his room with a lot of effort every couple of weeks and having a son who keeps a tidy room.

As we will discuss, sustaining 5S can be extremely difficult for information Lean because information flow is much harder to see, and therefore it's harder to determine whether the changes are being maintained, and the kinds of people who do information intensive work are harder to manage in a measured, prescriptive sense. It's not just herding cats; it's herding absent-minded cats who resent too much management scrutiny of their professional and too-complicated-to-measure work.

Table 9.1 5S

	Topic	Nature	Key Takeaway
1.	Sort	Project	These three elements feel the most natural to project managers. Most projects get "put in order" like this for progress reviews or handoff meetings. This project polishing is standard operating procedure (SOP). The important thing is to not celebrate it with a mission accomplished announcement because you have only just begun.
2.	Sweep	Project	
3.	Straighten	Project	
4.	Standardize	Process	This feels most like process improvement work: visualizing, creating, and documenting the end state.
5.	Sustain	Culture	This is the critical step and is dependent on leadership and the reporting/measurement tools that are necessary to demonstrate and track the straightened performance. This is where previously murky or anecdotal progress is made visible and unambiguous.

Table 9.1 highlights the roles of each S and visually demonstrates that not all Ss are created equal. The first three, while not easy (identifying and trying to cull underused sacred cows is always a challenge), are the blocking and tackling of 5S. Their critical challenges are in identifying candidates for elimination and risking that the team will declare victory and promptly revert. The process changes needed to support the fourth S can be technically challenging or may involve significant change management effort to satisfy certain stakeholders resistant to change. Most organizations have done process improvement work of some kind, so it has a familiar feel.

The fifth S is, by far, the most difficult as it requires a systemic cultural shift. Many office workers have learned that "this too shall pass" is an excellent strategy for coping with process improvement projects. After the redesigned process is rolled out amid congratulatory fanfare, they can go back to doing their (thankfully invisible) information work as before. Therefore, it is critical that the fifth S include assessment and reporting sufficient to monitor performance against the fourth S. Previously murky items like project completion dates, risks, design and content evolution, worker handoffs, knowledge sharing, and so on need to be elevated to the same at-a-glance visual management system as that employed by Lean in the factory.

5Si

To illustrate 5Si, we will begin with a negative example.

Case Study

Not too long ago, in a professional services firm, one of the client invoices was aging and, this being a tightly managed firm, the accounts payable manager called the project manager and asked him to expedite payment from his client. The project manager agreed to try even though he knew his client was having trouble with their new SAP system and many payments were late. He asked for a PDF of the invoice so that he could forward it to his client. That's when the fun started.

This professional services firm was very proud of the tailored accounting system it had written for itself years ago. One of the "features" of this system was that it could only send invoices to a printer. This was fine in support of the official policy, which stated that invoices should be mailed or faxed. To the project manager the idea of printing and faxing an invoice and then following up with phone calls to make sure it had been received made as much sense as sending it via carrier pigeon. "I can't call a senior vice president and ask him to stand by the fax machine. If he needs to forward it to someone in his organization, how is he going to do that? Do I tell him to walk around and hand-deliver it? Let me just e-mail it." That is when he learned that you weren't allowed to e-mail invoices, partly because of some legacy notion about fraud prevention, and partly because the accounting system could not generate an electronic file, only a printed document. "No problem," said the project manager. "PDF software looks just like a printer to your accounting system; just tell the accounting system to print to it and, *voilà*, it generates the PDF file, which I can e-mail."

At that point, the project manager was treated to a long and depressing lecture about adhering to company policy, fiscal responsibility, the dangers of independent thinking, and a slew of other things that depressed and still haunts him, I can tell you, to this very day. The (other) sad thing about this story is that every single project manager and secretary in the professional service firm knew that e-mailing was a more efficient way to expedite payment than faxing. Therefore, what they would do after printing the invoice was to retype it in a word processor, being careful to match all the accounting codes and dollar values, so that they would have a soft copy that they could e-mail to clients. This introduced wasted work and the possibility for costly mistakes if any of the transcribed data was wrong.

This little story illustrates several of our 5Si points:

1. Information workers will find a way to get the information they need to do their jobs regardless of policy or official procedure. For one thing, it's just too easy, as the example demonstrates, to circumvent the accounting controls by retyping or scanning invoices.
2. This organization should have "sorted" through its equipment and procedures, and scrapped the accounting rules and fax machines that were in place since before the Internet era.
3. It did not "straighten" the process by redesigning a workflow that met all the requirements of accounting control as well as efficient client communication.
4. It lacked the Lean leadership and culture to "sustain" an attitude of continuous improvement in this workforce.

Instead, everyone found it easier to adopt a don't-ask-don't-tell approach to getting the job done while paying lip service to the procedural sacred cows. This is quite common. Isn't it surprising that a culture will more typically evolve to one that winks at little white business lies, rule breaking, and microfraud rather than listen to the change agents within its own ranks who dare to try to improve procedures? It's more accepted to cheat the system than to buck the system.

During one of our stays in Japan, we visited a company that had done a real turnaround by implementing 5S. Actually, they just practiced 3S. The CEO was obsessed with 3S and demanded perfection. The most difficult obstacle was to continue and sustain the practice of it. "One person needs to be the bad guy, that's me," he said.

On a voluntary basis, most all employees spent their first 30 minutes at the start of the day cleaning their offices. When we came into the reception area that early morning, We saw the CEO on his knees scrubbing the floor. He said you only needed to focus on the first 3Ss; the two other Ss would come automatically. He had implemented what he called a stand up Lean office in which all the staff was standing up while working. "This will keep us on our toes and it's also healthy." Like in the factory, he had marked all the working areas in the office with plastic tape to visualize what should be done where.

The CEO had marked the area on his desk where his computer went, where his mobile phone should be placed, and even where he should place his reading glasses when he was not wearing them. His 3S commitment had become an obsession and a goal unto itself instead of a means to drive efficient processes. We base our practice of 5S on the actual work process and ensure that 5S supports the flow of the process. It is the process that needs to sort, sweep, straighten, standardize, and sustain tidiness. Don't lose sight of the goal.

In the high-tech office, 3S means sorted, swept, and straightened information flow. Put your reading glasses wherever you'd like.

One of the challenges of applying 5S to the high-tech office is failing to make the transition from physical tidying to information tidying. The manufacturing cell might stress standardization in the placement and layout of tools, but does this really mean anything to an office worker? While we have seen it proposed and tried, we can't imagine telling a group of scientists that if they just put their phones on the left side of their desks and their keyboards and coffee cups on the right, in a standardized way, things will improve. A standard cubicle layout is not part of the answer because office shift work is not really part of the problem. Our bright young knowledge workers might collaborate with their colleagues, but those colleagues don't come in, sit at one another's desks, and quickly need to find the pencils and paper clips.

Certain changes to the physical layout would contribute to information flow, for example, clustering workers with mutually dependent activities as close together as possible because physical closeness might be an additional aid to ad hoc communication.

However, in a larger sense, the very task of the 5Si Lean designer is to make a hard-to-see information flow visible regardless of location. This is because it is unlikely that all the participants in a modern high-tech environment will always occupy the same physical location when we have large organizations with multiple offices, telecommuters, open innovation, business process outsourcing, and project teams comprised of companies, vendors, and systems integrators. We cannot rely on information being exchanged at the water cooler. The only way to provide equal access to a distributed workforce, and to make the invisible office visible, is to put in the cloud. Only by taking advantage of the ubiquity of Internet access in creating a system that is every bit as visual as the factory worker's pegboard system, and doing it with 5Si principles including process monitoring and management, will we enable sustainability.

See if any of the following information office wastes that could be addressed by such an approach seem familiar:

- John needs some information that Mary already has on her hard drive, but he has no idea that it's there, just 10 feet away. He wastes time doing the research.
- Bill can't find any information on the chemical industry work for his proposal even though he's certain the company has written proposals like this in the past.
- Steve can't find out who in the organization has had previous financial project management experience when he's staffing his team for a banking project.
- Jeremy can't monitor the day-to-day progress of his outsourced team.
- Mathilde can't coordinate the work of her telecommuters effectively with the rest of her team.
- Jonathan suspects that a certain project will be late though the official status is "green." Should he prepare for it or keep his team working on another project?
- Oswald has just had a brilliant breakthrough that will improve the design he is working on. Nobody else will learn of it until next month's review meeting when it will come as a surprise and invalidate some of his colleagues' work.
- Gillian is about to spend several hours recreating some analyses and graphs that have already been created.
- Alan and his team of three or four analysts have been e-mailing a large and complex PowerPoint deck back and forth for weeks. Version control has been a nightmare and many edits were made to slides that had already been superseded. They are currently on version 40 of the presentation.
- Marie cannot find a graph of survey results that she saw presented at a meeting just a few weeks ago.
- Will doesn't know if all the expenses have been submitted on the project, so he can't issue the client invoice and get paid.

- George can't demonstrate the firm's credentials to a prospective client because the last six project managers never finished their case studies or, if they did, he can't find them because nobody finished formatting them and loading them into the system.
- Philip is about to cancel a project, but he doesn't know if doing so will free up critical or underutilized resources.
- Mary Jane's project survived the cutbacks, but she hasn't realized that one of her tasks was dependent on a deliverable from another project that was cut.
- Suzanne is about to change project priorities again, because one client yelled louder than the others did.
- Raul was about to finish a project when he was redirected to a higher priority one. When he returns to the first project in a few weeks, he will waste time getting back up to speed.

The list could go on. These are just examples of information management, maintenance, and flow—5Si—wastes (we will discuss more insidious and complex office wastes later).

What's that you say? These aren't so bad; they feel like our daily experience. We should just suck it up and get down to work. Don't you think we could do better? The fact that they are each relatively minor irritants or time wasters—and that we are familiar with and have overcome them several times—is no reason to ignore them. Quite the opposite is true. We should eliminate them so that we don't have to spend our valuable time dealing with minor irritants and dedicate that time to the high-value work that we enjoy doing and that we are paid for.

Sustaining Information Age Lean Using a Visual Management System

We have emphasized that the key difference, from a Lean perspective, is that while process flow is visible and you can learn to see waste, information flow is largely invisible. Therefore, we have to find ways to make it visible.

Simple visual management is one of the hallmarks of Lean. This applies to all the diagnostic and awareness lessons in learning to see waste as well as to some of the major tools used to manage and sustain Lean such as kanban, 5S, and heijunka. Figure 9.1 illustrates the simple heijunka box technique, which we will build on in our information management tool set.

There is a handy lesson in Outlook, the popular e-mail application, which we can also build on. Outlook provides calendar visibility and most users know how powerful it is for scheduling meetings. Far better than the multiple back and forths of "Is Tuesday good for you?" "What time?" and so forth, colleagues can look at one another's calendars and suggest a meeting time that seems to accommodate both parties. This is useful for two-person meetings, but the utility

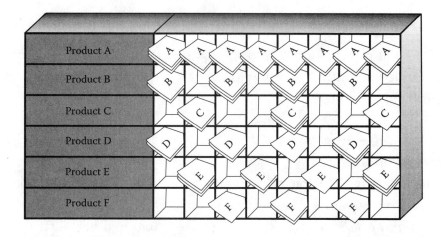

Figure 9.1   The heijunka box is a simple visual production scheduling technique from Factory Lean.

increases dramatically as the number of people attending the meeting increases. The first suggested meeting time is one that seems to be available for all parties. If you were to try this process by e-mail (and who hasn't?) and the participants pare down the desired options to two or three dates and times, someone, who perhaps is traveling and not able to participate in the first few rounds of discussion, will inevitably have a conflict. All the prior scheduling work is wasted.

We need to do for information flow and project status what Outlook does for the scheduling of meetings:

■ An Information Lean visual management system should provide at-a-glance status, support content collaboration, and serve as an aide in long-range management planning and evaluating process change options.

■ If it is not simple and powerful enough to support the at-a-glance reporting, it will never be adopted. It must compete with high-level status reports, however laboriously assembled, that management now uses to check status information.

■ If it does not support the actual work, become part of the workflow, it will be seen as just another management watchdog tool and overhead for the actual knowledge workers. The tool and the work should be as intertwined as "using Outlook" and "doing e-mail"; the two phrases are practically synonymous.

■ The tool must incorporate reality—risks, issues, dependencies, projections, accurate "percent complete" information, and so on—making its status information more valuable than the "plan of record" schedules generated without all this detail.

The high-level requirements for information visual management fall into two groups: (1) those that provide very fast feedback and information (thus saving all the time associated with learning and reporting on status) and (2) those that are useful for strategy and planning. You can think of these two as short- and long-range management.

Short-Range Management

These are the requirements for delivering useful at-a-glance status in support of tactical issues such as status reporting, changing requirements, resource allocation, and problem solving.

- *Visual tracking*—Progress must be conveyed very quickly and updated dynamically in a simple way.
- *Drill-down details*—This provides the user with the ability to peek into each project or work stream to verify that the status is correct, the "show me" feature.
- *Planning and predictability*—This supports situational visibility. Downstream groups can learn when to expect a handoff; specialists (such as the testing lab, shipping, or legal) have a much better view of the upstream pipeline so they can schedule and plan their work.
- *Content collaboration*
  - Peer review—The work product at each step should be visible. Documents, even drafts, should be available for insight and comment. Keeping work in progress locked in your drawer until the final unveiling leads to mismanaged expectations, rework, and poor resource planning. Since it is often a way to mask true progress, it can generate suspicion among the team and support a culture of inflated progress reporting (and the attendant last-ditch wasteful scramble to complete).
- *Information details*—A blog or other running commentary is very useful. Comments are made all the time, but since they happen in point-to-point e-mails or casual water-cooler remarks, their value is lost to the rest of the team. A comment such as "We did this before, check the Acme Project files, it'll save you a lot of time" could be invaluable. These are very detailed comments that belong at the document, deliverable, or Infel level. Only knowledge workers interested in the details of the specific task should see them when they dig to that level.

Since we need status quickly, the tool should be designed to provide it immediately. Since we will need more details, we can build them in as links or databases that can be queried below the surface. We can also incorporate streamlined work rules and all the lessons of KWL such as tracking information flow and actual information deliverables rather than activities. Since we're Lean, we believe this should all be in one tool.

Figure 9.2 is a sketch of a visual management system for information flow. It obviously shares DNA with the at-a-glance simplicity of the heijunka box, but it also leverages the current wiki and blog technology to allow for collaboration, planning, and risk management.

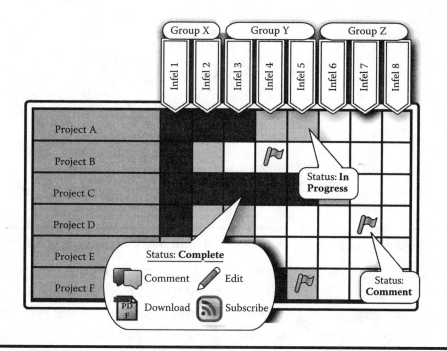

Figure 9.2 Our Web-based visual management version of the heijunka box adds a database behind the status presentation to allow for more detail, file management, and collaboration.

Long-Range Management

In addition to the at-a-glance tactical uses of visual management such as status it can also aid in broader scale or strategic management, areas characterized by a longer time horizon. A good visual management system should be holistic enough to provide decision support at the portfolio and enterprise levels. Some basic examples are:

- *Resource leveling*—One of the most common errors in a multiproject environment is the overallocation of key resources. Project management software can identify overallocation and redraw schedules based on resource constraints, but this is rarely done. Most project schedules are limited to one project and fail to consider the systems or "information factory" level constraints. Attempting to redraw hard outputs, such as project milestone dates based on soft inputs such as percent of time a resource will allocate to a specific project, rarely works. The soft data, such as percent of time per project, is ignored, even when the implications are dramatic and highly improbable utilization levels for key resources.
- *Risk management*—There are several types of risk in an information project and they come into effect at different times in the project life cycle. Since most projects are completed, "risk" really translates into schedule risk, not completion risk of finishing the design, software code, and so forth, that is the content of the project.

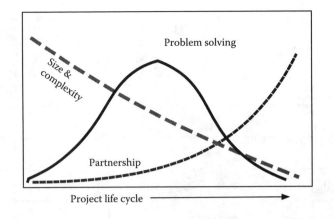

Figure 9.3 The drivers of project risk peak at different times of the project life cycle.

Schedule risk can be broken into three subcomponents (see Figure 9.3):

1. Inherent complexity risk—The more things to do in a project, the more things could go wrong. This risk decreases as the project progresses and tasks are actually completed.
2. Problem risk—In information projects, there is often a challenging problem, such as design or solving a software coding problem. This risk, that is the ability to effect or extend the schedule, is greatest in the middle of the project when potential alternatives are being weighed and their effectiveness is being evaluated.
3. Partnership risk—Technology and design projects, in particular, have risks associated with collaborating with a vendor, component supplier, or other delivery partner. This risk only becomes knowable toward the latter part of the project when the external input is received and evaluated. The risk peaks at the end when you need to integrate work product that has been developed independently.

Tool Tip: We developed the notion of different risks that vary through different stages of the project and the guiding principle that (almost) all risks actually translate into some form of delay. We may have done this independently, but we are not alone. FogBugz is a predictive tool that uses a Monte Carlo–based approach called evidence-based scheduling (EBS) to do much the same for software development. FogBugz displays a probability curve of ship dates that indicates the probability that you'll ship on any given date.

■ *Effective replanning*—A portfolio view of projects includes accurate assessment of status, risks, and resource dependencies as well as a clear understanding of how the projects tie into each other. Shifting resources to a project that will be delayed by an external source and cannot benefit from additional resources is a waste. Moving key resources from a project entering its riskiest phase may lead to project extensions. The big picture is comprised of many accurate little ones, all in context.

The Mechanics of a Visual Management System

We suggest three ways to apply these principles in creating a Lean visual management system for a multiproject organization.

Approach 1: Excel and SharePoint

We can use the natural tabular layout of a spreadsheet and, of course, its ability to easily perform calculations with the document storage and organization abilities of SharePoint to create a simple Lean visual management system.

As you can see from Figure 9.4, the layout is relatively straightforward. The first series of columns contains project names and (experience tells us) unique project numbers. Project sponsors, managers, and key resources are identified, and projects are grouped by similar type or interconnectedness.

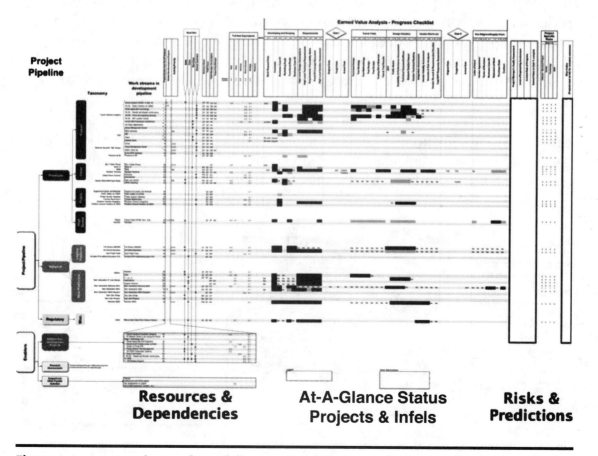

Figure 9.4   Lean project and portfolio status visualization using an Excel-based tool.

The middle section lists the discrete deliverables each project is expected to develop. At the time of acceptance, the project manager selects which of these deliverables are actually required based on the nature of the project. The earned value automatically adjusts so that the sum of these deliverables constitutes 100 percent of the effort. Using conditional formatting in Excel, you can represent completed deliverables as a solid cell and deliverables currently being worked on as a gray cell. Anyone looking at the project can instantly see which parts are complete as well as the general left-to-right progress of dark cells. Any project document represented by a dark cell can be found on the appropriate SharePoint site. Blogs and discussions about the document as it develops are also available.

The final section contrasts the plan of record due date with the predicted due date. This latter calculation is based on the current earned value of completed documents, the calculated risks, and the current staffing levels. The automatically predicted completion date can be very useful. Many projects suffer from optimistic schedules that are not debunked until the last minute. The projected date is a very clear way to highlight potential slippages; any explanation should be incorporated into project reviews.

Approach 2: Intranet Status Board

The evolutionary step from the aforementioned system to a customized database application is a short one. Today's technology and Web tools make it relatively simple to customize an application that does all the above with the important addition of building it into the day-to-day work process.

Figure 9.5 represents such a next evolution. The middle diagram is recognizable: project in rows and deliverables in columns with dark cells representing a completed document. The difference in this approach is that we can make the cells directly clickable to take you to the document detail page where document history and control metadata exists, as along with a comment history and the ability to see and download the document directly.

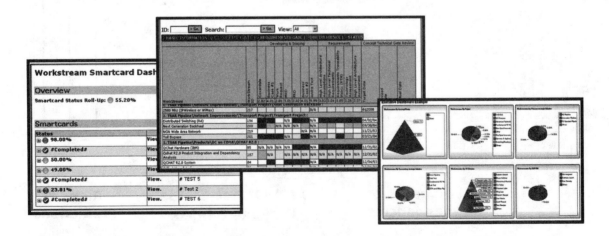

Figure 9.5   A Web-based visual management system.

Work rules can be customized to provide e-mail alerts to any document interested parties subscribe to so they don't miss comments or updates. Peer reviews are easy to build into the work process. Rather than have the document owner update the document directly, this update can trigger an Outlook form with accept/reject buttons that goes to the designated subject matter expert or line manager. Peer review guidelines can be customized depending on the skill or experience of the author. Peer reviews are one way to ensure that project quality and downstream activities, dependent on this deliverable, are less susceptible to rework.

The Web site approach, based on databases, provides tremendous flexibility and allows you to tailor such things as custom reports. These examples demonstrate simple colored status indicators (red, green, yellow are most common; shown here in grayscale) as well as several views of project portfolio progress.

Approach 3: Customized-off-the-Shelf (COTS)

Although we have developed bespoke solutions, there are also excellent commercial applications in this functional space that can be readily adopted or customized. As always, it is difficult to stay ahead of the collective innovation and skill of the marketplace. The rush of talented new startup companies developing collaborative tools—whether they specifically refer to themselves as Lean or not—is one of the surest indications that this is a healthy future direction.

Tool Tip: We found and tested several tools. One of them, Intervals from Pelago, is billed as hosted project tracking for small business and made us immediately feel comfortable in its approach, tools, and structure. If we'd had this years ago, we wouldn't have found it necessary to build tools like the ones described earlier.

As Pelago says, "Intervals is about getting work down, empowering knowledge workers to have every piece of information they need to work efficiently, tracking that work, communicating openly with clients, having real-time status of what's going on, and getting meaningful reporting from the whole cycle." We could not agree more. We have no financial, personal, or any other stake in Intervals; we simply identify it as an example of an approach with which we happen to agree.

Another excellent tool is Mingle from ThoughtWorks, which personifies that balance between powerful and simple that we think of as critical Lean DNA. This tool is aimed more at software development and is a little less generic than Intervals, but more than worth a look.

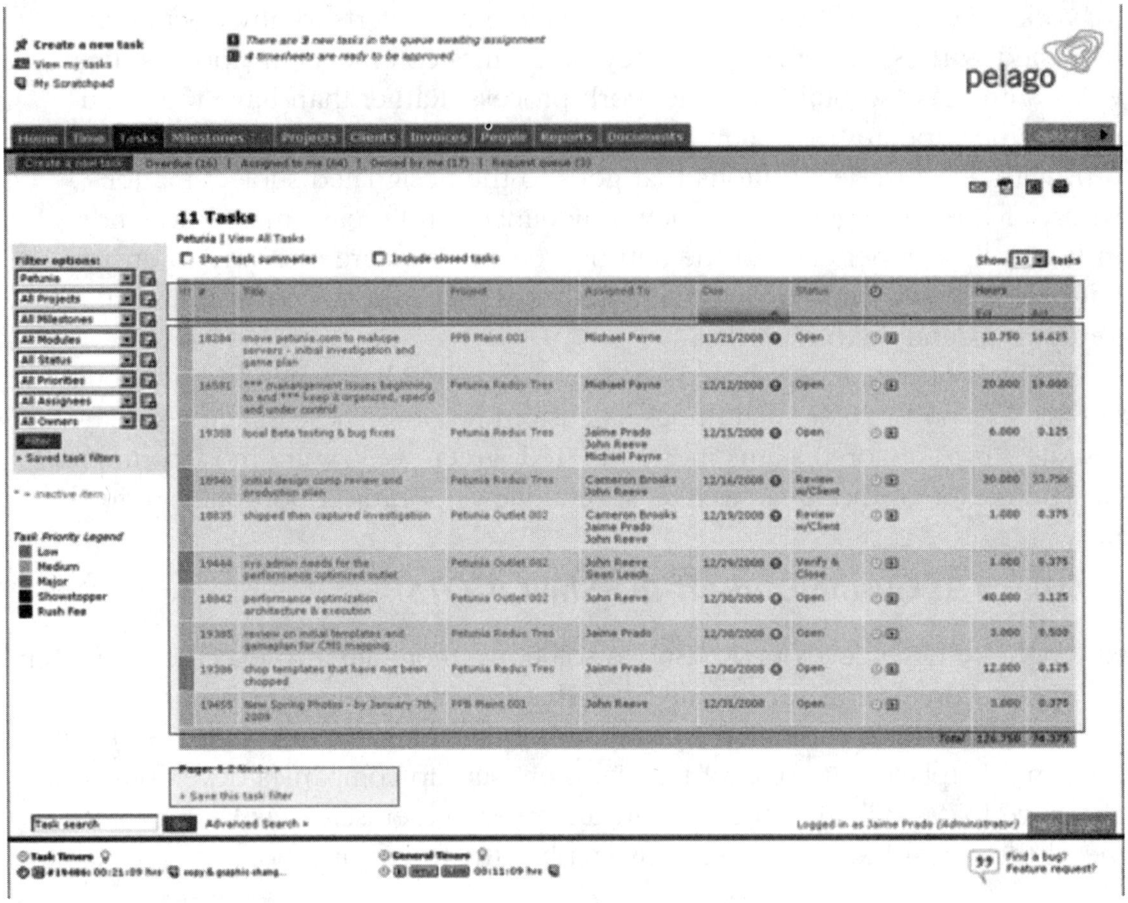

Figure 9.6   A example of a Web 2.0 collaboration and project management tool.

Figure 9.6 and Figure 9.7 illustrate some of Intervals' look and feel. We used Intervals, in part, as a collaboration approach for this book. Overkill for two people, we know, but illustrative and useful.

Intervals supports document uploading and building workflow into its centralized project management. It does a particularly good job of task management and time reporting. We don't emphasize time reporting in our view of Lean because work and efficiency so often becomes subordinated to budgetary performance and cost project overruns, but in some applications it can be extremely useful.

Like most database applications Intervals shines once you have enough data to get value out of the reports sections. See Figure 9.7 for an example of this. Most project management today is what we term "parallel project management." The only way to get status is for resources to collect information—interviewing project personnel, gathering meeting minutes, evaluating progress, and so forth—then presenting the information in, typically, a custom PowerPoint report. From a Lean perspective, all this is waste. The very act of project status reporting, once you have moved your projects to a collaborative visual management system (as modern vendors and we suggest), just falls off the spoon. The work is captured because it is interwoven with the workflow (like e-mail and

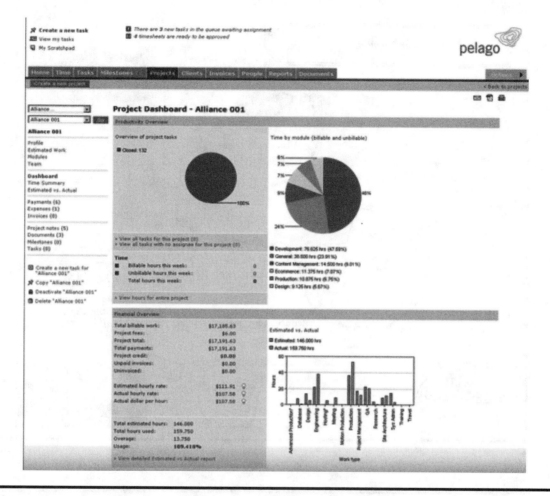

Figure 9.7 A key advantage of the Web 2.0 collaboration tools is the ability to quickly provide up-to-date status, clearly influenced by business intelligence trends; whereas legacy planning tools are relatively static, however accurate at inception.

Outlook). The reporting tools can then provide customized, accurate views in real time.

This does not mean that project management is obsolete. It only means that there are far more effective ways to gather, format, and report the data feeding the project management function. The result moves project managers up the value curve of activities and focuses them on analysis and planning rather than wading through old information and optimistic schedules to learn true status.

The Lean Journal

In Chapter 6, we represented the Lean journey as movement along a two-dimensional grid of quality and efficiency. We used this device to explain the benefits of Lean and its superiority in many ways to other improvement methods. We also wanted to strip the idea of the "Lean journey" of any vestige of metaphysics or Eastern philosophy. We are talking about quantified movement on a Cartesian

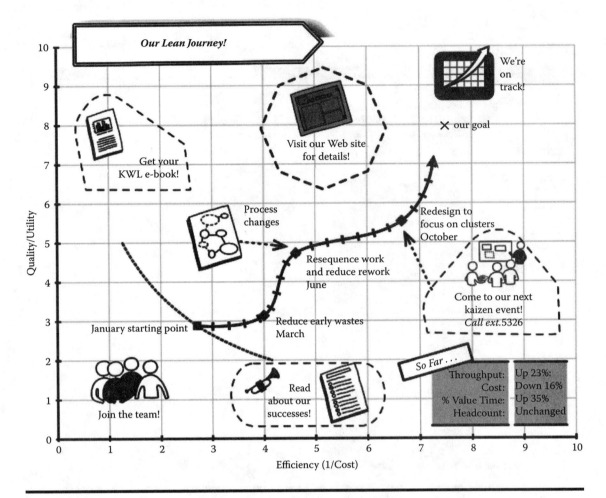

Figure 9.8   An example of communicating and celebrating the ongoing Lean journey.

coordinate system where one axis is hard cash and the other is critical performance. Nothing could be more hard-bitten Western management than this. Note that in Figure 9.8 we are graphing a process performance against objective quantifiable metrics of performance and cost. We are also using changes in the x and y values to tell a story of improvement and change, and illustrating that story with tangible examples. We are appealing to both sides of the brain as well as addressing the important so-what questions of both management and process workers.

After all, Lean must spread in order to grow. One or two pockets of Lean will not survive long, if for no other reason than because Lean is so tied to the attitudes of the workers and the workers are mobile. You can't step into the same river twice, and the Lean process will regress as new knowledge workers, who were not a part of the journey, join the group. However, if we spread it throughout the organization and make everyone a part of the journey, then we'll be replacing Lean workers with other Lean workers.

Chapter 10

Change Management: Practical Lessons from Monks, Generals, and Fashion Models

Lean adoption must be broad and deep. It is often at odds with legacy processes and attitudes, and, therefore, change management is the essential part of making your Lean journey successful.

> Nobody ever listened themselves out of a job.
>
> **—Calvin Coolidge**

President Coolidge has a point. The assignment of the Lean evangelist or proponent can be a risky one. In the right environment, you are poised to be an innovator, a leader, a successful change agent. In the wrong environment, you are a nonconformist, a troublemaker, or at best a starry-eyed worker who spends all of his or her time dreaming up improvements instead of getting the job done.

Anyone undertaking Lean in the latter workplace should think long and hard about his or her approach, gain support from upper management, build a support structure, and have a way to promote or evangelize your successes. Start small and build, but not so small that your efforts get lost in the details.

Three Ways to Lead Lean

We call the three most common paths to Lean implementation in the United States and Europe the path of the monk, the general, and the fashion model.

Those who choose the path of the monk study Lean. They read books about Lean, take training courses, and perhaps gain a certification. Their knowledge of the theory grows and eventually they find themselves participating or leading a

Lean effort. Like the monk, they are focused on studying and developing their own understanding and skill rather than concerning themselves with the worldly community at large (the rest of the company). Few of their coworkers have their depth and breadth of understanding or their command of the language and tools of Lean. Even if their project is a success, it is not likely to spread or sustain itself. It has been too insular and isolated. Perhaps there has been too much emphasis on theory and the purity of Lean and not enough on just going out there, getting started, and enlisting the contributions and insights, even the untutored ones, of others.

Generals decide that there shall be Lean. They develop a strategy and detailed operations plan, carefully select a team, set objectives, provide funding and resources, and launch their attack. It is highly likely that they will succeed—at first. They have too much talent, resources, and publicity to fail. "Mission Accomplished" banners pop up in the corporate communications documents. A year later, most likely, it will be forgotten and people will have moved on.

The general has made the fundamental mistake of turning Lean into a project. It is not. Lean is a way of working and, unless fully inculcated into the right workforce, it will not be sustainable. The handpicked team of hotshots selected will get a tick in the box and paragraph on their resume and move on to new challenges. Even if the managers and workers retain the Lean improvements that were developed, they are not likely to build upon them and make that a fundamental approach to work. They will be trying to support the next big project.

The fashion model's approach is the right way to see a Lean project. They, and their attire, are ahead of the trends. Fashion models very publicly display these leading concepts. No coercion, no management fiat—a simple subtext that you, too, could be like this if you try. Fashion models are highly networked influencers. If others adopt their fashions, they will not quibble about the correctness of their interpretation. What matters is that they try to actively seek continuous improvement.

The Rules of Success: People, People, People

Thus far, we have written about methodologies, tools, and Lean background, and have developed some new approaches. That's the easy stuff. We have never had a project come up empty handed in terms of improvement ideas or in discovering meaningful as-is improvement potential. However, we have had projects fail and Lean journeys cut short. It is always a change management issue, sometimes with the sponsor, sometimes with a rival stakeholder set, but usually with the rank-and-file and middle management, although they stood to gain the most from Lean.

We like to think this situation will improve, the demographics are in our favor as a younger workforce has grown up embracing new tools and, much more important, expecting that change will happen because they have seen so much change in such a short time. The big Motorola "brick" cell phone that receives so much fanfare in the movie *Wall Street* seems to have the size and feature set of a small refrigerator next to an iPhone. Perhaps by the time you read this the iPhone too will have been superseded to the point of quaintness.

Most managers today think of e-mail as state of the art; maybe not all in high tech do, but certainly managers in industry. Their workers are already sharing files on Google Docs and posting minute progress reports on Twitter. We look forward to working more with them.

People are critical: Pick them carefully and never let the neat technical solution cause you to lose sight of them.

Performance Management

Everyone at all levels should have a good understanding of company and area-related issues, and should be capable of contributing to all the issues on which they feel qualified. Organizations should consider the following:

- What—Effective meetings only discussing relevant information and issues based on actions and feedback.
- How—Log data using effective visual displays, that is, handover logs and control boards, which are updated every day at all levels of leadership. Major issues and performance from the previous day should be reviewed, expectations for the coming day discussed, and follow-up investigation and countermeasure activity applied when necessary.

Process Tip: Use the Socratic Approach

Learning is truly great when it harmonizes with these ideas, that is, harmonizes with the nature of the knowledge worker. The chief challenge for an organization is to put the ideas that are common to the knowledge worker into the office environment. No one can talk us into these common, primary ideas. No lecture can plant these in our minds. They are already there—the accumulated experience, hunches, and innovative thinking of your resource team. The task is to bring them out.

Here, dialogue between individuals in the organization is vital, but we also use words to make our own thoughts clear to ourselves. Without words, we would be hard pressed to understand anything. Dialogue with a fellow knowledge worker in the office often helps us clarify to ourselves just what we really do mean, especially when the colleague has asked the right questions. A good coach is able through the right questions to make us aware of our most basic ideas in the light of which we are able to make judgments about other things.

There are two ways to gain knowledge—either through discovery or by being taught. To be taught presupposes that someone has discovered the knowledge already, which the person later may communicate to another. When knowledge workers learn from one another, they are in effect led to relive the discoverer's experience, and they may indeed avoid the many blind alleys the discoverer undoubtedly followed, but they must necessarily see the first truths just as the discoverer did.

It may be a truism that the office workers are the primary actors in their own learning, but nowhere is it truer than in the beginning of the Lean journey. Lectures hardly help. Something more is required; something that turns awareness back on itself. This is why Socrates searched the souls of his disciples with questions. If any responded saying, "I have heard such and such …," he would invariably reply, "But what do you think?" He was not asking for their opinions; he was asking what they thought and knew about things.

It is not easy to say accurately what we really think. Often upon hearing a response, Socrates would ask, "Don't you also think such and such about it? How do these two ideas fit together?" The discussion would continue until the disciples began to harmonize their own thoughts. Socrates was not ready to quit until disciples delivered their own brainchild by their own labor, for until disciples could bring their own concept out and into the light of day, they would never know what they really knew.

There are no shortcuts to real knowledge. Neither sophisticated information technology, nor audiovisual techniques, nor even lectures can make us see. An office worker may be able to take up technology in its latest form without having to go back to the first inventions and repeat all the labors of their ancestors. Over 2,000 years ago, Socrates saw what was crucial to human learning. Funny enough, this is still more than valid for the knowledge worker practicing Lean.

- Why does Nathalie have such a backlog? Because she has more open work than the rest of her team members.
- Why does Nathalie have so many open work tasks? That is because Joe, Peter, and Ann route many of their tasks to her.
- Why do Joe, Peter, and Ann route many of their tasks to Nathalie? Because Nathalie is the only one in the team who can do complex insurance calculations.
- Why is Nathalie the only one who can do complex insurance calculations? Because she is the only one who has taken the course on complex insurance calculations.
- Why is Nathalie the only team member who has taken the course on complex insurance calculations? Because the training department allocated training for one team member for this year based on the projected workload of incoming insurance requests based on information from the current business plan done by corporate.

This line of reasoning is known as the Socratic method. It has five readily distinguishable characteristics:

1. *It is skeptical.* It begins with Socrates' real or professed ignorance of the truth of the matter under discussion. This is the Socratic irony, which seemed to some of their listeners an insincere pretense, but which was undoubtedly an expression of Socrates' genuine intellectual humility. Socratic skepticism is tentative and provisional rather than definitive and final; Socrates' doubt and assumed ignorance is an indispensable first step in the pursuit of knowledge.
2. *It is conversational.* It employs the dialogue not only as a didactic device, but also as a technique for the actual discovery of opinions. There are truths with which all can agree, and Socrates proceeds to unfold such truths by discussion and question and answer. Beginning with a popular or hastily formed conception, Socrates subjects the notion to severe criticism, and, as a result, a more adequate conception emerges. The method brings other people's ideas to birth.
3. *It is conceptual or definitional* in that it sets as the goal of knowledge the acquisition of concepts, such as the ethical concepts of justice, piety, wisdom, courage, and the like. Socrates tacitly assumes that truth is embodied in correct definition. Precise definition of terms is held to be the first step in the problem-solving process.
4. *It is empirical or inductive* in that the proposed definitions are criticized by reference to particular instances. Socrates always tested definitions by recourse to common experience and to general practice.
5. *It is deductive.* A given definition is tested by drawing out its implications, and by deducing its consequences.

Change Management: The Soft Part Is the Hard Part

The only true competitive evolutionary advantage is not size or speed but the ability to handle change. The soft part is the hard part, a quote ascribed to Dr. Michael Hammer stated in his and James Champy's best-selling book: *Reengineering the Corporation: A Manifesto for Business Revolution.* "The technical problems are the easy problems… the soft suff is the hard stuff," accurately describes the Lean practitioner's true challenge: change management. Lean is much more about the cumulative effects of a large number of practical, typically small-scale improvements than it is about a major redesign. The latter comes with significant investment and risk, and warrants study, business cases, and so on.

Lean improvements are quicker, simpler, tactical, and involve less risk. The governing philosophy is something like "Let's try this." If the proposed improvement fails to prove itself, it can be reversed or modified. Another change is tried, perhaps several in parallel. To some people this is the definition of a motivated team working hard to take waste out of the business, improve performance, and continuously improve. To others it looks like reckless chaos. There is no such thing as an organization exclusively peopled by one or the other kind of individuals. You have to decide which type describes you or, to be more accurate, where on the spectrum between these two points you lie. Of course, you also have to ask this of the other stakeholders, your boss, or your client. The same question is true for the process owners, their colleagues and direct reports, their upstream and downstream process owners. The list goes on. This is the starting point for the "hard part," and it will dictate your entire engagement plan: how fast to go, how broad to go, level of documentation or financial justification to support each idea, and where to start.

We have never been lucky enough to work in or for an organization that had a plurality of eager change agents. A typical change project often has two major challenges: (1) a limited budget and (2) a high risk-of-failure aversion. Both these forces tend to keep the change agents focused on the space delimited within the four corners of their proposal or work plan. Trying new things or deviating from the work plan or methodological book creates financial and reputation risk that is often far larger than the engagement itself. It is like a chess player who memorizes a great many standard openings. This is an excellent, indeed ubiquitous, approach, and everything goes fine until your opponent moves "out of book." Sadly, sponsors or process owners have an annoying tendency to do just that. It would seem to be their specialty. So the ability to think quickly on your feet, and use initiative and improvisation, becomes critical to the Lean practitioner. We stress this because it is probably even more important for the Knowledge Worker Lean project than it is for Factory Lean.

In a sports team it is nice to have a great coach, excellent training facilities, a solid game plan, and so forth, but we would argue that the single biggest driver of success is the quality of the players. If Lean is all about change, then the most important quality your team can have is changeability. A journeyman or even an apprentice who is eager to improve will become more valuable than a highly experienced resource who doesn't think things should change or feels you have nothing to teach him or her.

We are reminded of a popular story in the MIT (Massachusetts Institute of Technology) oral tradition. During World War II, the U.S. Army desperately wanted a radar system small enough to fit into a night-fighting airplane. The Army approached the brilliant Norbert Wiener, sometimes referred to as the father of cybernetics. Wiener was asked to head up a lavishly funded program, and he replied by submitting a list of talented graduate students he wanted for his team. "You don't understand," replied the flustered officer in charge of the program. "You can have whomever you want, department heads, the top men in the field...." But Wiener had his reasons. "What you are asking me to do is impossible. The experts you cite already know this. I need a group that doesn't know it's impossible and will go out and do it." Experience is an excellent teacher, but sometimes it is too good at teaching what won't work. After all, these Lean innovations are public, significant, involve others, and are meant to contribute to the success of the corporation. Failed projects might imply a lack of leadership, instinct, implementation, what have you, and become the negative career baggage that nobody wants to lug around.

The more fanfare surrounding the Lean project, the greater the expectations and visibility, and, often, the greater perceived risk of failure. Two common results of this are (1) low expectations surrounding Lean, setting the high-jump bar too low, and (2) the compromise selection of safe projects. How many times have you seen a presentation on Lean or a set of guidelines suggesting a very carefully chosen pilot study, one that can safely be expected to deliver a positive result? This combination of forces tends to deliver a yawn-inducing result. If you want to impress people with the capabilities of your new computer, you don't show them how it can balance your checkbook. You can make many stronger selling points. As any change agent or salesperson with a new thing knows, there are danger signs to watch out for and questions to ask.

Drivers of waste include:

- Unnecessary hierarchy
- Unclear roles, responsibilities, and authorities
- Inadequate knowledge and skills
- Undesirable interruptions
- Projects taken on or started for appearance rather than efficiency or need
- Unused talents
- Rigid and heavy worked hierarchy and structure
- Poor or inappropriate recruiting
- Lack of clear objectives and strategies or disintegration of these

Questions to ask include:

- How long has the business process been in place in its current form?
- How long have the process owners been working there?
- How personally vested are they in the design, development, and execution of the process?
- Has the process been under attack from other parts of the organization and have the process owners already successfully fended off such attacks?
- Are the performance metrics missing, or vague, or complicated enough to allow for more than one interpretation?
- How hierarchical is the culture?

Case Study: The Reengineer, His Mother, and the Coffee

While home on vacation one morning, the reengineer strolled into the kitchen and found his mother making coffee. Since he drinks a lot of coffee, this normally would have been a good thing, but he was a bright-eyed process reengineer and his mind was still on work and not using the very different part of the brain he used for family interactions. Rather than saying something pleasantly innocuous or talking about the weather, he found himself making process observations.

"Mom," he said, "instead of pouring coffee, adding milk, and then stirring it up, why don't you put the milk in first?" This epiphany had come to him in a flash and he grew more and more animated as he described all the advantages of his reengineered coffee-making process.

"You see, when you add the coffee to the milk in the bottom of the cup it mixes itself so there's no need for stirring. This makes the whole thing two steps instead of three steps, so there is inherently less risk of a failure, and two steps are faster than three, so you reduce cycle time. It also makes a better quality product because sometimes when you add milk you haven't left enough room to get the coffee color you are looking for. I'll bet that the topping-off process leads to spills, so it improves on safety performance as well."

As all these unassailable arguments were mounting in his head, the reengineer was growing more and more convinced that he was really onto something.

"Even more, since there's no stirring, you no longer need spoons or stir sticks. Think of the advantages. There is no spoon procurement, spoon inventory, spoon maintenance. All those processes have been eliminated, plus you free up inventory space in your cabinets and you don't have money tied up in spoons that you don't need. All of that is true for stir sticks as well and you eliminate hazardous waste disposal from the used stir sticks. It's really the perfect process redesign: improves speed, reduces costs, eliminates waste, increases quality and safety, and it can be put into effect immediately with no training or investment. It's brilliant."

Throughout this evangelism, his mother stood impassively, patiently absorbing all this with few outward signs of emotion. Any hope that he was scoring big points, not to mention justifying a long and expensive educational investment, was soon put to rest. Rather than comment on each point piecemeal, his mother cut to the chase. "I've raised an idiot," she calmly declared and walked from the room.

Now the point of this (painfully true) story is not to comment on the relationship between the reengineer and his mother. The point of the story is not that the client, played in this case by the mother, had failed to appreciate the Lean suggestions, but rather that the reengineer had failed to understand the situation. Every experienced practitioner will tell you that the challenge in most process redesign work lies in the change management and acceptance of the new design and not in creating the design itself.

What is illustrated by this story is that process owners will naturally consider themselves to be experts. Your revised process can easily be interpreted as an argument that they are not. This is rarely a welcomed thought. Any good practitioner understands that change management has to be built into the redesign. Lean efforts put that change in the hands of the workers; after all, it is natural to adopt a change that you created yourself. The difference between Lean and business process reengineering (BPR), among others, is that the former treats the process-owning stakeholders as an engine to be harnessed rather than an audience to be convinced.

Information Lean Is A Man-Machine System

An old military adage says something like, "Amateurs focus on tactics, journeymen on strategy, but masters concern themselves with logistics." The parallels to our challenge are easy to make.

It is simpler and easier to look at off-the-shelf software tools and explicit methodologies—magic bullets like templates and checklists of procedures—and expect to apply Lean to knowledge work.

A broader view would be to look at enterprisewide drivers: the adoption of spiral or agile approaches at the high level, building progress management into the workflow rather than keeping it as a parallel function, the effects of work in process and the way you manage your portfolio of work, and the redesign of your organization to support throughput rather than budgets. This would include bringing IT into the Lean fold to provide the visual management tools but also to modify their interaction with the other business units to emphasize fast response rather than project controls.

As a parallel to logistics, we would suggest that the people element should be the master class point of focus. Technology is making communication both faster and broader by increasing the size of the individual worker's one-touch-away network. Ever-increasing communication speeds and a broader contact list makes for exponential growth in the networked complexity of communications. As information transfer networks increase in complexity and speed, the negative feedback of miscommunication (missed e-mails, unread attachments, comments on already outdated information, etc.) increase. The situation is already becoming unsustainable as attested to by the widespread carping about e-mail overload and the rush by software companies to develop better teaming solutions. The resources need to see these techniques as valuable rather than as additional procedural overhead. They must adopt shared/collaborative views, with true progress reporting that is so evident that a newcomer can get an accurate sense at a glance. If your team sees the speed and simplicity of e-mail as the best of all possible worlds then your challenge is simple.

Information Lean is a man-machine system, but a great tool or an agile process delivered to the unprepared or unwilling either will be an instant failure or, over time, will regress to the old ways. It will drive home the message that this stuff doesn't work, or at least doesn't work here. You need a long view: bring new resources into the organization, develop pilots and broadcast their success, provide training, shunt the obstacle resources aside, and do it all in plain sight so the messages can propagate throughout the organization as undiluted as possible.

Overcoming Resistance to Lean

We firmly believe that the fundamental driver of Lean and the greatest predictor of success is the attitude to change held and exhibited by the process owners, their superiors, and the corporate culture they inhabit. Change is strongly tied to strong emotional and rational drivers. The emotional ones take the form of resistance for what seems like either obstinate or peevish reasons. You've heard them all before. If you are a change agent, they are old friends, the banes of your existence, but well known nonetheless: We've always done it this way. That's the way I was taught. Nobody's told me I could change this. This is our policy and procedure. If it isn't broke, don't fix it. We shouldn't try to change too many things too soon. The rational ones are covered in the fabric of business-case type thinking: We don't have the budget for it. I don't have time to learn, install, or develop a new system. It'll take too long to see results. The potential benefits are exaggerated or may never materialize.

We don't mean to make light of this. Even if the expressed arguments are paper thin, they are only the expression of resistance that may be rock hard. The Lean leader or change agent needs to address each one. The emotional resistance arguments are often addressed through the executive sponsorship, the team majority working on the Lean problem, and the design of the implementation or test adoption plan, which can be structured to ease some of these concerns. The rational objections have to be addressed using the return on investment logic they are couched in. The problem with most of the rational objectors is that they have done the analysis without doing the analysis; they are expressing the theory of return on investment without developing the details and working through the answer. A little data, a value stream analysis, some illustrations of the as-is process's weakness all go a long way toward convincing the rational holdouts.

Tool Tip: A Lean business case must be simple and basic:

"We can do this in three steps instead of eleven."
"Let's stop checking the same calculation three times in different
   stages of the process."
"Our works sits idle most of the time."
And so on.

In fact, the need to write a detailed business case, certainly one with spreadsheets and time-value-of-money components, is a fair indicator that it's not really a Lean idea at all.

Nonlinear Risk Aversion

The important, and far more interesting, third type of resistance is a combination of the emotional and the rational. This "emo-rational" element is a modification of the rational return on investment approach. It overlays the fear component of the emotional approach, which gives greater weight to bad results than it does to good results, particularly large results, good and bad. The result is a nonlinear risk aversion curve, and understanding nonlinear risk aversion is essential to developing and deploying your Lean initiative as well as one of the strongest reasons for selecting Lean.

Anyone who has ever played a few hands of poker has felt these nonlinear effects. If you are playing for pennies or matchsticks, you are curious to see the last card. Does the man in the black hat really have a flush? The situation is very different when you are playing for real "hurt-to-lose" stakes. In fact, there is not much point to playing poker unless the stakes are in that vicinity. Even if the risk you are avoiding is not financial but emotional because you're playing against your buddies, there's not much point in making the call or fold decision unless there are consequences. Otherwise, you could just turn over the cards or play solitaire. A characteristic that to varying degrees top poker players have is the ability to not be affected by the scale of the bet. If the cost of seeing the last card is X (investment at the margin) and the chance of winning is Y percent (OK, good poker players are also better at determining this number), and the return (size of the pot) is Z, then the question should be is $X > (Y \times Z)$. But does it?

Case Study: Nonlinear Risk Aversion

Assume you are discussing strategy and risk to a room full of people, and you introduce a simple game to illustrate the point. The game is to hypothetically auction off a ticket to the highest bidder. There is a 50/50 chance of winning the prize, say $20. Whoever submits the highest bid walks to the front of the room for a coin toss: heads the winner gets the $20, tails the person gets nothing. The audience is to write their bids and names on slips of paper, which are collected and brought to the front.

You graph the bids on a coordinate system along a horizontal line representing 20. Now, presumably everyone in the room can calculate that 50 percent of $20 is $10, but what is the point in bidding $10? The point is to get a bargain; otherwise, you have participated in an elaborate game to exchange things of the same value. On the other hand, there would seem to be no point in bidding too low, a nickel, for example, because you could not possibly win the competitive auction. Depending upon your audience, bids vary widely. Many people bid extremely low; the number of bids diminishes as they approach $10.

Next, repeat the exercise but instead of a $20 hypothetical prize, increase it to $100. Again collect the bids and graph them on the 100 value line. You will find that people did not increase their bids fivefold and some hardly increased their bids at all. Nobody bid $50, or $49. The high bid is about $45 and there are several in the $30 to $40 range. You can repeat this at $300 or higher and as you draw a line though the main cluster of points, you'll see how it matches up. The perceived risk outweighs the perceived gain even though they are mathematically the same.

But this is all just talk. Next, savvy facilitator that you are, hold up real money, three crisp $100 bills, and invite the group to bid. This time it is for real, highest bidder pays up front and never sees his or her money again. If the coin comes up heads, the bidder gets the $300, tails the bidder sits down. You will notice significantly fewer bids, usually only from about half the audience, and you will be lucky if you get a $100 bid as an outlying high value.

Personality differences add a lot of noise to the data, that is, objections to any type of gambling, showing off, and so forth. We wouldn't recommend using this as an instrument to graph a group's actual risk aversion curve (believe me, we learned the hard way), but it's an excellent way to drive home the lesson that high risk trumps high gain *every* time. There are some curious industry differences. Finance and Wall Street audiences, for example, skew far to the right. You would think that professional money people would never bid above the evaluated contract price, but the winning bids are usually above it and a very high percentage are clustered near it. Competitiveness and extreme confidence are largely to blame. Win or lose, they want to be the player at the front of the room, the one who eats risk for breakfast, which has an out-of-exercise reputation value that they take into account when they bid.

Assuming that your Lean process is not a high-stakes money trading operation or the like, you have to consider the risk aversion curve. Remember, too, that Lean is really owned by the process workers. In our experience, that tends to shift the curve even further down. The departmental vice president may be used to working with large budget numbers, but the line workers are used to keeping their head down. We were working on a Lean accounting project where one of the issues we were dealing with was that too much time and money was spent reviewing very small invoices. The process owner pointed out that recently a $5 invoice had been handled several times by senior clerks. This company is large and multinational and many millions pass through its invoice-handling process. When we asked the process owner where to draw the large to small invoice demarcation that would trigger greater attention and review, the owner thought about it for a moment and said $20. As an accounting professional, the owner was more focused on the idea of a mistake than the dollar impact. We were able to produce statistics on the invoices showing that $20 would not exclude very many and that the invoices above $1,000 represented only 10 percent of the work but 90 percent of the value. We eventually, in a group setting with reinforcements, compromised on $500.

Our suggested approach for the Lean team is to own and deliver against multiple small projects simultaneously because they can cope with the risk/reward ratio, to only do one or two medium projects, and to present the larger projects to the executive sponsorship.

The takeaway from this discussion of risk is that individual Lean ideas are smaller in scope than BPR or Six Sigma, so they have a relative perception advantage since they are on a lower part of the risk aversion curve where benefits and risks are more likely to be balanced. Because of the risk aversion curve, you can take long shots on the smaller projects but not the larger. Small Lean ideas can be risky, medium ones need to be far less risky, and large ones need to be very safe or their risk has to be underwritten by the executive sponsors.

Turning Your Lean Project into a Lean Culture: Measuring Performance

Just think for a minute of all the process-oriented methodologies that have contributed various insights over the last century. They include all the efficiency improvements of scientific management, which were then followed by the mass production efficiencies of specialization and scale from Ford and Sloan, and others that were the backbone of heavy industry and big business: statistical process control and the total quality management movement, just-in-time manufacturing, business process reengineering, Six Sigma, the Toyota Production System, and Lean.

During this time, while the understanding, analysis, and improvement of business processes was undergoing revolutionary change, the accounting tools that might be used to quantify and display these improvements have been largely stagnant. The generally accepted accounting practices (GAAP) have been largely unchanged since Gilbreth's day.

How can Lean process improvements be appreciated or evaluated when they broadcast FM results in a world of only AM receivers?

Until now, white collar processes have used cost as a key performance metric, probably the dominant one. Table 10.1 illustrates the necessary shift in metrics and guiding principles.

Table 10.1 The Necessary Shift in Guiding Principles

Rank	Traditional Guiding Metrics	Lean Guiding Metrics
1	Low operating costs	High throughput
2	Fat pipeline of projects	Low work in process
3	High utilization, high input	Balanced line, high output

Don't Rely on the 100th Monkey: Planning for Lean

There is a new-age legend that supposedly describes a paranormal dimension to the dissemination of new practices. It's based on some field studies in the 1950s with Macaw monkeys. As the story goes, monkeys scattered across several islands were nonetheless able to spread cultural development. If monkeys learned to wash sweet potatoes before eating them, they would pass this on to others in their group and teach it to the younglings. Mysteriously, once the new skill had spread to about 100 monkeys, the new knowledge would somehow leap across the water to monkey populations on other islands.

Take our word for it. Do not rely on this phenomenon with your office Lean project. Spreading Lean is hard, carefully calculated work. Like all such work, when it is done correctly it appears effortless and people working on other projects seem to spring up and request advice or assistance in bringing Lean to their processes.

The first Lean success tends to spawn imitators, either self-sown weeds or carefully cultivated gardens; both are good. These Lean spinoffs tend to drain resources from the original Lean group. Keeping the original Lean colony thriving is very important or else Lean will take on a project flavor rather than a cultural flavor. We believe that spreading Lean to the next generation of teams and processes is vital; the positive feedback and knowledge sharing from these later Lean "colonies" will support and reinforce the original one. Soon you will have a network of Lean leaders not only improving their processes, but also sharing and building upon one another's successes.

If they receive the proper credit and support, then you should be well on your way to your Lean tipping point. There are too many shoulds in this approach. Successful Lean office implementation has to be its own advocate and prove its contribution. In today's business world, that means prove its return on investment.

The PDCA Cycle

PDCA is a cycle of activities—plan, do, check, act—designed to drive continuous improvements. Initially implemented in manufacturing, it has broad applicability in business. The benefits are:

- Plan—Establish the objectives and processes necessary to deliver results in accordance with the specifications.
- Do—Implement the processes.
- Check—Monitor and evaluate the processes and results against objectives and specifications, and report the outcome.
- Act—Apply actions to the outcome for necessary improvement.

Setting the standards is the most important activity within the PDCA circle.

Change management is a structured approach to transitioning individuals, teams, and organizations from a current state to a desired future state. The current definition of change management includes both organizational change management processes and individual change management models, which together are used to manage the people side of change.

Many of the traditionally designed and executed approaches to managing change fail to address the complexity of today's business world. Often too one-dimensional, they struggle to cope with the nuances of changing human attitudes and behavior. The increasing power of information and communications technologies and faster communications have allowed the life of the knowledge worker and the highly information intense processes to be disaggregated.

Managing change means managing reality, not just a plan. A strictly linear, monochrome approach to change is bound to fail as a result of the complexity and diversity of today's knowledge worker environment. We need to recognize the inherent weakness in driving change via a simple linear project approach. It is rare indeed for the project office and a Gantt chart to bring about a shift in human behavior.

The fashion model analogy emphasized viral spread as the preferred approach to create interest and drive adoption of improved ways of working. Lean can only be done by involving the line organization. People are much more likely to be engaged and energized by a change process in which they are actively participating and when they clearly understand the benefits for themselves and the organization as a whole. Engaging and enabling people at all levels across the organization is the key to creating commitment through shared understanding, overcoming potential barriers to change, and building momentum for the new vision.

In Japanese factories you find that the machines are built around the humans. They are there to support the humans. The humans are not there to support the machines, which sometimes is suspected to be the case in U.S. or European factories. To build your capabilities to the point where you can deliver Lean successfully, you need to focus on the humans.

However it may be achieved, change management always boils down to embedding new behaviors. Organizations often revert to old, familiar ways of working once the initial energy of the change program has passed and there is no longer a focus on these activities. A new software or hardware system may survive this loss of human focus but it negates the benefits of improvement, which relies on behavioral change, such as people interacting differently with customers and their colleagues, following new priorities, or working with new processes. Therefore, sustainable *behavioral* change becomes the key ingredient to achieving long-term benefits. This is one of the reasons we emphasize collaboration tools and visual management: to support social reinforcing behavior. As a Lean practitioner, your success comes when the term *project* is no longer used in connection with Lean in your organization. Projects have beginnings and ends, improvement does not.

Chapter 11

Knowledge Worker Lean: The Takeaway

What practical advice and hard-won tips can we share about the application of the tools and techniques needed to implement Knowledge Worker Lean? What's the inside story?

In theory, there is no difference between theory and practice. But in practice there is.

—Jan Van de Snepscheut

We have discussed a lot of theory and background, reviewed many tools and techniques, and described step-by-step procedures for applying them. Now it is fitting that we stop and put some of these things into context. What really works? What are the two or three things that always gum up the works? In this chapter, we walk through a Lean implementation at a very high level and stop several times to create journal entries. Keep these close by. They are the tips and hints, critical success factors, and warning signs. They have all been learned the best way—the hard way.

Challenge 1: Getting Up and Getting Going

Unless the company in question has Lean well established as an operating principle, your Lean journey is likely to begin with some kind of a problem statement from senior management. This is true regardless of whether you are an internal resource leading a Lean effort or an external consultant, though in the latter case you are likely to be describing the problem to the executive and in the former it is the other way around.

In the case of the external consultant, the problem statement and overall scope and timetable are matters covered in the proposal (though sometimes services are proposed on a run rate or the scope is only specified through an early phase of work to mitigate risk). Internal Lean leaders have a tougher job. They will neither be capable of codifying the project upfront in the same detail that an external consultant would nor afforded the luxury of a "diagnostic phase," because they are already part of the organization. There is also the possibility that their backgrounds may suggest some predetermined or prejudicial position to some of the other stakeholders.

Step 1: Meet the Boss; Obtain Buy-in

The important thing, for both external and internal Lean resources, is determining the degree of executive sponsorship that exists. Is senior management truly undertaking a Lean journey, with the long-term view and dedication that this implies, or are they looking for a process redesign project? Worse, are they looking for a cost reduction effort with some Lean fairy dust sprinkled on it? The easiest way to tell, from our experience, is from the commitment in resources, reputation, and time that senior management is willing to dedicate to this effort. Translated, this means that they are willing to free up top resources (not just those currently "unassigned"), they will have a visible role in representing Lean to the organization, and they have a horizon view of continuous improvement.

Step 2: Meet the Process Owner; Assess Commitment

Next, you must gauge the commitment of the process owner. Is this person's problem statement even close to that of senior management? In our experience, "close" is more than good enough. Two people in the same organization rarely attribute the same fundamental explanation to a problem, especially if one of them owns the problem. The process owner's reaction will tell you a lot about the Lean challenges to change management that lie ahead.

What if the process owner sees this as an attack on his budget? Is it an indictment of his performance? Does he express the problem in terms of people or relationships (they give us poor material, or late deliveries, etc.) or does he have a systems view? Is he speaking in terms of the customer needs or of his budget? Is he using the same evaluation criteria as senior management or his customers? Some may be worried about quality, others about cycle time and throughput, and others about overall cost. Are they aligned?

You can also learn a lot by how the process owner talks about his peers upstream and downstream in the internal process and in the supply chain. Does he see them as obstacles or partners? How strongly does he value the internal customer role?

By the way, your Lean work is not likely to succeed without the cooperation and support of the process owner. By definition, process owners should be leading the Lean efforts as they relate to their particular process. If Lean leaders are successful, they soon will be and that will be a key element sustaining Lean. Therefore, work hard to get process owners on board, give their ideas a prominent place, transfer Lean principles, and provide whatever background and training they may need. In other words, the Lean leader's job is to make process owners succeed and to make themselves redundant. Above all, you must ensure that process owners see waste in their organization as a positive finding leading toward future success, and not as a discovery and documentation of past faults.

Step 3: Get a Feel for the Process and the People

In the very early days of the Lean journey, you will develop some high-level feel for the process. Perhaps you are involved in the process and already have this; perhaps you will get your first impressions by going to gemba and experiencing the process firsthand in detail.

What are your initial impressions?

- Does your team's process expert feel that it is an up-to-date approach or is it a generation behind in technology or methodology?
- Do the direct contributors feel they are doing a good job or are they quick with excuses and mitigating factors to explain weak numbers or customer complaints?
- Is it somebody else's fault? The supplier, the union, the field, the upstream group, and so forth.
- Are the direct contributors able to use the full IT set of tools?
- Is performance measured and monitored by the direct contributors or is there a parallel project management organization? Does the latter report to management or collaborate with process owners?
- How do they see change? Is it an unfair imposition on their time to make them learn something new or are they excited about doing things better?
- How are you and your team received in the workplace? Are you outsiders causing disruption? Are you the "downsizers"?
- Do people seem interested in sharing their ideas about making improvements?
- Do you get the sense that some of the workers plan to ride this storm out by keeping quiet, keeping out of the way, and waiting for the effort to peter out?

During the early phases of Lean, we often find workers who are intensely relieved to have an official outlet for their suggestions and ideas. The absence of this, or in its place the existence of reticence, skepticism, or denial, is indicative of a tough change management problem. Even if your team develops great ideas, they will be a hard sell at the very place where they should be embraced, at the direct contributor level. If you are an external consultant, now is the time to reread the section in your proposal titled "change orders." If you are an internal Lean resource, settle down for a longer haul and make sure your sponsor is aware of this.

Finally, how can you measure or represent success? Within the culture and systems of this process, what data can we use and what data will be convincing? Were these process workers interested in value stream measurements, cycle-time reductions, customer feedback, or something else?

The Takeaway: How to Begin

The key questions to ask before you begin are:

- Are we really doing Lean? Or do "they" envision something else?
- Can our culture (workers, managers, stakeholders) adopt Lean?
- How much time do I have to show progress? This will help you prioritize your ideas to, if necessary, show some quick wins on which to build Lean acceptance and momentum.

What Can Go Wrong

This early phase is critical. In keeping with Hammer's dictum, "the soft part is the hard part," and this early phase is where the tone is set for all the soft parts. It is critical that you have the right executive sponsorship, strong working partnerships with the process owners and other key workers, and enough process improvement potential to serve as grist for your Lean mill.

Understanding the charter

- ☐ Is there a clear problem statement?
- ☐ Is the problem view shared by management and process owners?
- ☐ Is there executive sponsorship and support for true lean and continuous improvement?
- ☐ Do we have resources (team, IT, time...)?
- ☐ Do we know the extended stakeholders' positions?
- ☐ How quickly can our culture adopt a Lean view?
- ☐ Do we need quick wins to sustain the initiative?

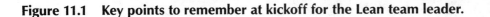

Figure 11.1   Key points to remember at kickoff for the Lean team leader.

Challenge 2: Creating a Lean Team

The key thing in selecting and forming a winning team to support a Lean journey is to bear in mind that the individuals must be subsumed by the team. In other words, don't try to create a team packed with the stars of the organization (OK, this would probably be a great team, but you will never get it) but rather an all-star team where each of the members contributes something. The ingredients for a successful Lean team are:

- At least one member well-versed in Lean (two would be better).
- One team member expert in the process. It is even better if the person's expertise is in the same process somewhere else, for example, a former employer or competitor.
- At least one expert communicator. This does not mean an Ivy League vocabulary or killer PowerPoint skills. This means likability, empathy, trust, credibility, and so on—all the things necessary to get straight answers and smooth ruffled feathers.
- One strong analytical jack-of-all-trades: VSM, spreadsheet, statistics, and Web site–building skills.

Of course, if you have a larger team you may have more than one in each category, but you need to have each category covered. Five point guards are not going to win the NBA championship; you need a well-rounded team.

Picking & Coaching the Lean Team

☐ Convince them — "There is no plan"
☐ Focus on their Strengths, not Weakness
☐ It's about Systems, not people
☐ Mistakes are ok -- don't play it safe
☐ No sacred cows
☐ Learn to see waste -- would customers pay?
☐ Persistence & Sustainability trump Big Breakthroughs

Figure 11.2   Key points to communicate to the Lean team in the early stage.

Preparing Your Team

All of your team members will have failings. Some of them may feel unqualified because they lack special training or certifications and don't know how to use fancy tools like Minitab. Your process expert may be on the crusty or curmudgeon side, and your first job may be to convince him or her that there is something to this Lean stuff after all (this seems to happen a lot). The most common issue is that the team members haven't worked in the consulting or process leadership role before and they may be worried about their credibility or the effect this will have on their working relationships.

As the team leader, you must get them to focus on the real strengths they contribute rather than on their perceptions of their own weaknesses. "You don't have to be a Minitab expert Mary, because Dan will cover that, but I need somebody that accounting respects, and that's you."

From the very first meeting you have to establish that it is not about you. Or them. Or those guys. You have to take personalities out of the problem diagnostic phase and focus on a pure systems view. If group A delivers an incomplete document to group B, it is not because of incompetence or laziness; that must not be your initial hypothesis even if that is the way the interviewee expresses it. The answers are more likely to be time pressure, a prioritization of schedule over completeness, or a perception that the deliverable still met group B's requirements.

Try to get your team to make some mistakes. Yes, we know that sounds odd, but if you are trying hard, if you are being creative, if you are challenging the established norms, you are going to make some mistakes. Enjoy them. Make some excellent ones that show daring imagination. Sometimes we tell teams to aim for 20-percent mistakes. This ensures the presentation of some good ideas that might never otherwise see the light of day because they are too risky or wild. Certain auto manufacturers today are not in trouble because they produced a few outlandish designs. They are in trouble because they produced many boring ones. We have seen Lean fail to take root in organizations because they could not develop powerful success stories within a certain time. Sometimes this is because they played it too safe, and the organization was expecting more.

At the same time, don't focus only on big breakthrough ideas that can actually move the bottom line. These are great, of course, especially early in the Lean journey, as they will help establish the process and, even more important, color communications to the rest of the organization. However, you are in this for the long haul. The cumulative effect of many practical improvements, maintained and sustained for years, will far outweigh any one big splashy improvement. Our automobiles today are better in every way than those of our father's generation— far more features and amenities, better performance, far better reliability, and the list goes on—but you can't point to any one big breakthrough to explain this. Cars are still made of steel and run on gasoline, but thousands of small design and quality improvements throughout every aspect of modern cars account for this difference.

Don't be afraid of the sacred cows. Sometimes it is clear that some Lean ideas will face fierce opposition. Imagine telling the business case team that you want to replace Excel? Or telling IT that usability is more important than security after all. It is fine to capture and discuss these ideas; the point is not to try to force them on others. Build and present your case rationally; let others approach it emotionally. Be prepared to move on. The best way to have good ideas is to have lots of them. Some will not be good enough and others will be violently opposed. That's OK. We have lots of them.

Get your team to focus on metrics. Some workers give you the right behavior because it is in their nature and they desire to be the best they can be. Some workers give you what they think you want because that's what you're measuring. Good metrics that tie into Lean principles, which, in turn, tie into the strategic goals of the organization, address both these groups. Throughout your interviews, ask the workers how they think they are being measured and what they would do differently if they were measured differently. Collating these results will be invaluable.

Some of your team will be new to Lean and you will spend some time providing background. The good news is that Lean concepts are not difficult, only different, for example, recognizing that in-process inventory is a waste rather than a comfort is the opposite of what most people believe. The best rule of thumb is to always ask yourself, "If we were itemizing this activity on our bill, would our customers be willing to pay for it?"

Doubt is an unpleasant condition but certainty is absurd.

—Voltaire

In our experience, the single hardest thing to communicate to your team is that there is no plan. The cynics on the team may assume that there is a hidden management agenda such as a headcount reduction. It is imperative that you be clear on this point: "We are undergoing a Lean journey of improvement and not cost reduction or a headhunting initiative. We do not have targets or force reduction quotas."

The other equally important, but rather more frightening, explanation is "We do not have a blueprint. We are on a voyage of discovery, not of implementation. We don't know what the answers are, and we don't know what the root causes of the problems are. At best, we have a hazy view of the symptoms." Although this might be self-evident, it can also be very disconcerting to team members who are used to being on projects that are defined by a detailed task list, an explicit schedule, and so forth. The implicit definition of a good project manager is one who understands where the project is now and exactly where it is headed.

Don't worry; this concern is usually a fleeting one. Facts are gathered, hypotheses are developed, and ideas are generated. Soon your team will have much to work on, and plans will be redrawn many times. Success in running a Lean initiative is based on adaptability and many course corrections, not on rigorously executing a predetermined plan.

The Takeaway: How to Build a Lean Team

The high-level issues around creating your Lean team are:

- Do I have the right mix of skills and experience for this process and environment?
- Will my team be credible enough for these workers?
- Will they be daring enough for success?

What Can Go Wrong

If your Lean team has the right elements, little can go wrong. Most organizations operate in an opportunity-rich environment. The right team will find many exciting improvement ideas. However, if you don't have the right team, you have to make changes. It is usually easier to change *people*, than to *change* people. Now is not the time for training or indoctrinating team members. Get your executive sponsor to back you on a change of personnel.

Challenge 3: How to See What You See; Fact Finding

The most common challenge we face in Lean fact-finding is data rich and information poor (DRIP). There are usually file cabinets, hard drives, printed reports, or Web sites filled with data, but there are no metrics or management reports that have distilled this data to answer the questions, such as percent value time, process speed (throughput, cycle time), or internal customer satisfaction, we are interested in.

Sometimes the process owners are gathering the wrong metadata and measuring the wrong things. For example, it is very common to find measurements such as the number of work orders received, the amount of work (projects, invoices, whatever the workload driver is) currently on hand, or the percentage of on-time delivery or completion. In each of these cases, you are measuring input instead of output. To take an extreme example, if you collected all the work and produced nothing, your metric would be very high—not exactly the Lean approach. In the case of the very common "on-time completion" metric, it should be obvious that a key driver of this is the original estimate itself. Padding estimates to ensure a higher on-time completion is as old as project management itself.

This means that the Lean team will be doing some digging and constructing its own information from available data. The key to success here is not to be bogged down in detail. There is a wealth of information—some of it contradictory, incomplete, or confusing. A detailed analysis to create an elegant and exhaustive "proof" will not only get you sidetracked and consume your time and effort, it will also cause the discussion to default into details and numbers rather than ideas. The important thing to remember is that Lean itself is Lean. The process owners or customers will generate some hypotheses, and you can quickly design a simple experiment to gather data and test it. Conversely, an examination of the data may suggest hypothesis, and now the test becomes a discussion with the process owners to see if these hypotheses ring true. Rule of thumb: If you need to make an elaborate business case, it is no longer a Lean idea.

If you don't have good data on meaningful metrics, you'll just have to make some. Here are some simple data gathering exercises:

- Gather samples of a work product (job orders, specifications, design documents, etc.) and extract time-stamp information such as date received or date completed. Represent this data as a histogram, line graph, cumulative flow diagram, or whatever works best to reveal patterns and trends.
- Explore this data using the 5 Whys or another root-cause analytical technique. Is the pattern cyclical (end of month quota surge, phase shift from schedule deliveries, seasonality, etc.)?
- Data mine and graph. Sometimes the right graphical representation can do wonders. For example, a scatter plot of invoice processing times that shows a fat cluster of data points just outside the 30-day payment target drives home a powerful point. A histogram of processing time per supplier may start a root cause analysis showing that some have many more errors than others and, therefore, should receive training or feedback.

Searching for Clues Indicating Waste

In an information-intensive modern office environment, waste may be harder to see than in the physical environments of paper handling or factory assembly. However, there are still many hints that might be the tips of icebergs. For example:

- Is there a lot of project management hustle and bustle?
- Does it take a lot of effort to create status reports and hold status meetings? Is this because the status of things is fundamentally hard to determine?
- Is there a lot of multitasking?
- Can the workers give you a quick answer about cycle time and performance?
- Can the workers tell you how long tasks take or is the answer always "it depends"? Do internal customers or upstream groups, such as marketing or management, often interfere with or inquire about timetables and deliverables?
- Is there a lot of expediting or special handling? What percentage of the projects or work receive expedited treatment?
- Are things done via escalation to management or by worker collaboration?

- Do internal customers feel the need to exaggerate the priority of the project to get it done on time?
- If projects or work have official priority designations, do they have a normal distribution statistically or are they heavily skewed towards "top priority"?

The Takeaway: Dig Deep

As you probe, always remember:

- It's not about you or them. Take a systems view; no personalities or feuds allowed.
- Beware of a culture of multitasking. Remember being busy is a side effect, not a goal. A very full plate of past due work or work in progress is not a sign of capacity or importance. It is a waste.
- Excessive status gathering and reporting is a waste in itself and a key indicator of other wastes. Is all this parallel reporting needed because projects are slipping and affecting other areas? Is it an indication that status is inherently hard to know, perhaps because the information is locked up in a few hard drives and heads rather than openly available. Is it valued because it allows workers to highlight themselves in front of management?

What Can Go Wrong

Your findings and the cultural perception have to be somewhat in sync or quickly get there. If you tell a group that has always been told they are stars that 95 percent of what they do is waste, you are facing a challenge. Chances are they

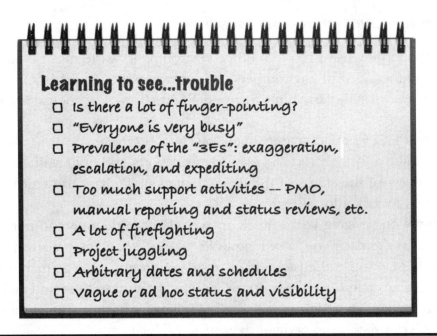

Learning to see...trouble
- ☐ Is there a lot of finger-pointing?
- ☐ "Everyone is very busy"
- ☐ Prevalence of the "3Es": exaggeration, escalation, and expediting
- ☐ Too much support activities -- PMO, manual reporting and status reviews, etc.
- ☐ A lot of firefighting
- ☐ Project juggling
- ☐ Arbitrary dates and schedules
- ☐ Vague or ad hoc status and visibility

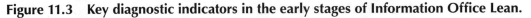

Figure 11.3 Key diagnostic indicators in the early stages of Information Office Lean.

will soon see you as the problem. Make sure that the intuitions, perceptions, and belief systems of the process workers are front and center in your list of hypotheses—even if you don't believe them. You need to address them head on, and either disprove them or explain them in light of an interesting twist or cause that has eluded exposure until now. Besides, the workers may even be right and your initial observations or the sponsor's problem statement may be wrong. Don't do the analysis before you do the analysis!

Challenge 4: How to Build the Lean Case; Doing the Analysis

You have to ask yourself, "What does the data suggest?" Experience shows that with sufficient data of reasonable quality, some trends or views are discoverable, which, if not immediately representing a finding, can at least suggest the next steps. The advantage is that most workers in process-lite environments do not bother too much with their own data. You have an opportunity for real discovery simply by flogging your spreadsheet or statistics package a little—tempered by experience and guided by your soft interview findings.

Some more simple data tests are:

- Do delivery or completion dates often shift? If so, does this tend to happen just before the original promise date? This green–green–red phenomenon is a sure symptom of low status visibility, firefighting, and overall poor information flow.
- Conversely, are target dates somewhat arbitrary? A never-failing indication of this is the comparison between project length and early completion. If an activity or project has a natural low value time ratio (in other words, several weeks have been scheduled to do a few days' work) and these projects are almost never completed early, then it's safe to assume that these distant dates are highly conservative guesses. The real work doesn't begin until the due date approaches.
- How well do theory and practice compare? Recreating one "typical" project work item can be a very useful exercise. Comparing a theoretical person-hour curve derived from a project plan against an actual one based on interviews and estimates usually highlights the hurry-up-and-wait syndrome very well. It is also an excellent exhibit when describing continuous flow or pull-based systems later in the Lean effort.

These two views—the statistical summary and the recreated typical project—represented by these questions are the broad and deep views. They should be mutually supportive representations of the same issues.

Breaking the News: How to Report Your Findings

The early analytical findings are pointers to root-cause issues or problem drivers. They are not answers by themselves. Many of them are well established in the belief system that existed before the Lean team ever arrived—the famous "They borrowed my watch and then told me the time" criticism of consulting. The fact that you are also disproving other dearly held beliefs will not help your credibility much. Still, you will need to tell your Lean story to management and to the workers, so this information should be kept and polished.

A common approach is to list the things workers or managers believe, and to comment on each with added data and analysis reinforcing some, discrediting some, and leaving others as plausible. This legacy belief structure cannot be ignored and may be an excellent place to start. We suggest displaying this list of "beliefs" as a working document; either as a poster or a Web site element, whichever works best for this team. As these beliefs are fleshed out, more folks will come forward to provide insights and evidence. It is important to keep this communication simple: drawings and illustrations, a few graphs, no equations or complex analyses. People will gather around a story far more readily than they will around a geometric proof.

The Takeaway: If You Build It, They Will Come Around

- Don't get bogged down in details. There is enough data to support many different points of view; the devil can quote scripture.
- Communicate clearly; be honest and up to date. When workers see your evolving hypothesis on the wall chart or Web site, they should know that their comments or contributions will be timely and useful.
- Lean is Lean—keep it simple, keep it fast. A detailed diagnostic with all its required proof, verification, and documentation will cost more time and effort than the entire Lean effort; don't go down that path.

What Can Go Wrong

Don't do the analysis before you do the analysis. Be objective; work with your team in kaizen and brainstorming sessions; follow all the leads; and be sure you can defend your numbers, assumptions, and methods. Sometimes an entire team can be seduced by an exciting idea or discovery, and continue to pursue it despite mounting evidence or opinion to the contrary.

Challenge 5: How to Evaluate Information Flow

We recommend using dependency (or design) structure matrices (DSM) software, discussed in detail in Chapter 7. This is an area with an important distinction

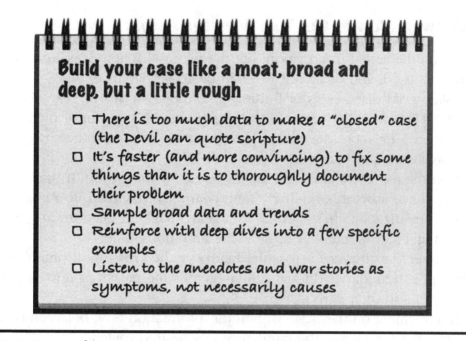

Build your case like a moat, broad and deep, but a little rough

☐ There is too much data to make a "closed" case (the Devil can quote scripture)

☐ It's faster (and more convincing) to fix some things than it is to thoroughly document their problem

☐ Sample broad data and trends

☐ Reinforce with deep dives into a few specific examples

☐ Listen to the anecdotes and war stories as symptoms, not necessarily causes

Figure 11.4   Ensure that your Lean arguments are themselves lean.

between theory and practice. Are the software tools necessary or effective in this environment and culture? We think the answer should be yes in most information age, white-collar environments, but we have occasionally been surprised at the lack of acceptance given to new analytical tools by experts who don't want their expertise challenged by a black box.

Remember to focus on the information elements (the nouns) rather than on the tasks or process steps (the verbs). This mind shift from verbs to nouns is critical. It is analogous to focusing on outputs rather than inputs, and it simplifies the data representation tremendously. We find that five to ten process boxes in a flow diagram can be condensed to a single document or Infel representation. For example, the verb approach might be: (1) gather test procedures, (2) reserve lab space, (3) write test plan, (4) perform test, and so forth, whereas the noun view might be test results.

Reporting Your Findings

Sometimes the representation of the information matrix itself, which provides a very dense and detailed view of the situation, coupled with a soft discussion of some of its implications is enough. Of course, we don't suggest that you ignore the clustering and tearing algorithms at the heart of DSM, only that you consider the context. The comfortable hybrid solution is to do the analysis in the back room and to come to the team meetings with two or three suggestions without indicating that they came from DSM analysis. These alternate designs, identifications of waste, and other ideas can be easily put into words so you don't have to resort to matrices. In fact, if they cannot be, it is probable that you do not understand them well enough to present them.

The Takeaway: How to Get Your Message Across

- Focus on the actual information, not the process. Where is it created, retrieved, used, and deleted (CRUD, in database parlance).
- Translate DSM discoveries or findings into the lay terms of Lean. The Infel matrix is just another analytical technique like a histogram or pie chart. It may suggest far more detailed improvements than these others do, but they still have to be put into words.
- Choose the representation that makes sense for this group. If they like Gantt charts, create a before-and-after Gantt chart. Overlay the information flow on the organization chart (similar to a Lean spaghetti diagram in a factory) to highlight a large number of handoffs and inbox time.
- Remember that distance across the matrix or the crossing of organizational/geographic boundaries dramatically increases the delays or rework penalties represented in the matrix.
- Seek agreement on the desired path for information flow between two points. Try to eliminate the parallel or less desired routes.
- Emphasize the surprising discoveries such as the expensively created but never again used information element, the cut-and-paste pass through of information, and so on.

What Can Go Wrong

The information flow techniques are rich in ideas and flexible enough to support many different and creative representations of those ideas. The two most common adoption challenges are the unwillingness to give up the "just in case" parallel flows

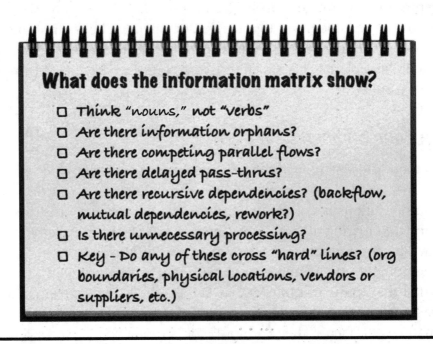

What does the information matrix show?

☐ Think "nouns," not "verbs"
☐ Are there information orphans?
☐ Are there competing parallel flows?
☐ Are there delayed pass-thrus?
☐ Are there recursive dependencies? (backflow, mutual dependencies, rework?)
☐ Is there unnecessary processing?
☐ Key – Do any of these cross "hard" lines? (org boundaries, physical locations, vendors or suppliers, etc.)

Figure 11.5 Use the information matrix to develop your initial hypotheses.

of information and the organizational challenges associated with resequencing tasks. Even if a manager admits that it makes sense for Bill to work closely with Mary, the manager may not be willing to give up head count in his group to accommodate it.

Challenge 6: Turning Lean Ideas into Results

There are three separate entries against this challenge. The first is the implementation strategy and the other two are the very different tactics associated with simple versus complex implementation tactics.

How to Create a Plan

The good news about a well-run Lean initiative is that it generates a great many ideas. The bad news on the implementation side is—well, you guessed it—pretty soon some of the team members or process owners are asked to stop generating ideas and move on to an implementation and break-in phase. After that, management would like the dust to settle for a while and get the hang of things before moving on to new ideas.

Before you know it, somebody is creating implementation teams, drafting schedules, identifying milestones, and the imagination soup of kaizen brainstorming starts to look like a staid project management organization. While to some of us to stop generating ideas is a psychological impossibility, the good news is we can finally tell the team that we do have a plan. We didn't know what it was when we started but we have a good idea now.

The Takeaway: Moving Forward

- You do not need, nor should you have, distinct phases. At no time should the organization say stop brainstorming and start building. Of course, you will do exactly that for individual ideas being implemented, but the Lean team itself will always be developing, evaluating, and implementing ideas.
- Resist the temptation to build elaborate project plans that sequence and prioritize all the ideas. Keep it simple; keep it Lean. Some of the ideas are so simple they will be completed and delivering value before you can figure out how to apply resources in the new Gantt chart program you are using.
- The beauty of continuous improvement is that it goes on forever. One approach that we like is to implement ideas in a spiral program. First, you select some candidates because they are easy or highly visible or high value. Start work on those and set the rest aside for the time being. You will learn far more about how to make Lean work in a given organization by actually implementing one idea than by planning 100. Once you are smarter and wiser, you can do a better job of planning and executing against the next batch of ideas.

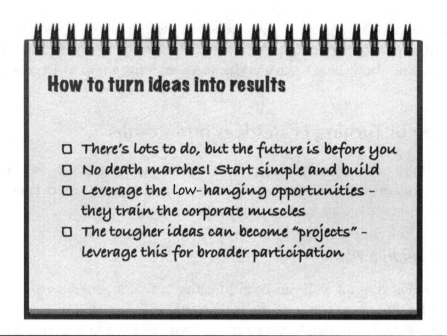

Figure 11.6 Carefully prioritize and pick implementation initiatives to build Lean momentum.

What Can Go Wrong

All the classic change management challenges come into play here: turf issues, legacy process issues, organizational conflict, fear of change. An entire library of management science books is dedicated to these issues. The advantage you have lies in the baby-steps nature of Lean. This minimizes the perception of change and develops the change management muscles of the organization.

Start with the Quick Win: Low Hanging Opportunities

The low hanging fruit or quick-win projects are key elements of success. In some organizations, the viability and survivability of Lean as a management improvement methodology depend on them. Fortunately, DSM techniques do an excellent job of highlighting quick-win opportunities.

The situational visibility provided by the matrix starts generating a chorus of "I didn't know that's what happened," which in turn fuels brainstorming and improvement ideas. The identification and elimination of orphaned information and parallel flows are easily represented not as the elimination of fuzzy office "wastes," but as real tangible savings.

What Can Go Wrong

Not much, really. If there's one class of ideas that is fairly safe and readily accepted, it is these. Naysayers might complain that the ideas are too small, but it's

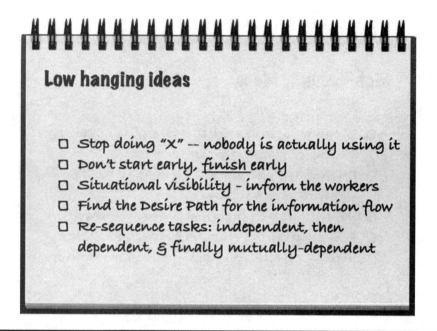

Figure 11.7   Leverage the information matrix's ability to highlight quick wins.

an easy argument to refute because you have captured their value at little cost and if you did so across the entire organization the effect would be anything but small.

Scoping and Prioritizing Projects

The larger ideas generated by the Lean effort will require special handling. Sometimes this is because more detailed study is required, or special skills are needed, or additional information such as vendor quotes and specifications have to be gathered. Usually the reason is that these ideas are too big to be done without creating a project team and a project manager. Not surprisingly, this happens most often in companies that have a strong project management culture.

This is fine. The organization needs to adapt and adopt Lean in a way that makes sense to it. Their interpretation is not a deviation, but rather an enabler to adoption.

What Can Go Wrong

There can be resource issues, both personnel and budgetary. There will be some effort to delay the ideas until the next budget cycle or until resources are available. Your executive sponsor can make a decision to prioritize some of the larger Lean initiatives or to have them handled via the organization's normal mechanisms. The Lean team can continue working and continuous improvement can proceed, even as some of these individual projects must wait until a later time.

The two things that most commonly delay information redesign ideas are IT and changes to the organizational chart. IT of course will have its own experts, budgets, and security concerns that must be satisfied. Organizational chart issues can be quite difficult. In some organizations, the very definition

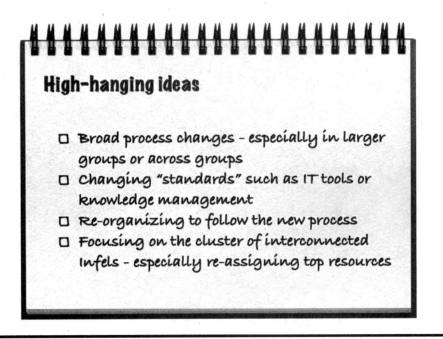

Figure 11.8 **The Lean team will benefit from uncovering large ideas even if additional resources are required to fully implement them.**

of a manager's grade is dependent on how many direct reports he or she has. In a situation like that, a decision to move some head count to another part of the organization to support a more efficient process is a tough one for the manager to make. Sometimes the DSM resequencing will balance resource shifts between two organizations. The resulting horse trading can be to everyone's benefit.

Challenge 7: Sustaining Lean; Communications and Collaboration

During the Lean Discovery Phase: Team Talk

During the early stages, communication and collaboration is largely among Lean team members and the process workers contributing to the Lean effort. The key elements of a Web-based tool, if you decide to go with one, are:

- ◼ Scheduling
- ◼ Document sharing (including coauthoring, editing, and commenting)
- ◼ Some basic "mission statement" material, such as a letter or charter from the executive sponsor
- ◼ Some description of the scope and what the process worker or stakeholder can expect, or how this project may affect them, for example, interviews, data requests, and participation in brainstorming sessions

The Takeaway: Fundamentals of Early Success

The fundamental principles enabling early success are:

- Transparency and visibility—What are you doing and how is it going?
- Frankness and honesty—What does our data show? What ideas are on the table?
- Usability and value—This tool or forum is easy to use and provides visitor value.

Tool Tip: A Lean Web site can be constructed by a midlevel Web designer. If you don't have one, or if there's too much paperwork involved, you can use a Web 2.0 site such as Intervals or Onehub. Indeed, there are so many of these sites cropping up, and evolving rapidly, that we know we are onto something with this approach. If you don't like these sites, try Campfire, WorkZone, Box.net, Sosius, or Backboard. Some of these young companies may go casters-up by the time you read this. No matter. If there are 30 or so now (at our last quick count), there will be plenty in the foreseeable future and using them will be more a matter of course than an interesting new concept.

During the Sustain Phase: Ongoing Communication

During the sustain phase, the emphasis shifts from a tool that enables the development and implementation of the first few Lean ideas to one that rallies and reinforces Lean, and addresses all the rumor mill and change management issues. Since you have made it to the sustain phase, presumably you have something to sustain, and it is not some of the Lean changes but the Lean culture itself.

The best way to sustain the Lean culture within a group or process is to facilitate its spread and adoption to other groups and processes. This can be done through your Lean Web site. Thus, you build to some tipping point where not having Lean initiatives becomes the outlier behavior.

The Takeaway: Use Your Web Site to Sustain Lean Culture

- The Lean site must tell a good Lean story: before-and-after pictures and diagrams, before-and-after performance/metrics, success stories, positive statements from the executive sponsors, endorsements from the Lean team members and the process owners who have contributed.
- The Lean site must be fit for multiple users and use cases.
  - Lean workers. It must continue to effectively support the ongoing work of the Lean teams: collaboration, idea generation, scheduling, progress management.

- Lean tourists. It must smooth the pathway to adoption for other workers and other processes. There should be
  - Links to general Lean training and materials
  - A place to ask questions or request more information
  - A place to volunteer for participation in future kaizen events
  - A place to ask questions about how to apply Lean to the visitor's processes
- ■ Senior management. It must answer the so-what question for management in whatever way is meaningful to them. In some organizations, a hearty "thank you so much for listening to my ideas" by one of the workers will be seen as a huge win by management. In others, they won't be satisfied unless they can trace the effects of these ideas down to the bottom line and notice an impact on strategy or their financials. Do not ignore this! Too often Lean practitioners wave their arms and say, "Don't worry; it'll all come out in the wash, as long as we're improving throughput the other numbers will follow." We may be all right with that as a philosophical principle, but it's unreasonable to expect that by-the-numbers managers will be embracing that view.

What Can Go Wrong

It's easy to come across as a propagandist in developing Lean communication platforms. Sometimes there is too much emphasis on selling the sizzle and not enough on selling the steak. Keep it simple, quantify benefits where you can, explain your reasoning for why the new solution is better than the legacy solution, and don't be afraid to list your failures. If your organization is like most,

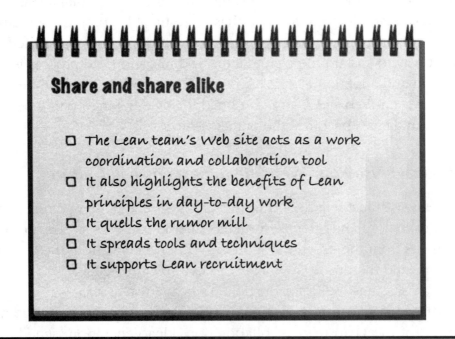

Share and share alike

- ☐ The Lean team's Web site acts as a work coordination and collaboration tool
- ☐ It also highlights the benefits of Lean principles in day-to-day work
- ☐ It quells the rumor mill
- ☐ It spreads tools and techniques
- ☐ It supports Lean recruitment

Figure 11.9 Communicating, even evangelizing, is critical to sustain Lean efforts.

everybody will know about your failures already. Be upfront about them, but be sure to explain what you have learned or how you have grown from them.

Challenge 8: Sustaining Lean; Policies, Procedures, and Metrics

If your Lean initiative is to be an effective management and operations tool, more than just communications will be needed. Lean approaches such as visual management, continuous flow, pull, and so forth must be an equal part of process management, scheduling, and coordination efforts.

Policies and procedures must be viewed as in perpetual beta rather than carved in stone. It is common for one part of the organization to be dragged (the professional office version of kicking and screaming) to a redesigned process or end state. At this point they dig in their heels and say this far and no farther and issue an updated operations manual, or new policies and procedures statements. The implicit position is that now that these have been updated, there will be no need to touch them for some time. In this fashion, one rigid policy has been replaced, with great effort, by another rigid policy.

An interesting approach is to build the frequent updating of policies and procedures into the policies themselves. For example, you could create a quarterly checklist: Has this policy been updated? If so, how? Or you could devise a performance metric for the administrators and keepers of the policy manual comprised of the feedback of the process workers who rate themselves on their willingness to support continuous improvement efforts.

It is both disruptive and confusing to replace existing performance metrics with a new set of the performance metrics in toto because you lose continuity of performance and you start talking about the metrics BL (before Lean). In fact, a transition period where both the legacy metrics and the new Lean metrics exist side by side is most effective. Watch all these metrics for some time to understand which ones are reinforcing, redundant, or less meaningful. Soon you will winnow the group to a small set of mostly Lean metrics that focus on speed, cycle time, and throughput, and a few legacy metrics that provide budget or financial performance and fit into the legacy accounting perspective.

Sustaining Lean with Visual Management Systems

Visual management systems (VMSs) are a vital component in sustaining Lean. They work hand in glove with the new performance metrics to help drive Lean behavior. They really bring home the importance of continuous flow and throughput and they provide situational visibility. The good news is that with the advent of Web sites and all the bells and whistles such as RSS feeds, e-mail workflow integration, wikis, blogs, document tagging, and so forth, they are easy to use and incredibly powerful. In fact, we think they are at the center of a coming surge in office worker productivity.

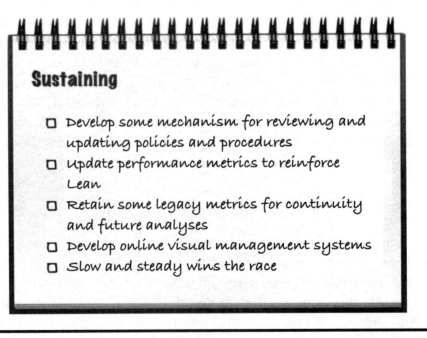

The Takeaway: Use Policies, Procedures, and Metrics to Sustain Lean

- Grow and spread Lean broadly but slowly. Your Lean stories, Web sites, and tools should be so good as to be pulled—never pushed—by other groups into their work processes.
- Tie Lean results and initiatives to corporate strategies or financial results. Consider developing Business Intelligence-type capabilities on your Web site to allow for tracing contributions from high-level strategies, through organizations, to discrete Lean ideas.
- Wrap your day-to-day operations around Lean by using reinforcing measurements and metrics, and ensuring that "changing policies" is something that is seen as a natural side effect of growth and continuous improvement rather than a suspicious activity that should be carefully reviewed.

What Can Go Wrong

Lean by management fiat can be a real problem. The difference between sponsorship and mandate can be the difference between successful Lean adoption and a short-term window dressing project. In the latter case, the workforce spends its time trying to figure what management wants and delivers something that approximates that. They get their tick in the box and move on to the next fad or crisis. In the former case, the workforce tries to develop the right thing in an objective sense, they enjoy doing it and telling others about it, and they keep doing it.

Sustaining

☐ Develop some mechanism for reviewing and updating policies and procedures
☐ Update performance metrics to reinforce Lean
☐ Retain some legacy metrics for continuity and future analyses
☐ Develop online visual management systems
☐ Slow and steady wins the race

Figure 11.10 Continuous improvement implies revisiting metrics, routinely updating policies, and developing unambiguous visual management systems all as a normal way of doing business.

IT can block the deployment of or take too tight control of the Web sites and tools. Try to get an implicit agreement that they will be hands-off within certain parameters or timeframes. One approach is to couch this as a user specification phase; the Lean team is developing and honing what it wants in the Web site and visual management systems, and then IT can step in and do it right.

Index

The Authors

George Gonzalez-Rivas has been a process improvement consultant for most of his life and has worked with several consulting companies, most recently as a partner for PA Consulting Group. He has advised telecom, energy, and product development organizations, and is the inventor of the Infel Matrix approach to information modeling. He is continuously improving his Lean skills. He is currently the national director of AnyLogic America. He lives in New Jersey with his wife and two children.

Linus Larsson has advised large international corporations on strategy and performance improvement for more than 20 years. He has worked with high-performance companies in a range of industries including manufacturing, financial services, health care, and business services. He is a leading thinker, writer, and speaker on how to apply the philosophy of Lean in a non-factory environment. Linus has held several senior management positions within several global business services corporations. Linus is currently working on business ventures with The Quest Group and writing a book. He was formerly a partner at PA Consulting Group. He is based in Stockholm, where he lives with his wife and three children.